T0330178

The Evolution of Social Innovation

The Evolution of Social Innovation

Building Resilience Through Transitions

Edited by

Frances Westley

J.W. McConnell Chair in Social Innovation, Waterloo Institute for Social Innovation and Resilience, University of Waterloo, Canada

Katharine McGowan

Assistant Professor, Bissett School of Business, Mount Royal University, Canada

Ola Tjörnbo

Adjunct Professor, Waterloo Institute for Social Innovation and Resilience, University of Waterloo, Canada

Edward Elgar
PUBLISHING

Cheltenham, UK • Northampton, MA, USA

Published by
Edward Elgar Publishing Limited
The Lypiatts
15 Lansdown Road
Cheltenham
Glos GL50 2JA
UK

Edward Elgar Publishing, Inc.
William Pratt House
9 Dewey Court
Northampton
Massachusetts 01060
USA

A catalogue record for this book
is available from the British Library

Library of Congress Control Number: 2017947101

This book is available electronically in the **Elgar**online
Social and Political Science subject collection
DOI 10.4337/9781786431158

ISBN 978 1 78643 114 1 (cased)
ISBN 978 1 78643 115 8 (eBook)

Typeset by Servis Filmsetting Ltd, Stockport, Cheshire
Printed and bound by CPI Group (UK) Ltd, Croydon, CR0 4YY

Contents

Contributors

Erin Alexiuk, PhD candidate, University of Waterloo, Canada.

Nino Antadze, Visiting Assistant Professor of Environmental Studies, Bucknell University, USA.

Jaclyn Blacklock, Researcher, University of Waterloo, Canada.

Sean Geobey, Assistant Professor, University of Waterloo, Canada.

Daniel McCarthy, PhD, Associate Professor, University of Waterloo, Canada.

Katharine McGowan, PhD, Assistant Professor, Bissett School of Business, Mount Royal University, Canada.

Michele-Lee Moore, Associate Professor, Department of Geography, University of Victoria, Canada and Deputy Director, GRAID, Stockholm Resilience Centre, Stockholm University, Sweden.

Per Olsson, Research Theme Leader, Stockholm Resilience Centre, Stockholm University, Sweden.

Ola Tjörnbo, Adjunct Professor, Waterloo Institute for Social Innovation and Resilience, University of Waterloo, Canada.

Frances Westley, J.W. McConnell Chair in Social Innovation, Waterloo Institute for Social Innovation and Resilience, University of Waterloo, Canada.

Acknowledgements

We would like to acknowledge the support of a number of people who commented on this book or whose ideas helped shape the content, especially Tim Brodhead, Ken Coates, Thomas Homer-Dixon and Steve Quilley. We are grateful to the J.W. McConnell Family Foundation and Suncor Energy Foundation for their generous support of the researchers and research throughout. Lastly we would like to thank Meg Westley for her excellent and efficient editing and thoughtful comments, and Nina Ripley for keeping us organized. We are grateful to our families for their love, patience and understanding throughout what sometimes felt like a long journey.

Waterloo
March 2017

1. The history of social innovation

Katharine McGowan, Frances Westley and Ola Tjörnbo

INTRODUCTION

They are far from the usual suspects: an early modern trader of the Dutch Golden Age, an economics professor from the 1970s quantifying risk, a post-war Utopian hippy computer programmer working in the belly of the US Defense Department, a female clinic owner warning against venereal disease in the First World War, a prolific and eloquent 19th-century hiking and nature enthusiast, early 20th-century psychologists testing more than a million army recruits, and the modern inheritors and stewards of the Haida nation and its land. Yet we posit that all these individuals and their actions can contribute to our understanding of social innovation in a meaningful way, and that many of them were explicit and purposeful in trying to disrupt their circumstances and move their societies towards greater resilience. They were engaging in social innovation before anyone articulated terms to describe their projects and goals.

Conversations about social innovation frequently start in the present and look towards the future: what are we doing today to achieve the future we want to see tomorrow? This is partially why scholars and practitioners have agonized over social innovation's permanency and relevance. Is it just a new buzz term (Pol and Ville, 2009), popular with funders, governments and the private sector because of the word "innovation", intensely popular across many fields and disciplines at the moment? Is it riding roughshod over more established disciplines and practices like community-based action research and community service learning? With this collection of cases, we seek to establish that work on social innovation provides a new lens for examining social transformation, and that looking back through history can illuminate the complex processes of transformation and innovation.

In truth, we are not the first to venture backwards to explore social innovation; Geoff Mulgan explicitly places the origin of social innovation in the industrial revolution. As people moved into cities en masse, the new human geography overwhelmed the traditional civil society and religious institutions that provided many basic services, and the need for social innovation was born (Mulgan, 2006). In addition, several social innovation, systems-informed and transition-informed case studies have used history to explain or explore the dynamics of a complex system over time, but they are often limited to one or a few cases (Mumford, 2002; Mumford and Moertl, 2003; Bures and Kanapaux, 2011), focused on social-ecological systems (Gunderson et al., 1995), primarily concerned with socio-technical transitions (Van den Ende and Kemp, 1999; Van Driel and Schot, 2005; Geels, 2006; Geels and Schot, 2007) or simply science (Thagard, 2012). In contrast to these and other similar works, our study is a broadly constructed series of case studies of social innovation over time. Although our cases are concentrated in the 19th and 20th centuries, and in North America and Europe, we consider several problem domains, from conservation to economic tools, from Indigenous nation-building to reproductive technologies. Additionally, to support and expand on the cases' utility in discussing and understanding social innovation, we include three bridge discussions diving deep into key theoretical elements, specifically self organization, attractors and adjacent possible, agency and opportunity contexts, and cross-scale dynamics. These theory chapters are meant to supplement the cases and facilitate comparison. We conclude with a chapter that summarizes our insights into the nature and dynamics of social innovation, insights that we feel have important implications for the study of contemporary initiatives.

HISTORY "OF" VS. HISTORY "AND" SOCIAL INNOVATION

This collection uses an explicitly historical approach to explore cases of social innovation through time. The concept of social innovation itself seems to emerge in the early 20th century in sociology (Ward, 1903), and then appears more and more frequently in the post-Second World War period. This does not necessarily mean all those using social innovation employed the term in a common or even mutually intelligible way. It was often employed in the context of social policy and social action, in relation to issues surrounding race, employment and urbanization in the United States. In these instances, the term often refers to some sort of improvement in the social (as opposed to medical, ecological or economic) realm. Until the 21st century however, the term was rarely used critically: it was employed descriptively rather than analytically.

The increase in use of the term "social innovation" from the 1960s to

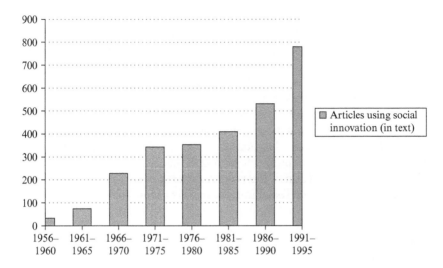

Note: This figure is based on a Google Scholar search of the discrete term "social innovation" excluding citations, patents and indexes. It is meant as heuristic, not definitive.

Figure 1.1 Uses of social innovation in academic articles, 1956–95

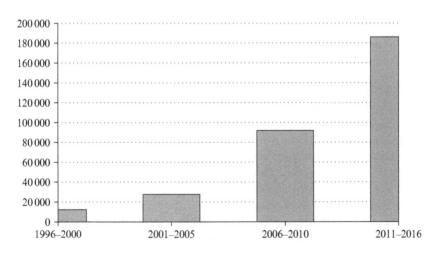

Note: See Figure 1.1. Note the changing vertical scale between Figures 1.1 and 1.2.

Figure 1.2 Uses of social innovation in academic articles, 1996–2016

today creates a false sense of unity and progression in the field. In fact, few scholars are trained in social innovation. Instead they come from the distinct intellectual traditions of sociology, political science, complexity, ecology, business (and especially entrepreneurship), non-profit studies, social work and even, increasingly, Indigenous studies. It is a concept that still attracts people more for its promise than its certainty.

This book arises from a very specific tradition within the broad and fuzzy social innovation canon, combining resilience theory (Gunderson and Holling, 2002), complex adaptive systems theory (McElroy, 2002; Berkes et al., 2003), and innovation process theory (Quinn, 1985; Pascale, 1984; Nonaka, 1995; Kanter, 1984) to create a relatively robust and analytically useful definition of social innovation. We define social innovation as *a new program, policy, procedure, product, process and/or design that seeks to address a social problem and to ultimately shift resource and authority flows, social routines and cultural values of the social system that created the problem in the first place* (Westley et al., 2011; Westley et al., 2006). Unlike many of the term's historical (and even contemporary) uses, here "social" is not merely a qualifier of a novel invention (differentiating it from the technological or the material), but a descriptor of process and of ultimate goal: to transform social institutions at all scales (from micro to macro). In this, our approach is also closely tied to structuration theory (Giddens, 1984).

The origins and content of our definition of social innovation inform our case selection (see the Methodology section below); some of our selections may initially surprise readers. Contemporary actors in our cases rarely if ever used the term "social innovation" (it was not in common use during many of the historical periods we considered), so we looked for several key elements to determine whether a social innovation was actually part of the transition under consideration. First: was there a new program, process, procedure, product, policy or design that could be directly tied to the transition in question? Did it deliberately or inadvertently seek to shift authority and/or resource flows, social routines or cultural values? Was the architect(s)' and/or advocate(s)' specific goal, at least at some stage of development, to disrupt a system and transform it? This is a high bar, based directly on the University of Waterloo's Waterloo Institute for Social Innovation and Resilience (WISIR)'s definition of social innovation (Westley et al., 2006). Importantly however, the actors in these cases appear deeply intentional in their actions, generally displaying an understanding and attention to systems dynamics and scale.

THEORY AND TERMINOLOGY

This project began with an insight and a moment of juxtaposition between technological innovation and social innovation. In *The Nature of Technology*, complexity theorist Brian Arthur argued that the discovery of new natural phenomena (through scientific advances), and new ways of capturing/exploiting such phenomena, catalyzes the creation of a cluster of new technologies (2009). The combination of existing technologies within or between domains or regimes can also create new technologies. So, according to Arthur, novelty in technology originates in new or different understandings and exploitation of the natural world, which in turn results in path-dependent combinations and recombinations of elements.

For the researchers at WISIR, already committed to a complexity perspective, this led to the question: was a similar process at work in many transformative social innovations? And, if so, were the number and types of phenomena broader than just those commonly associated with science and technology? Could, for instance, new social or political philosophies be considered as examples of phenomena that have the same catalytic effect? If so, it solved a challenge presented by our own definition: how does the researcher interested in the transformation of social institutions determine which novel ideas, designs or initiatives, identified in the early stages of their development, are most likely to have transformative impact?

And so we began a journey of discovery using historical examples. We chose historical innovations rather than contemporary or ongoing ones because we wanted to be able to trace the entire process from successful scaling/transformation back to new phenomena. Many promising or popular current innovations may still be in the process of scaling, or the consequences of their mass adoption are still emerging. The failure of social innovations to have a lasting impact is common. An historical approach to these phenomena gives us a different perspective on how and why some social innovations do in fact result in the transformations to which they aspire.

TERMINOLOGY

Specialized terminology, drawn from the theoretical traditions of complexity theory, resilience theory, innovation theory and structuration theory may not be familiar to all readers. Here we have chosen to focus on defining concepts we believe to have explanatory or theoretical significance to the overarching story we seek to tell surrounding social innovation and systems shifts. They are as follows:

Social Phenomena/Social Fact

Social phenomena are socially created concepts that a discrete group (a culture, a sect, a political group) believes to be true and that guide their behavior accordingly. This concept is derived directly from Durkheim's social fact – ideas that are real in their effects (we believe them to be true and therefore act accordingly) (Durkheim, 2014 [1938]). As noted above, Arthur saw the discovery of new scientific phenomena as being the cata-lyst for new technologies. For example, the discovery of the light spectrum stimulated innovations from lenses to original styles in painting. In the social sciences, it would appear that social philosophies and religious beliefs have a similar capacity for stimulating cascades of social innova-tion. Take for example Martin Luther's break with the Catholic church and his belief that all men should have direct access to the word of God, which meant not only that the Bible should be translated from Latin to the local language, but also that all men should learn to read. This may be said to be the "social fact" which stimulated mass education. In our cases, the phenomena at the root of social innovation are extremely diverse, ranging from mathematical formulas governing financial transactions (see Chapter 9), to legal rulings on Indigenous rights (Chapter 6), and new technological innovations in computing and telecommunications (Chapter 7).

Adjacent Possible

The term "adjacent possible", first coined by Stuart Kauffman (2000), refers to:

> a kind of shadow future, hovering on the edges of the present state of things, a map of all the ways in which the present can reinvent itself . . . captures both the limits and the creative potential of change and innovation . . . its boundaries grow as you explore them. Each new combination opens up the possibility of other new combinations. (Johnson, 2010, p. 11)

Adjacent possibles are the range of alternative social arrangements just beyond the horizon of the prevailing possible (the current reality) (Johnson, 2010, p. 31). Arthur indicates that the adjacent possible defines the various possible trajectories along which an innovation develops. Social facts or phenomena, such as the belief that all men should read the Bible, may start initially with the education of a few. However, depending on what other inventions or innovations occur in the adjacent possible, the trajectories may take very different directions. The discovery of the printing press, for example, accelerated access to reading and to education.

Had such an invention not been available, other trajectories would have developed. Chapters 6 and 10 showcase two different adjacent possibles in the history of the relationship between the Canadian government and Canada's Indigenous population, one that had tragic consequences, and one that now gives cause for renewed hope for the future.

Elective Affinity, Bricolage, Paradox and Basins of Attraction

Four additional concepts are useful for enriching our analysis of how adjacent possibles are formed, and how they impact social innovations. First, elective affinity, a concept developed by Max Weber (1922), helps us to understand why certain adjacent possibles become more likely to succeed than others. As Weber indicated, of the sets of available adjacent possibles, some will be more likely than others to form a mutual attraction with the developing social innovation. Weber noted, for example, that the economic form of capitalism and the Protestant ethic had a kind of natural fit in which "they mutually favor one another's continuance or conversely, hinder or exclude one another – are 'adequate' or 'inadequate' to one another" (Weber, 1992, p. 138). We see an example of this in Chapter 3, where the intelligence test had an unfortunate elective affinity with the then popular concept of eugenics. So too, as social innovations develop over time, they attract elements of the adjacent possible and in doing so create a kind of *bricolage*, a coming together of elements not previously juxtaposed but which nonetheless fit together to form something new and generally coherent; for example, in Chapter 7 the World Wide Web is not only an amalgam of three different inventions, but also builds on the inventions of the Internet, email, hypertext and several others. Once formed, the elements continue to reinforce and amplify each other, creating a coherent, consistent and stable pattern of interaction to which the system returns even when perturbed, such as the modern derivatives trading market described in Chapter 9, which survived the 2008 recession largely unaltered. Complexity theorists refer to this as a basin of attraction (Walker et al., 2004). The fit is never perfect, however. Over time, the social innovations in this book go through further transformation, in response to tensions between the original, disparate elements. *Paradoxes* become part of the dynamic that drives the continuing evolution of the innovation. For example, as we will see in the chapter on national parks, some of the tensions that characterize today's parks system are a result of the dynamics of combination and recombination, the process of bricolage which is essential to successful social innovation. Nonetheless, as we shall also see, the sensitivity to initial conditions which some complexity theorists have gone as far as to call prophetic, continues to characterize the innovation, despite those permutations and transformations. An innovation's basic DNA – the values and hopes of its earliest architects and advocates – may be easy to obscure but are very difficult to eradicate.

Agency and System/Institutional Entrepreneurship

In these historical cases, identifying individuals associated with our innovations was an invaluable means of bringing focus to the details of our narratives, allowing us to see how actions at the smallest scale of the systems related to the broader trends associated with the adjacent possibles (for example, in the case of the intelligence test, the role that key actors played in getting the test launched at a massive scale despite limited peer review). Institutional or system entrepreneurship is used to describe a particular form of agency associated with social innovation. The creators of social innovation ideas are often described as social entrepreneurs. Social entrepreneurship has been defined by three components:

1. identifying a stable but inherently unjust equilibrium that causes the exclusion, marginalization or suffering of a segment of humanity that lacks the financial means or political clout to achieve any transformative benefit on its own;
2. identifying an opportunity in this unjust equilibrium, developing a social value proposition, and bringing to bear inspiration, creativity, direct action, courage and fortitude, thereby challenging the stable state's hegemony; and
3. forging a new, stable equilibrium that releases trapped potential or alleviates the suffering of the targeted group, and through imitation and the creation of a stable ecosystem around the new equilibrium ensuring a better future for the targeted group and even society at large (Marten and Osberg, 2007, p. 35).

To this list we add a focus on and connection to the institutional resources required to assist in destabilizing the "unjust equilibrium" – what writers such as DiMaggio describe as "institutional entrepreneurship" ("when organized actors with sufficient resources see in them an opportunity to realize an interest they highly value" (DiMaggio, 1988, p. 14)). Institutional entrepreneurship adds to the definition of social entrepreneurship in that it identifies a category of actor whose role is to secure, resource and scale the social value proposition created by the social entrepreneur. The social entrepreneur and institutional or system entrepreneur may be the same person, or they may be different people operating at different phases of the dynamic process through which an innovation moves from phenomenon to institution. The two roles each require a different skill set (Westley et al., 2013). Certainly the latter is highly dependent on the opportunity context.

Windows of Opportunity and Opportunity Context

For institutional/system entrepreneurs to succeed in securing, resourcing or scaling a social innovation or social value proposition, the opportunity context must be right. Opportunity may here be defined as "the likelihood that an organizational field will permit actors to identify and introduce a novel institutional combination and mobilize the resources required to make it enduring" (Dorado, 2005, p. 391). Opportunities can be defined as opaque, hazy or transparent. Opportunity contexts are hazy when there is such uncertainty or turbulence and change in the organizational/institutional field that it is hard to predict where resources will come from and how to stabilize the value proposition. Opportunity contexts are opaque when the "unjust equilibrium" is firmly established, highly integrated, and complacent. Finally opportunity contexts are transparent when multiple competitive institutional frames of reference and resources coexist for their support (Dorado, 2005, p. 394). In such contexts novel combinations and recombinations are possible and system entrepreneurs can broker new arrangements. It is in transparent opportunity contexts that social innovations are most likely to flourish. The options open to system entrepreneurs in opaque contexts are more restricted, often limited to creating small disturbances and equally small wins or at best destabilizing the status quo. In hazy opportunity contexts, system entrepreneurs need to focus on sense-making to create the shared problem definition required to stimulate new solutions (Westley et al., 2013). Opportunity contexts were key in the formation of Dutch joint stock companies, as explained in Chapter 11.

Scale/Cross-Scale Dynamics

Of course, system change involves not only time but what we refer to as cross-scale dynamics. This is best captured in the structuration theory of Giddens (1984). Giddens postulated that for analytic purposes social structure could be divided into three structures: legitimation, domination and signification. At the highest institutional scale (macro), structures of legitimation are reflected in the laws of any country, structures of domination in the economic system and political/authority system and structures of signification in the widely shared beliefs and values that define a culture. These institutions are reproduced at the level of organizations or communities (meso scale) and in the ways we interact with each other in everyday conversation (micro scale). Most social innovations are born at the interactional (micro) level, people imagining together novel social arrangements or technologies based on new ideas and social facts. As the innovations move from idea to substance and are then launched as programs, processes, products and so on, an organization or community forms to support the innovation (meso). Finally, a successful innovation at the community or organization level will encounter the broader system dynamics and institutionalized barriers (macro) of the system that created the problem in the first place. For example, someone creates a new educational program that challenges the broadly held assumptions about how children learn mathematics. The inventor may begin by forming an organization and trying to sell the program to individual schools. In the long run, however, he/she will need to take on the broader educational system (including policies and laws, economics and beliefs) if the new programming is to really achieve its objective: transforming how we believe children learn mathematics and responding with appropriate programming.

One framework based on Giddens's structuration theory is the Multi Level Perspective (MLP). MLP uses the terms "niche", "regime" and "landscape" to refer to, respectively, the micro scale where innovations are developed and nurtured, the meso scale where they are introduced to a broader organizational and inter-organizational field and the landscape scale, defined as exogamous to the institutional context of the problem regime and rarely influenced by actors in that regime. While we take some exception with the treatment of this "highest" scale, preferring to treat this scale as the broadest institutional context, we did use this framework as an initial organizing device to help visualize the unfolding of social innovation over time.

METHODOLOGY

Strictly speaking, this is not a collection of histories or historical case studies. Historians who engage with our cases may find them unsatisfactory in the traditional sense; we are following the evolution of specific ideas over time and landscape, acknowledging rather than challenging path dependence, seeking to trace the origin and direction of that path. Hence it is closer to the works of Charles Tilly, Douglass North or David Byrne, who use historical events as rudimentary laboratories to explore and propose hypotheses about important phenomena that disrupt and transform societies. We acknowledge the risk of looking back and seeing ourselves reflected in our data, but we have tried to use history as a check on our thinking, following Byrne's assertion that, "historically, we can see what happened" (1998, p. 4) to test our thinking.

This project emerged from the research team at the Waterloo Institute for Social Innovation and Resilience at the University of Waterloo in Ontario, Canada, an interdisciplinary team of graduate students, post-doctoral researchers and faculty members, including sociologists, economists, historians, planners, systems theorists, political scientists and engineers. This team co-collected, co-designed and co-developed the cases over more than two years.

Despite the number of cases contained here – eight in total – this is still very much an exploratory study, which is reflected in the case selection and development. We began by working backwards from the moment when we felt a transition had occurred; the introduction of a new law or the mass adoption of a new program. To be frank, this moment is usually one of the final stages of the transition itself. We worked backwards from that point as a group, asking two key questions. Did one or several discrete social inventions trigger this eventual transition? And, could we trace the invention's origins to a new phenomenon or combination of phenomena, as per Brian Arthur? At this early stage, we hypothesized three general categories of phenomena: Arthur's naturalistic, and also technical and social, phenomena (the former being new technological capabilities and the latter new "social facts", as per Durkheim). Over time we focused most on social phenomena, although we did not abandon naturalistic or technological phenomena and these appear in at least one case (technological most often folded into naturalistic as an expression of the former).

Not all possible cases discussed were selected for significant considera-tion; often the link between phenomenon, innovation and transition was too vague or ambiguous. This does not mean we chose the obvious stories, and in fact we sought out uncomfortable stories such as the intelligence test and derivatives market, but as we were exploring largely uncharted territory, we sought the paths that were clearer to follow and that we found most personally intriguing. We hope and anticipate that others will take up this work and discover paths we have not.

Once selected, we began not by writing cases but by mapping them visually using the presentation software Prezi (these have been inserted in image form through the book and are available online in their original dynamic form). We used a few basic framework tools to aid this process, although we deliberately sought to minimize structure at this stage of the case construction process, to leave us open to emergence. First, we employed a basic three-scale approach: landscape, regime and niche – our direct debt to MLP – to follow ideas, institutions, organizations and innovations over time. We indicated moments of definitive agency (eye), bricolage (funnel and Venn diagram) and phenomena (light bulb). Where relevant we also marked external shocks like war, and internal shifts like court cases and new laws.

These prezis formed the basis of our conversations and cases. It was through comparison that we appreciated the importance of prophetic starting conditions, the constant interplay between bricolage and the adjacent possible, and the importance of war in the modern era as a huge shock and shift in opportunity context and windows of opportunity. We also found that the MLP framework, while very useful for more technical and commercial innovations, became less useful as we expanded the problem domains. In particular, the regime space became more and more difficult to employ, and MLP frameworks for transition became less helpful. We have kept landscape and niche, both of which are used beyond MLP, as descriptive rather than explanatory categories.

The prezi comparisons informed the case writing process, where we explored in depth the role of agents and networks, the shifts in opportunity contexts, occasions of bricolage and the adjacent possible, and how prophetic starting conditions could affect the path of a phenomenon and/or its related innovation even decades later. We also explored the dark side of innovations, how attempts at social engineering, no matter how well-intentioned, can create terrible consequences for many of society's most vulnerable. What was most surprising in these cases was how similar they were to some of the more celebrated examples of social innovation – with the exception of those prophetic starting conditions that disenfranchised and disempowered the target populations.

The results of that iterative process are the cases in this book. We want to reiterate that this is an exploratory study; we sincerely hope readers will see these eight cases as a challenge. What cases have gone unexplored, what agents have been underappreciated and what phenomena still beg for attention?

BOOK OUTLINE

The book contains eight cases, three synthesis chapters and a conclusion. The three synthesis chapters focus on the themes of agency, adjacent possibles and critical transitions, and cross-scale interactions. The book is organized to intersperse these synthesis chapters with case-based chapters, but each synthesis chapter draws on the numerous chapters that are the backbone of the book. The focus of these cases is as follows:

National Parks in the United States

The American national parks system is a story of distributed networks of agents transforming how Americans saw their natural landscape from an exploitable resource to a national treasure in need of preservation and pilgrimage. The adjacent possible of the parks was a visceral experience for many early architects and adopters; they walked the American wilderness and could easily see its many splendors – then they had to strategically convince those across American society and up to the highest offices. The elective affinities of such unusual partners as railroads and conservationists and the exceptional importance of scaling, as the parks were trapped for decades as individual parks and not an effective conservation and tourism system, are key to this case.

The Intelligence Test

Different elective affinities can draw a social innovation in different directions at different times and the intelligence test provides our first example of this. In its early history, the idea of testing individuals' intelligence was attractive to proponents of eugenics, and spoke to contemporaneous concerns about the challenge of the "feebleminded". The success of the intelligence test in this domain at that time was due in no small part to the efforts of an extraordinary network of social entrepreneurs who used the opportunity of the First World War to launch intelligence testing on a mass scale. It is also interesting to see how the test bore the marks of these individuals' biases and preconceptions. In the aftermath of the Second World War, the intelligence test instead became a tool for educational and social mobility, but still carried with it some of this earlier baggage.

The Legalization of Birth Control in North America

The case of birth control is an odd one, in some ways not so much a social innovation as a social rediscovery, as a practice that had been considered relatively normal became scandalous, then illegal, before re-emerging in a modern guise. Truly this case is a demonstration of how social forces can reach a tipping point that causes a system to reconfigure into one adjacent possible and then another. In both instances, social entrepreneurs worked tirelessly to transform our understanding of reproductive technology and our views on the morality of reproduction and women's health issues, and in both cases they were aided by broader developments in the religious, scientific and economic arena. This case also provides a timely reminder of how fragile some of the freedoms and rights we take for granted truly are.

The Duty to Consult and Accommodate in Canada

This case shares a historical origin with the Indian Residential Schools (Chapter 10) – that of treaties between First Nations and the Crown. They are another reminder that social innovations may be pulled into different adjacent possibles by different elective affinities at different times.

The treaties were a form of bricolage of European and Indigenous worldviews, although the two adjacent possibles emerged at different times. The first, a wholly European view, justified residential schools as an assimilation tool; the second, a more Indigenous-informed view, sought to balance and reconcile cultures and sovereignties within Canada. Slowly, over the second half of the 20th century, social entrepreneurs, especially in the legal sector, have worked to replace the wholly European view with a more balanced perspective, and recent breakthroughs in the courts have profoundly shocked the institutional landscape of Canada, a critical transition which has yet to mature fully in its consequences.

The Internet: A Dynamic History

Although the Web is one of the most contemporary cases, intriguingly, this modern technology is powerfully shaped by the prophetic starting conditions of the 1960s, when it was first conceived. The Web was a coming together of the US Defense Department's desire to have a reliable (nuclear bomb-proof) information network after the Second World War and a group of computer scientists and programmers who were largely inspired by a Utopianism in favor of open technology and an open society. This tension between security and openness rears its head repeatedly in the Internet's development, scaling and utilization today. The shift in authority flows imagined by those early programmers has not disappeared as the network scaled to become what we now know as the Internet.

The Global Derivatives Market as Social Innovation

The derivatives case is a prime demonstration of how dependent innovations are on a convergence of factors across scales at the right time. In this case we see how academic ideas about economics, tied to a social philosophy, arose early in the 20th century but were out-competed by another adjacent possible, Keynesianism, in the immediate aftermath of World War II. It was only later in the century that a convergence of macro-economic factors, political shifts, and crucially, the emergence of new technology with the right elective affinity, allowed the derivatives market that still exists today to dominate global finance.

Indian Residential Schools

This case study is undoubtedly our darkest and most distressing example of how social innovation can have disastrous consequences. The residential schools were born out of a centuries-old European belief about the superiority of European civilization, and an insight into the power of education as a tool for assimilation. However, they only took on this role because of the steady, violent domination of Indigenous North America by two settler nations, the US and Canada. An alternative adjacent possible existed, glimpsed in some of the early treaties and in the aspirations of some early Indigenous advocates, who hoped that their people could learn from the settlers the tools needed to survive in the new landscape, while remaining part of their own culture. Instead, the social innovation was captured by a mixture of church and state forces which used them as a means to divorce Indigenous peoples from their culture, with the coercive power of the state backing them up.

Dutch Joint Stock Companies

Changes in perception are key to the story of Dutch joint stock companies, changes brought about by shifting worldviews and socio-economic conditions at multiple scales. The trigger for the innovation was the realization that the Portuguese/Spanish Empire was fallible, but only the Netherlands was able to take full advantage. This was due in part to the unique combination of urbanization, religious reformation and rebellion against Spain in the Netherlands. The combination of these variables, acting across sectors and through time and space, is essential to understanding why a small northern country was able to do what Italy and England were not.

We will conclude with a chapter summarizing our learnings from the cases and the projects and suggesting how these are useful for recognizing early social innovations with transformative promise.

REFERENCES

Arthur, W.B. (2009). *The Nature of Technology: What It Is and How It Evolves*. New York: Free Press.

Berkes, F., Colding, J. and Folke, C. (2003). *Navigating Social-Ecological Systems: Building Resilience for Complexity and Change*. Cambridge: Cambridge University Press.

Bures, R. and Kanapaux, W. (2011). Historical regimes and social indicators of resilience in an urban system: the case of Charleston, South Carolina. *Ecology and Society*, **16**(4), 16.

Byrne, D. (1998). *Complexity Theory and the Social Sciences: An Introduction.* London: Routledge.

DiMaggio, P. (1988). Interest and agency in institutional theory. In L.G. Zucker (ed.), *Institutional Patterns of Organizations: Culture and Environment.* Cambridge, MA: Ballinger, pp. 3–21.

Dorado, S. (2005). Institutional entrepreneurship, partaking and convening. *Organizational Studies*, **26**(3), 385–414.

Durkheim, E. (2014 [1938]). *The Rules of Sociological Method.* New York: Free Press.

Geels, F.W. (2006). Major system change through stepwise reconfiguration: a multi-level analysis of the transformation of American factory production (1850–1930). *Technology in Society*, **28**(4), 445–76.

Geels, F.W. and Schot, J. (2007). Typology of sociotechnical transition pathways. *Research Policy*, **36**(3), 399–417.

Giddens, A. (1984). *The Constitution of Society: Outline of the Theory of Structuration.* Cambridge: Polity Press.

Gunderson, L.H., Holling, C.S. and Light, S.S. (1995). *Barriers and Bridges to Renewal of Ecosystems and Institutions.* New York: Columbia University Press.

Gunderson, L.H. and Holling, C.S. (2002). *Panarchy: Understanding Transformations in Human and Ecological Systems.* Washington, DC: Island Press.

Johnson, S. (2010). *Where Good Ideas Come From: The Natural History of Innovation.* New York: Riverhead Books.

Kanter, R.M. (1984). *The Change Masters.* New York: Touchstone.

Kauffman, S. (2000). *Investigations.* Oxford: Oxford University Press.

Marten, R. and Osberg, S. (2007). Social entrepreneurship, the case for definition. *Stanford Social Innovation Review*, Spring, 28–39.

McElroy, M.W. (2002). Social innovation capital. *Journal of Intellectual Capital*, **3**(1), 30–39.

Mulgan, G. (2006). The process of social innovation. *Innovations*, **1**(2), Spring, 145–62.

Mumford, M.D. (2002). Social innovation: ten cases from Benjamin Franklin. *Creative Research Journal*, **14**(2), 253–66.

Mumford, M.D. and Moertl, P. (2003). Cases of social innovation: lessons from two innovations in the 20th century. *Creative Research Journal*, **15**(2,3), 261–6.

Nonaka, T. (1995). *The Knowledge-Creating Company: How Japanese Companies Create the Dynamics of Innovation.* New York: Oxford University Press.

Pascale, R.T. (1984). Perspectives on strategy: the real story behind Honda's success. *California Management Review*, **26**(3), Spring, 47–72.

Pol, E. and Ville, S. (2009). Social innovation: buzz word or enduring term? *The Journal of Socio-Economics*, **38**(6), 878–85.

Quinn, J.B. (1985). Managing innovation: controlled chaos. *Harvard Business Review*, **63**, May–June, 73–84.

Thagard, P. (2012). *The Cognitive Science of Science: Explanation, Discovery, and Conceptual Change.* Cambridge, MA: MIT Press.

Van den Ende, J. and Kemp, R. (1999). Technological transformations in history: how the computer regime grew out of existing computing regimes. *Research Policy*, **28**, 833–51.

Van Driel, H. and Schot, J. (2005). Radical innovation as a multi-level process: introducing floating grain elevators in the port of Rotterdam. *Technology and Culture*, **46**(1), 51–76.

Walker, B., Holling, C.S., Carpenter, S.R. and Kinzig, A. (2004). Resilience, adaptability and transformability in social–ecological systems. *Ecology and Society*, **9**(2), 5.

Ward, F. (1903). *Pure Sociology: A Treatise on the Origin and Spontaneous Development of Society*. New York: Macmillan Books.

Weber, M. (1922). *Wirtschaft und Gesellschaft*. Tübingen: Mohr.

Weber, M. (1992). *Economy and Society: An Outline of Interpretive Sociology*. Berkeley, CA: University of California Press.

Westley, F., Tjörnbo, O., Olsson, P., Folke, C., Crona, B., Schultz, L. and Orijan Bodin, O. (2013). A theory of transformative agency in linked social-ecological systems. *Ecology and Society*, **18**(3), 27.

Westley, F., Olsson, P., Folke, C., Homer-Dixon, T., Vredenburg, H., Loorbach, D., Thompson, J., Nilsson, M., Lambin, E., Sendzimir, J., Banerjee, B., Galaz, V. and van der Leeuw, S. (2011). Tipping toward sustainability: emerging pathways of transformation. *AMBIO*, **40**(7), 762–80.

Westley, F.R., Zimmerman, B. and Patton, M.Q. (2006). *Getting to Maybe: How the World is Changed*. Toronto: Random House Canada.

2. National parks in the United States

Nino Antadze

INTRODUCTION

Regarded as "America's best idea" (Keiter, 2013, p. 261; Duncan, 2009), national parks evoke images of vast scenic beauty – the place where man can meet wild nature (Keiter, 2013). As naturalistic phenomena, the areas that are currently national parks have existed for thousands of years. At the end of the 19th century and start of the 20th, with increased urbanization, industrialization and population expansion, the idea of preserving nature gained momentum. This paradoxical historical coincidence has its explanation: the idea of national parks was nurtured by individuals and influenced by larger historical developments. Starting in the early 19th century, the context within which pristine wilderness was viewed changed rapidly. America's active westward expansion and increased rate of industrialization and urbanization revealed a sharp contrast between the untouched natural landscape and the one explored by man. National parks (or the areas that would later become national parks) turned into social phenomena as soon as they, as naturalistic phenomena, were acknowledged and appreciated.

The literary and intellectual movements of the 19th century, the emergence of science, and the political process of colonization created a gravitational field within which the national park idea gradually gained its present shape and content. Altruistic sentiments and political and economic interests merged, leading to the establishment of the first national park in 1872. In the next decades, the number of national parks drastically increased and in 1916 the National Parks Service was created (see Figure 2.1). This case study explores how historical developments, coupled with the efforts of individuals, turned the national parks idea into an institutionalized reality.

A NEW IDEA

In 1864, as the country was torn apart by the Civil War, a senator from California, John Conness, introduced a bill in the Senate chamber. The

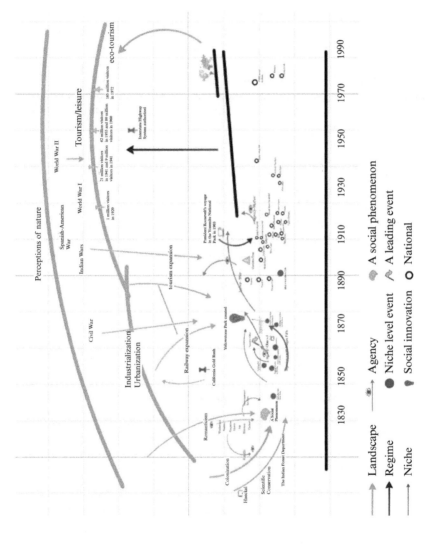

Figure 2.1   The emergence and maturation of national parks as a social innovation

bill offered something unprecedented: to preserve a large area of land for the enjoyment of everyone. Without much deliberation or questioning, the Senate passed the proposed bill. It was then also passed by the House and signed by President Abraham Lincoln. Thus beautiful Yosemite Valley and the Mariposa Grove of Big Trees were donated to the state of California for preservation and public use (Duncan, 2009).

This initiative, however, did not belong to Senator Conness. The idea of having land set aside for preservation and public enjoyment had been nurtured over many years. The first travelers to the area were stunned by the breathtaking beauty of the Yosemite Valley. Word spread about Yosemite's powerful waterfalls, high cliffs and giant trees. Artists and photographers came to witness firsthand the beauty of Yosemite Valley and to depict it in their paintings and photos (Duncan, 2009). The first recorded idea of a national park belonged to artist George Catlin (Jones, 2012) who described it as a place "containing man and beast, in all the wild and freshness of their nature's beauty" (Duncan, 2009, p. 11). In 1832, after studying and observing the Indians and their environment on the Great Plains in South Dakota, Catlin was struck by the idea that this pristine wilderness, including the native Indians and their way of living, could disappear forever (Duncan, 2009; Miles, 1995; Jones, 2012): a powerful glimpse of an adjacent possible. Herein lay the seed of a new social phenomenon that sought to conserve nature as pristine.

DIVE 1: AN IDEA IS GESTATED

Three major influences shaped the idea of national parks as we know it today: literary and intellectual movements of the first half of the 19th century, scientific advancements of the time, and colonization. Each had its role in creating both the social phenomenon of conservation that underpins the parks and the basin of attraction within which the idea of national parks was forged.

Literary and Intellectual Influences

Catlin's ideas and aspiration to preserve natural beauty in the face of destructive human activities fall within the broader literary and intellectual movements of that time. Romanticism and romantic environmentalism, which originated in Europe at the end of the 18th century and reached their climax in 1800–1850, were partly a reaction to the industrial revolution and scientific rationalization of nature. As Jones notes, romanticism "advanced the worship of the wild" (2012, p. 34). This was most visible in England – both a cradle of industrialization and the birthplace of the strongest opposition to it. Rapid industrialization and urbanization in the 19th century transformed not only towns, but also the quiet English countryside. These changes fueled negative reactions, especially within artistic circles (Guha, 2000). Among the poets, William Wordsworth voiced the strongest opposition:

> For I have learned
> To look on nature, not as in the hour
> Of thoughtless youth; but hearing oftentimes
> The still, sad music of humanity. (Wordsworth, 1985, p. 37)

Wordsworth's poetic sentiments were echoed by John Ruskin, an artist, art critic, art patron and influential thinker. Ruskin wrote that every river in England was polluted and turned "into a common sewer, so that you cannot so much as baptize an English baby but with filth, unless you hold its face out in the rain, and even that falls dirty" (as cited in Guha, 2000, p. 13). He believed that modern man had desacralized nature by viewing and treating it only as a source of raw material and failing to find the divinity in it that pre-modern man had seen (Guha, 2000).

Active environmentalists of this time were William Morris (poet, architect, designer, socialist) and Edward Carpenter (mathematician and priest). Ruskin's and Carpenter's writings influenced Mahatma Gandhi, as he wrote in his book *Indian Home Rule* (Guha, 2000). Gandhi rejected industrialization as a future option for India and noted that "the world has enough for everybody's need, but not enough for one person's greed" (as cited in Guha, 2000, p. 22). The writings of Wordsworth, Ruskin, Morris and Carpenter inspired the establishment of several environmental societies in the late 19th century, including conservation societies (Guha, 2000).

In addition to the intellectual influence of romanticism, powerful voices were raised in the United States. One of them was George Perkin Marsh, a scholar and diplomat from Vermont, whose 1864 book *Man and Nature: or, Physical Geography as Modified by Human Action* became an international bestseller. Marsh "was a lonely voice" who warned about the destructive force of human activities and careless growth (Cronon, 2000, p. x), noting that "man is everywhere a disturbing agent. Wherever he plants his foot, the harmonies of nature are turned to discords" (Marsh, 1864, p. 36). He argued that the damage caused by men is impossible to predict or accurately evaluate, as our understanding of the complex natural environment is limited: "The equation of animal and vegetable life is too complicated a problem for human intelligence to solve, and we can never know how wide a circle of disturbance we produce in the harmonies of nature when we throw the smallest pebble into the ocean of organic life" (Marsh, 1864, p. 103).

Marsh's analysis was based on his study of the impact that environmental degradation and, particularly, deforestation had on the ancient civilizations of Greece and Rome. He warned that at the present rate of environmental degradation, the United States could experience the same bitter results as those ancient civilizations, but he remained optimistic about the possibility of reversing the trend (Cronon, 2000). Marsh's insights and powerful vision were the result of his multifaceted experiences and knowledge. A native of Vermont, he served as a member of the House of Representatives and an ambassador to Turkey and Italy, traveled extensively around the world and spoke numerous languages. Marsh actively advocated for state ownership of important resources (Cronon, 2000) (see Figure 2.2).

Other literary voices advancing national environmental thinking were those of Henry David Thoreau and Ralph Waldo Emerson. Both denounced the notion of nature as a source of material well-being and a major target for exploitation. Emerson saw nature as "the source and salvation of the human spirit" (Scheuering, 2004), and Thoreau wrote "in wilderness is the preservation of the world" (as cited in Scheuering, 2004, p. xviii). As

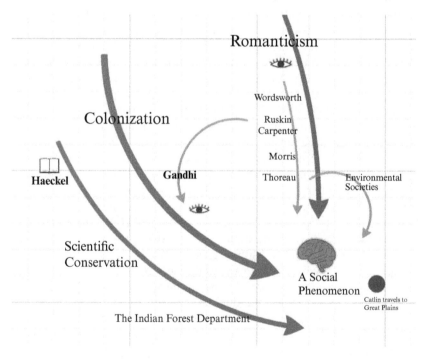

Figure 2.2   Dive 1: birth of the idea

important and influential as the writings of Marsh, Thoreau and Emerson were, they did not articulate a clear conservation policy (Scheuering, 2004). It was John Muir whose ideas launched the conservation movement in the United States (see Box 2.1). John Muir, a distinguished conservation activist, wilderness enthusiast, writer and philosopher, wrote:

> Thousands of tired, nerve-shaken, over-civilized people are beginning to find out that going to the mountains is going home; that wildness is necessity; that mountain parks and reservations are useful not only as fountains of timber and irrigating rivers, but as fountains of life (Muir, 1997, p. 721).

> God never made an ugly landscape. All that sun shines on is beautiful, so long as it is wild (as cited in Browning, 1988, p. 58).

> God has cared for these trees, saved them from drought, disease, avalanches, and a thousand tempests and floods. But he cannot save them from fools (Muir, 1997, p. 720).

Scientific Movement and Colonization

The 19th century saw unprecedented advances in science; science gained more popularity and prestige, and scientists became influential public figures. These processes indirectly influenced the promotion of the national parks idea. From the late 18th century, scientists started to explore the links between deforestation, soil erosion and drought (Guha, 2000). In 1866, German scientist Ernst Haeckel first introduced the term "ecology" in his book *General Morphology*. At the same time, the scientific conservation

---

BOX 2.1 PEOPLE BEHIND THE HISTORICAL EVENTS: JOHN MUIR

John Muir, the son of a Scottish émigré who spent his childhood doing hard labor on a Wisconsin farm, became one of the most passionate advocates of nature conservation. Muir was instrumental in promoting the idea of national parks through his writings. His prose was descriptive, eloquent and alive with the wonders of nature so much admired by the author (Sax 1976 [2013]). Muir's essays and books undoubtedly influenced public opinion and that of politicians. He worked together with the editor of *The Century*, Robert Johnson, to lobby for the creation of Yosemite National Park in 1890 (Gifford, 1992). President Theodore Roosevelt's three-day journey in the Yosemite National Park is regarded as a turning point in conservation history. It was John Muir who hosted the President in the open air of the Yosemite Valley (Gifford, 1992). The campsite conversations with Muir made a profound impression on Theodore Roosevelt, whose contribution to nature conservation has probably not been matched by any other President of the United States (see Figure 2.4).

movement was gaining momentum. For example, ideas about the limits of natural resources were often disseminated by scientists and botanists employed by large trade companies such as the French Compagnie des Indes and the Dutch and English East India Companies (Adams and Mulligan, 2012). Large, powerful institutions were established by scientists (involving irrigation engineers, soil conversationalists and wildlife managers) in the European colonies of Asia and Africa; there state systems were allowed to exercise scientific conservation unconstrained by parliaments, a free press, or the practice of democracy more generally (Guha, 2000) (see Figure 2.2). The institutionalization of nature protection was led by the colonial metropole through bureaucratic and legislative structures in the colonized territories. For example, during the 19th century, the Indian Forest Service was established and conservation legislation was adopted in South Africa (Adams and Mulligan, 2012).

The close affiliation of the spread of national parks with colonization is well illustrated by the following example. The first international environmental conference was held in 1900 in London and was dedicated to the protection of wildlife in Africa. There were no Africans present. The delegates were -foreign ministers of the colonial powers that controlled the continent: France, Germany, Belgium, Italy, Spain, Portugal and Great Britain (Guha, 2000). Soon after, the first multinational conservation society was established, called "Society for the preservation of the fauna of the Empire".[1] With colonization, the boundaries of the known world no longer existed. Resources beyond the frontier were now within reach, within the boundaries of the known and therefore could not be conceptualized as "unlimited" (Jones, 2012). It was also true that the destruction of wilderness and depletion of valuable natural resources was most visible and took place most quickly in the colonies. The establishment of national parks throughout the world was an attempt "to incorporate certain forms of valued nature into schemes of national or imperial development" (Jones, 2012, p. 8). However, the ideology that sought to preserve pristine and exotic wilderness was based on Eurocentric values. In this vision of nature preservation, aboriginal communities were ignored. This was the global trend employed by colonizing powers starting in North America and ending in New Zealand. The criticism of the preservation ideology imposed by the colonial metropole includes the initial idea of national parks as well. As Adams and Mulligan note:

> the language of biodiversity enshrined in the Conservation of Biological Diversity has come to drive a programme of action based upon the identification and protection of critical biodiverse areas – a "protected area" strategy based largely upon a US model of national parks and wilderness reserves. This

tradition tends to foster a conceptual separation between humans and nature, and between nature and culture, which creates both moral and practical dilemmas, especially in poor countries where human needs cannot be set aside in pursuing the "intrinsic" rights of nature. (2012, p. 10)

Adams describes the way the colonial mind perceived and portrayed nature in former colonial territories: since nature was always viewed as separate from human life, the colonial mind preferred "centralized and formalized ways of knowing nature over localized and informal ways" (2012, pp. 42–3) and established control over nature through bureaucratic apparatus.

Within the context of literary and intellectual movements of the 19th century, advancements in scientific thought, and the forceful colonization of previously unknown lands, the national parks idea emerged, developed and was finally made law. Thus, the establishment of Yellowstone Park in 1872 was not only fueled by local personal, commercial and political interests, but was also the result of a larger historical context, including the new social phenomenon of conservation of pristine wilderness.

SOCIAL INNOVATION

It took exactly 40 years for Catlin's daring idea to become a reality. In 1872, President Ulysses S. Grant signed a bill to create the first national park in the world: Yellowstone Park. In contrast to Yosemite, Yellowstone was not managed at the state level, but federally (Duncan, 2009). The establishment of Yellowstone Park ensured that this natural phenomenon would remain intact, protected from the rapid exploitation and extraction typical in the west during the Gilded Age (Sellars, 1997).

The national park idea may well have become one of the most popular and widely copied social innovations of its kind. The novelty was not only in the desire to preserve wilderness because of its intrinsic value, but also in the notion that the enjoyment of wilderness should be universally available. The national park idea encompassed a not-yet-articulated notion of social justice: parks were to be accessible to everybody, not only noblemen and the privileged (Duncan, 2009). "This democratic rationale distinguished the national park from the preserves of Old Europe, whose ornamental lakes and corralled environmental resources were tied to aristocratic purse strings" (Jones, 2012, p. 35). However, assigning the civic end of public leisure to green spaces was not new. By this time, many European cities had already set aside parks for public enjoyment (Jones, 2012). Nevertheless, the national parks that originated in the United States bore that country's particular "blend of natural iconography and democratic zeal" (Jones,

2012, p. 36). To better understand the latter, it is important to recognize that the idea of national parks also touched the patriotic sentiments of the relatively young nation. Some Americans viewed national parks as a way for them to position themselves as equals to the Old World, not in terms of ancient cultural monuments and historical sites, but of natural monuments of stunning beauty (Jones, 2012; Duncan, 2009).

DIVE 2: THE ESTABLISHMENT OF YELLOWSTONE NATIONAL PARK – PUTTING THE PIECES TOGETHER

The debate continues as to who first proposed converting the Yellowstone area into a national park. As early as 1868, Montana Territorial Governor Thomas Francis Meagher publicly suggested that the region should be under state protection. A similar suggestion is assigned to David Folsom, who together with Charles Cook and William Peterson explored the Yellowstone region in 1869 and produced the first careful survey of the area (Haines, 1996; Dilsaver and Wyckoff, 2005). Cook later recalled:

> The night before we came to this junction we camped a little way up the Firehole River. We had decided to make that the last camp on our exploration and to follow the Firehole down to the Madison River and home.
> In the camp that night we were talking over the great array of natural marvels we had seen and the scenic beauty of the area we had traversed.
> Peterson remarked that probably it would not be long before settlers and prospectors began coming into the district and taking up land around the canyons and the geysers, and that it would soon be all in private hands.
> I said that I thought the place was too big to be all taken up, but that, anyway, something ought to be done to keep the settlers out, so that everyone who wanted to, in future years, could travel through as freely and enjoy the region as we had.
> Then Folsom said: "The Government ought not to allow anyone to locate here at all."
> "That's right," I said, "It ought to be kept for the public some way."
> None of us definitely suggested the idea of a national park. National parks were unknown then, but we knew that as soon as the wonderful character of the country was generally known outside, there would be plenty of people hurrying in to get possession, unless something was done. (Haines, 1996, p. 103)

In 1870–71, Montana lawyer and writer Cornelius Hedges seemed to be gravitating towards the idea of creating a state park by proposing that the Territory of Montana should be put under protection similar to that of Yosemite Park (Haines, 1996). The last documented version of the proposal to create a national park appears in a personal communication to Dr Hayden from the Northern Pacific Railway Company, signed by A.B. Nettleton:

> Dear Doctor:
> Judge Kelley has made a suggestion which strikes me as being an excellent one, viz.: Let Congress pass a bill reserving the Great Geyser Basin as a public park forever – just as it has reserved that far inferior wonder the Yosemite Valley and big trees. If you approve this would such a recommendation be appropriate in your official report? (Haines, 1996, p. 155)

Not only did Hayden approve it, he became one of the most active advocates of creating the Yellowstone National Park.

The creation of Yosemite Park served as an experiment, testing and grounding an innovative idea. Not only did Hedges use Yosemite Park as an example to convince Hayden to support the preservation of what would later become the Yellowstone National Park, but Frederick Law Olmsted also based his Preliminary Report, outlining the theoretically justified rationale behind the need to create federally protected areas, on the case of Yosemite Park (see Box 2.2). Later on, the legislation establishing Yellowstone National Park was largely based on the bill that created Yosemite Park in 1864.

After the Civil War, the US government expressed interest in exploring the natural resources available in the western territories of the country. This interest was mainly dictated by the economic hardship of the post-Civil War period. By this time, it was already known that Yellowstone offered stunning scenery and could potentially become a major tourism destination. However, the US government wanted to see if Yellowstone could serve not merely as a tourism destination, but also as a source of valuable natural resources. In 1871 funds were designated to support an expedition that would document the natural resources in the west, particularly on the route of the transcontinental railroad that was under construction. The first transcontinental linkage, joining the tracks of the Central Pacific and Union Pacific railroads at Promontory Point, Utah, was completed two years prior to the 1871 expedition, paving the way for a more rapid and intensive development of the far west (Merrill, 1999). The 1871 expedition, led by Dr Ferdinand Hayden, the head of the US Geological and Geographical Survey of the Territories, was the first scientific expedition that studied and documented the territory of the present Yellowstone National Park (McNamara, 2014; Merrill, 1999).

The exploration of the west and the expansion of the railway network were intertwined. By 1871, railroad companies had become powerful empires and major land-administration agencies. During the period 1862–71, Congress granted about 174 million acres of public land to

BOX 2.2   PEOPLE BEHIND THE HISTORICAL EVENTS:
FREDERICK LAW OLMSTED

Olmsted, a wealthy, well-connected, intelligent gentleman, was a generator of ideas and a man capable of converting those ideas into political action (Sax, 1976 [2013]). He was a central figure behind establishing numerous city parks and park systems, including Central Park in New York City. Olmsted was not only a pioneer of landscape architecture, but also a thinker who formulated the philosophy behind national parks. His report that discussed the concept of national parks (especially Yosemite Park) was written in 1864, only to be lost and rediscovered after 87 years. In this report, Olmsted advocated that public green space should be equally accessible to everybody (Sax, 1976 [2013]). As Duncan (2009, p. 15) explains, "Olmsted had, in essence, delivered his own combination of a Declaration of Independence and a Constitution for the park idea – a lofty statement of principles coupled with the nuts and bolts of how to put them into action". Thus, Olmsted was not only a theoretician behind the national parks movement, but also a talented promoter of his ideas. His dashing public personality, social connections, and reputation as a high caliber professional helped Olmsted to access those in power and actively promote his vision of national parks. As Elizabeth Stevenson wrote (1977, p. xi),

> Olmsted is also very much a man of today. He was a maker and demonstrator of ideas which are today visible, present, and potent, even to the point of irritation and rejection by some, as well as advocacy by others. He is a dual presence: in ideas and in created places. These places demonstrate to us that he was also an artist in embodying his ideas.

(See Figure 2.3.)

construct transcontinental railroads. The Northern Pacific Railroad, which aimed to build a railroad line connecting Chicago to the west coast, actively promoted Yellowstone as a place of spectacular beauty (Merrill, 1999). The Northern Pacific adopted Judge Kelley's suggestion to protect the Yellowstone area as a company policy and started to actively promote it (Haines, 1996). This is not as surprising an elective affinity as first glance may suggest. The main financial backer of the Northern Pacific, Jay Cooke, famously publicized Yellowstone as "America's Switzerland", claiming that instead of traveling to Europe to see beautiful natural scenery, Americans would soon travel to the west, thus urging investors to fund the western line construction. The Northern Pacific was interested in seeing the results of Hayden's expedition. The company gave Hayden cheap rates and helped transport his horses and supplies. In return, he planned to survey the route for potential rail beds (Merrill, 1999).

The expedition that Hayden led in 1871 to explore the territory of the present Yellowstone National Park was one of the largest endeavors of its kind, with a budget of $40 000. The team of 32 people included a geologist, a topographer, a mineralogist, a zoologist, an ornithologist, an agricultural statistician, an entomologist, a physician, a support staff of drivers, waiters, cooks, general assistants, hunters and guides, a wagon master, a secretary, as well as painter Thomas Moran and photographer William Henry Jackson (McNamara, 2014).

After the expedition, Hayden prepared a 500-page report for Congress with detailed accounts of the expedition's findings. Moran produced paintings of Yellowstone scenery and Jackson brought back photographs (McNamara, 2014). The expedition produced a vast amount of material for scientific investigation: "forty-five large boxes containing more than one thousand specimens of minerals (including specimens from the hot springs), more than six hundred specimens of rocks, large numbers of mammal and bird skins, eggs, and other items had been sent during the expedition to the Smithsonian" (Merrill, 1999, p. 203) (see Figure 2.3). After receiving a letter from the Northern Pacific with the suggestion to set aside the area of Yellowstone as a national park, Hayden became one of the most active advocates of this idea (Merrill, 1999).

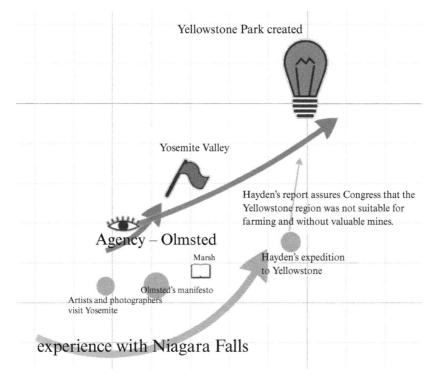

Figure 2.3   Dive 2: the establishment of Yellowstone National Park

The draft bill was prepared based on the Yosemite model and intro-duced in both houses of Congress on 18 December 1871. Hayden and his supporters actively lobbied members of Congress to create a national park. With enthusiasm, energy and a thorough knowledge of the subject, Hayden communicated to congressmen the importance of preserving the Valley of the Upper Yellowstone. Jackson's impressive photographs and Moran's watercolors proved to be indispensable to this process (Merrill, 1999). Hayden argued that aside from the unique scenery and geological features of the area, the entire Yellowstone would not be suitable for agricultural or mining purposes because of its altitude and geography. He advocated dedicating this land "as a pleasure ground for the benefit and enjoyment of the people" and if Congress would not pass the corresponding bill, Hayden warned that:

> persons are now waiting for the spring to open to enter in and take possession of these remarkable curiosities, to make merchandise of these beautiful specimens, to fence in these rare wonders, so as to charge visitors a fee, as it is now done at Niagara Falls, for the sight of that which ought to be as free as the air or water. (Merrill, 1999, p. 208)

The bill did not encounter much opposition, although there was an attempt to send it back to the Committee of Public Lands and the Committee on Territories. However, the representative Henry Dawes inter-vened. Dawes was one of the most influential members of the House at the time, and, more importantly, was a friend of Hayden and shared his strong conservation convictions. Dawes commented on the proposed legislation:

> This bill follows the analogy of the bill passed by Congress six or eight years ago, setting apart the Yosemite Valley . . . with this difference: that bill granted to the State of California the jurisdiction over the land beyond the control of the United States. This bill reserves the control over the land . . . to the United States . . . it will infringe upon no vested rights . . . treads upon no rights of the settler . . . and it received the urgent and ardent support of the legislature of that Territory [Montana]. (Haines, 1996, p. 171)

Yellowstone National Park's establishment did not unfold without opposition. The local residents of the area were against imposing strict restriction on economic development and settlements as they feared that these regulations would hinder the economic prosperity of the region. These groups advocated reducing the size of the park and allowing mining, hunting and logging activities. The opponents of the park were active and insistent. For example, Montana's Congressional representatives intro-duced bills to revoke the park's designation into Congress every season for twenty years (Wuerthner, 2007).

Yellowstone's creation was not solely guided by altruistic motives. A combination of forces triggered it. Aside from individuals hoping to preserve the natural wonders, the idea of creating a national park was also promoted by a powerful corporation with radically different interests. The Northern Pacific Railroad Company intended to monopolize the tourist traffic and trade corridors in the area. The fact that huge areas of land would be under federal control and free from private claims would limit competition and help the Northern Pacific establish its monopoly across the southern Montana Territory. However, in mid-1880 Congress denounced proposals by railroad and mining companies to construct a railway through the northern part of Yellowstone and reduce the area of the park (Sellars, 1997).

The other factor that contributed to realizing the national park idea was Niagara Falls' unfortunate transformation into a crowded and mismanaged tourist destination. At the beginning of the 19th century, the land around the Falls began to be privatized and by the mid-century practically all the land surrounding Niagara Falls was privately owned. Landowners changed the landscape based on their own interests and needs, with no consideration for the beautiful scenery. With the influx of tourists, everybody – landowners, self-appointed guides, drivers, vendors – tried to make money. By the 1860s it was impossible to view the falls without paying an entry fee to a landowner (Sax, 1976 [2013]) (see Figure 2.3).

BEING TRAPPED

As innovative as it was, the establishment of the Yellowstone National Park did not bring about the widespread adoption of national parks. As Sellars explains, "Yellowstone came close to becoming a historical anomaly rather than a trendsetter in public land policy" (1997, p. 11). Within the next three decades only four large national parks were created (Sellars, 1997). Although the national parks idea as social innovation did come into being, it did not mature and was not able to bring about a systemic change. Instead it seemed that this novel idea got trapped and could not develop further.

The reasons for being trapped, as well as the factors that helped to overcome this trap, were mostly contextual: Yellowstone National Park was created while Indian wars raged on the northern plains, making it an unwelcoming tourist destination. When the Indian wars ended and white settlements started to expand rapidly to the west, the inflow of capital and people gave new impetus to the rise of national parks as tourist destinations (Sellars, 1997). Broader historical developments gradually created conditions that encouraged the spread of national parks. Just as with any war, the Civil War opened up new opportunities and brought social transformations that changed the economic and social landscape of the country. The victorious North experienced an unprecedented immigration influx, emergence of the new forms of industrial organization, a manufacturing boom, and the construction of new railway networks. The post-Civil War period gave birth to the urban middle and upper classes, professionals and white-collar wage-earner workers (Foner, 1988), who were interested in traveling for pleasure, thus turning national parks into popular leisure destinations. Alongside the old commercial elite, a new social class of industrialists and railway entrepreneurs was born (Foner, 1988). As mentioned above, the latter played an important role in advocating for and promoting the national parks idea (see Figure 2.4).

Another important development that contributed to overcoming the trap unfolded on the legislative arena. In 1906 Congress passed the Antiquities Act that enabled the creation of "national monuments". According to the

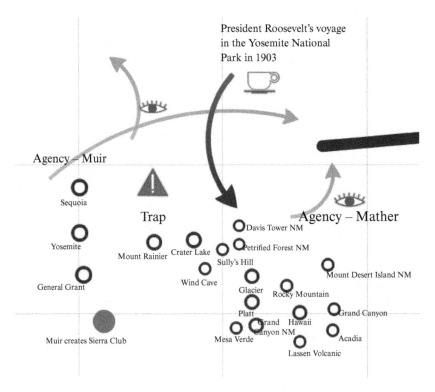

Figure 2.4   People behind the events: being trapped

Act, the status of "national monument" could be given by the President to an area of historic, prehistoric or scientific importance, without congressional authorization. During the period 1906–1908, five national monuments were established: Devils Tower, Chaco Canyon, Muir Woods, Mount Olympus and Grand Canyon. Over time, national monuments would be added to the national parks system (Sellars, 1997). These developments took place during the administration of President Theodore Roosevelt and represented the strong political support for the revived conservation movement and expansion of the emerging national parks system. As a result, beginning in 1903 the idea of national parks got second wind and between 1903 and 1916 nine national parks were established (Sellars, 1997).

Although the historical and legislative contexts were crucial in overcoming the trap and moving forward, micro-level developments were also important. The establishment of the first national parks was an important milestone for the emerging environmental movement of the 19th century. A new discourse began about the necessity of environmental protection and wise use of resources (contrary to the Exploitative Capitalist Paradigm of the time), which introduced the practice of outdoor recreation, and mobilized public and political resources to influence policy developments (Taylor, 2000). At the same time, more formalized environmental groups were founded, such as the Appalachian Mountain Club and the Sierra Club (Taylor, 2000). Taylor (2000) characterizes this period as the transition from the Pre-Movement phase to the better-mobilized and developed Early Environmental Movement period. Thus the discontinuity after the establishment of the Yellowstone National Park can also be related to the birth of the Early Environmental Movement, when actors started first to formulate and then to advocate for institutional changes. In order to do so, they needed to engage in sense-making, as the dominant rules, practices and values started to lose legitimacy and the formulation of new ones became necessary in order to overcome a possible "meaning vacuum" (Westley et al., 2013).

COMING OF AGE

The actual protection and management of the national monuments and natural parks raised concerns. The regulations for parks, as well as administrative and leadership responsibilities varied. With the establishment of more and more national parks and monuments, a certain "system" of national parks and monuments developed, but it lacked coordination or systematic management (Miles, 1995). In 1910, a campaign advocating for the establishment of a national parks bureau started. The campaign participants called for the efficient, effective and businesslike management of the existing national parks (Sellars, 1997). The proponents of creating a central agency called for improvements to the parks' infrastructure (for tourism development), better administrative practices, and coordinated leadership. As described, Stephen Mather played a central role in these events (see Box 2.3). The campaign proved to be successful and in 1916 Congress created the National Park Service by enacting the National Parks Service Act (Sellars, 1997).

The newly formed National Parks Service struggled to impose a common conceptual and administrative system over the existing 43 national parks and monuments. In the meantime, the American public increasingly traveled and took their vacations in national parks. Those involved in the management of the existing national parks and monuments started to realize that a new organization was needed to study and develop a management system for the national parks and monuments (Miles, 1995). Another

---

BOX 2.3 PEOPLE BEHIND THE HISTORICAL EVENTS: STEPHEN MATHER

Stephen Mather was a man of business and, as we would say today, a brilliant advertising executive. His work for Pacific Coast Borax Company in the 1890s was regarded as very successful (Strong, 1988). Later, together with his friend, Mather established his own borax distribution company. The business flourished and by 1914 Mather was a self-made millionaire (Sax, 1976 [2013]; Strong, 1988). Having acquired financial security from his successful business, Mather moved his attention to other projects he was interested in pursuing. One of his long-time interests was nature conservation. After traveling to Europe at the beginning of the 20th century, Mather became very impressed by Europe's parklands and protected areas. Later he became a friend of John Muir and an active member of the Sierra Club – an organization established by Muir. With his flair for business, Mather soon noticed that the existing national parks were very poorly managed – they lacked an administrative system and leadership. Mather became an active lobbyist for the establishment of the agency that would manage national parks throughout the country. Mather set out for the task of acquiring support of politicians and businesspeople, while conducting a lavish publicity campaign (e.g. the April 1916 issue of *National Geographic* was fully dedicated to the national parks). He often spent his own money without reservation. In order to gain support from congressmen, in 1915 Mather organized a mountain trip to Northern Sierra Nevada. He carefully selected guests and made sure they enjoyed the trip. Mather hired a Chinese cook to travel with them and did not spare money to make the trip unforgettable. The costs were covered from Mather's own pocket. The trip served the aim that Mather envisioned and the next year Congress approved purchase of the private tracks in the Giant Forest (Strong, 1988). In 1916 the National Parks Service was created and Mather was appointed its first director (Sax 1976 [2013]) (see Figure 2.4).

development also encouraged the creation of the new organization: the emerging conservation movement started to develop in two directions. The first direction called for "conservation" of natural resources for human use and consumption, while the other advocated the "preservation" of special resources simply because of their beauty and intrinsic value. The latter movement, led by the famous John Muir, implied that such special resources should be preserved in parks. Thus, "a need emerged for a powerful voice raised specifically for national parks" (Miles, 1995, p. 9). Such an organization, the National Parks Association (NPA), was created in 1919. NPA had three main objectives: to advance the educational agenda, to develop a rational and complete system of national parks, and to encourage scientific research and economic development (mainly to support tourism) within the parks (Miles, 1995).

With the creation of the National Parks Service and later the National Parks Association, national parks became not only one of the most widely adopted social innovations, but also one thoroughly institutionalized and deeply rooted in American society. The idea of preserving certain areas of land moved beyond US borders. In 1972, the Convention concerning the Protection of the World Cultural and Natural Heritage was adopted to recognize, protect and preserve cultural and natural sites of exceptional importance. Interestingly, the idea of merging the protection of both cultural and natural sites was initiated by the US and later supported by the International Union for Conservation of Nature (IUCN) (UNESCO, 2012). According to the Convention, natural heritage includes (Article 2):

> **natural features** consisting of physical and biological formations or groups of such formations, which are of outstanding universal value from the aesthetic or scientific point of view;
> **geological and physiographical formations** and precisely delineated areas which constitute the habitat of threatened species of animals and plants of outstanding universal value from the point of view of science or conservation;
> **natural sites** or precisely delineated natural areas of outstanding universal value from the point of view of science, conservation or natural beauty.

ALTERING THE LANDSCAPE

At the macro level, the changes in leisure practices during the last century can, to some extent, be attributed to the creation of national parks. Traveling and taking vacations in national parks became one of the favorite pastimes of Americans in the late 19th century. In fact, from their very inception, national parks were regarded as "pleasure grounds" or "public parks" that would be accessible to everybody, regardless of differences in

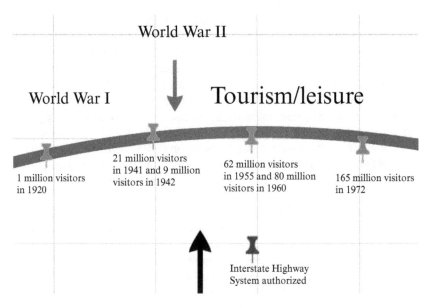

Figure 2.5   Landscape changes – tourism expansion in national parks

economic or social position (Keiter, 2013). Yet, given the financial and time expenditures required to travel by rail, only the wealthy could afford to visit the western national parks. With the end of World War II, the situation changed drastically. Post-war population growth, the availability of paid vacations, economic prosperity and more importantly, the construction of a highway system made it possible for millions of Americans to visit national parks. It was the automobile that made national parks a truly equally accessible pleasure and a "much more democratic institution than was true at their inception" (Keiter, 2013, p. 60).

Although increased interest in national parks fueled tourist influx, recreation "developed appreciation" of unique landscapes and beautiful wilderness (Cox, 1988, p. 6). What was taken for granted by the first settlers of the west became greatly appreciated and cherished (Cox, 1988). Today camping, hiking and bird watching in national parks remain among the most popular leisure activities in America (the vast industry of camping gear, appliances and accessories is perhaps the best illustration of the popularity of outdoor activities) (see Figure 2.5). Those who travel to national parks appreciate the possibility of distancing themselves from noisy, busy urban life and spending time in pristine wilderness.

On the policy front, the conservation movement of the 19th century and the emergence of national parks was crystallized in "the principle of ecological integrity". The principle of ecological integrity builds upon the premise that natural ecosystems, as biophysical phenomena, "are valuable to themselves for their continuing support of life on Earth, as well as for the aesthetic value and the goods and services they provide to humankind" (Westra et al., 2000, p. 22).[2] In Canada, ecological integrity became a central principle in 2001, when Parliament legislated that the preservation of nature, that is, the maintenance of ecological integrity, is the primary purpose of Canada's national parks (Fluker, 2010). In addition, the Canada National Parks Act specified that the "maintenance or restoration of ecological integrity, through the protection of natural resources and natural processes, shall be the first priority of the Minister when considering all aspects of the management of parks" (Section 8(2)).

As significant as they were, these changes came into being slowly. The developments at the micro and meso levels gradually caused macro-level alterations that we can observe today. Profound changes at the macro level were preceded by the wide adoption of national parks as social innovation. The widespread dissemination of national parks created a platform that supported further changes in upper scales.[3] The initial adoption of the national parks idea was triggered by a combination of forces: overall historical context, company interests, previous experience, and human agency. The initial adoption, however, did not create profound changes at the meso level that would lead to institutional reforms. Such changes could be observed only after a number of national parks were created throughout the country and the need to institutionalize management practices for numerous national parks became obvious. Moreover, the establishment of the National Parks Service may be considered the creation of a new institutional setting: hardly anything similar existed before. The widespread adoption of the national parks idea that caused institutional changes was realized after the trap was overcome. Although national parks as a social innovation had been successfully nurtured and adopted, it was not yet established at the higher institutional level. The latter happened only after the creation of national parks became not the rare exception, but the common practice of nature conservation policy.

NOTES

1. The first wave of national parks spread around the British Colonies: Australia (Sydney, 1879), Canada (Banff, 1885), and New Zealand (Tongariro, 1887) (Harper and White, 2012).
2. Ecological integrity is considered to be an emergent property of a complex system. Emergent, in this case, is explained as a property that "spontaneously connects its macro-properties (e.g. resilience) with its micro-properties (e.g. age composition of the

forest)." Ecological integrity, therefore, is a property applied to an entire system, rather than its particular components (Crabbe and Manno, 2008, p. 74).
3. Similar dynamics were observed in the case of social enterprises (see Westley et al., 2014).

REFERENCES

Adams, W.M. (2012). Nature and the colonial mind. In W.M. Adams and M. Mulligan (eds), *Decolonizing Nature. Strategies for Conservation in a Post-colonial Era* (pp. 16–50). London: Earthscan Publications.

Adams, W.M. and Mulligan, M. (2012). Introduction. In W.M. Adams and M. Mulligan (eds), *Decolonizing Nature. Strategies for Conservation in a Post-colonial Era* (pp. 1–15). London: Earthscan Publications.

Browning, P. (1988). *John Muir in his Own Words: A Book of Quotations.* Lafayette, CA: Great West Books.

Canada National Parks Act. Accessed 20 December 2014 at http://laws-lois.justice. gc.ca/eng/acts/N-14.01/page-3.html#h-5.

Cox, T.R. (1988). *The Park Builders: A History of State Parks in the Pacific Northwest.* Seattle, WA: University of Washington Press.

Crabbe, P.J. and Manno, J.P. (2008). Ecological integrity as an emergent global public good. In L. Westra, K. Bosselman and R. Westra (eds), *Reconciling Human Existence with Ecological Integrity* (pp. 74–84). London: Earthscan.

Cronon, W. (2000). Foreword: Look back and look forward. In D. Lowenthal (ed.), *George Merkins Marsh: Prophet of Conservation.* Seattle, WA: University of Washington Press.

Dilsaver, L.M. and Wyckoff, W. (2005). The political geography of national parks. *Pacific Historical Review*, **74**(2), 237–66.

Duncan, D. (2009). *The National Parks. America's Best Idea. An Illustrated History.* New York: Alfred A. Knopf.

Fluker, S. (2010). Ecological integrity in Canada's national parks: the false promise of law. *Windsor Review of Legal and Social Issues*, **29**, 89–123.

Foner, E. (1988). *Reconstruction, 1863–1877: America's Unfinished Revolution.* New York: Harper & Row.

Gifford, T. (1992). Introduction. In J. Muir, *John Muir: The Eight Wilderness-Discovery Books* (pp. 13–20). London: Diadem Books.

Guha, R. (2000). *Environmentalism: A Global History.* New York: Longman.

Haines, A.L. (1996). *The Yellowstone Story: A History of our First National Park* (rev. edn, 2 vols). Niwot, CO: University Press of Colorado.

Harper, M. and White, R. (2012). How national were the first national parks? Comparative perspective from the British settler societies. In S. Höhler, B. Gissibl and P. Kupper (eds), *Civilizing Nature: National Parks in Global Historical Perspective* (pp. 50–67). New York: Berghahn Books.

Jones, K. (2012). Unpacking Yellowstone. The American national park in global perspective. In B. Gissibl, S. Höhler and P. Kupper (eds), *Civilizing Nature: National Parks in Global Historical Perspective* (pp. 31–49). New York: Berghahn Books.

Keiter, R.B. (2013). *To Conserve Unimpaired: The Evolution of the National Park Idea.* Washington, DC: Island Press.

McNamara, R. (2014). Yellowstone expedition led to creation of first national park. Magnificent wilderness was set aside to be protected and preserved. Blog post, accessed 5 June 2015 at http://history1800s.about.com/od/thegildedage/a/first-national-park.htm.

Marsh, G.P. (1864). *Man and Nature; or, Physical Geography as Modified by Human Action*. New York: Charles Scribner.

Merrill, M.D. (ed.) (1999). *Yellowstone and the Great West: Journals, Letters, and Images from the 1871 Hayden Expedition*. Lincoln: University of Nebraska Press.

Miles, J.C. (1995). *Guardians of the Parks. A History of the National Parks and Conservation Association*. Washington, DC: Taylor & Francis.

Muir, J. (1997). *Nature Writings: The Story of my Boyhood and Youth; My First Summer in the Sierra; The Mountains of California; Stickeen; Selected Essays*. New York: Literary Classics of the United States.

Sax, J.L. (1976 [2013]). America's national parks. Their principles, purposes, and prospects. Accessed 2 December 2014 at http://www.naturalhistorymag.com/picks-from-the-past/271452/america-s-national-parks.

Scheuering, R.W. (2004). *Shapers of the Great Debate on Conservation: a Biographical Dictionary* (Vol. 4). Westport, CT: Greenwood Publishing Group.

Sellars, R.W. (1997). *Preserving Nature in the National Parks. A History*. New Haven, CT: Yale University Press.

Stevenson, E. (1977). *A Life of Frederick Law Olmsted. A Park Maker*. New York: Macmillan Publishing.

Strong, D.H. (1988). *Dreamers & Defenders. American Conservationists* (2nd edn). Lincoln, NA: University of Nebraska Press.

Taylor, D.E. (2000). The rise of the environmental justice paradigm injustice framing and the social construction of environmental discourses. *American Behavioral Scientist*, **43**(4), 508–80.

The Convention concerning the Protection of the World Cultural and Natural Heritage (1972). Accessed 15 December 2012 at http://whc.unesco.org/en/conventiontext/.

United Nations Educational, Scientific and Cultural Organization (UNESCO) (2012).The World Heritage Convention. Accessed 15 December 2012 at http://whc.unesco.org/en/convention/.

Westley, F., Antadze, N., Riddell, D.J., Robinson, K. and Geobey, S. (2014). Five configurations for scaling up social innovation: case examples of nonprofit organizations from Canada. *The Journal of Applied Behavioral Science*, **50**(3), 234–60.

Westley, F.R., Tjörnbo, O., Schultz, L., Olsson, P., Folke, C., Crona, B. and Bodin, Ö. (2013). A theory of transformative agency in linked social-ecological systems. *Ecology and Society*, **18**(3), 27.

Westra, L., Miller, P., Karr, J.R., Rees, W.E. and Ulanowicz, R.E. (2000). Ecological integrity and the aims of the global integrity project. In D. Pimentel, L. Westra and R.F. Noss (eds), *Ecological Integrity. Integrating Environment, Conservation, and Health* (pp. 19–41). Washington, DC: Island Press.

Wordsworth, W. (1985). *William Wordsworth: The Pedlar, Tintern Abbey. The Two-Part Prelude* (Vol. 1). Cambridge: Cambridge University Press.

Wuerthner, G. (2007). NREPA: Local interests and conservation history. Blog post, 15 November, accessed 2 May 2015 at http://newwest.net/topic/article/nrepa_local_interests_and_conservation_history/C38/L38/.

3. The intelligence test

Katharine McGowan

INTRODUCTION

What dynamic explains the different outcomes we see within society: nature or nurture? This debate is a truism, actually a red herring, but over time where we have found ourselves on the spectrum between these two poles has had significant effects on views about and treatment of individuals deemed above or below the socially constructed range of normalcy. The story of the early intelligence test is the confluence of an overly assured belief that nature was the root of intellectual incapacity, and by extension poverty and crime, and that scientific measurement could inform an unimpeachable approach to shaping society.

Measurement tools are powerful things: they help answer questions and track trends, inform policy and production, and as such they underpin many of our current public and private institutions. Additionally, they often occupy an uncomfortable space between the normative and the objective; frequently within these tools' design and application are telling assumptions about how the world works, how we can manipulate outcomes and even where we (as policy makers, marketers, agents, etc.) should try to engage and ultimately shift the systems we inhabit. These assumptions can have prophetic effects on the tools' use and impact. The intelligence test is one such tool, a rare "truly original assessment tool" (Becker, 2003, p. 1) that contained important assumptions about how society functioned, and should function under ideal conditions, and sought to advance ourselves from the former to the latter. It was also, in a way, a social innovation.

The intelligence test was a solution to a concern about how to arrange people in a modern meritocracy and industrial economy, grounded in the faith in scientific progressivism to improve society and individuals, built on an implicit (or explicit) belief in nature as a deterministic force. The particular scientific or pseudo-scientific basis for the tests relied on a combination of inheritance and Social Darwinism (here the nature in nature vs. nurture), as well as new methodological techniques that facilitated repeatable mass testing.

After decades of various labs experimenting with the potential of testing mental capacity, Alfred Binet debuted his thinking and his test in the years 1905–11. Henry Herbert Goddard, a psychologist who worked with the "feebleminded", and Robert Yerkes, a psychologist and chairman of the American Psychological Association (APA), both advanced the practice of intelligence testing before and during the First World War. These men worked in their niche laboratories while reading signals of potential landscape shifts as opportunities to advance the use of the intelligence test.

The test was born out of the emergent field of psychology, as researchers sought to apply theory to social problems (an early predecessor perhaps of George Fairweather's experimental social innovation approach) – in this case the concern that underperforming children were a burden on the educational system, and by extension on society generally. Advocates for the test took advantage of a window of opportunity created when America joined the First World War and needed to raise a modern army from a citizen population quickly. The test could not only be a tool for officers seeking to assess and assign recruits, but the war effort could refine and improve the test, making it efficient and proving to observers its utility in placing people in a complicated organization.

As an assessment tool, the test reflected the preferences and values of its time, and after the war it was used to validate medical interventions to remove the feebleminded from America's genetic pool and give apparently scientific weight to racial segregation. As such, the language and theories examined below are difficult for modern readers, so be warned. Indeed, this is more than a question of changing tastes. Landscape shifts demonstrated the ultimate risks of such combinations: the Holocaust was informed by scientifically "validated" racism and eugenics. But some assessment tools are flexible, and the intelligence test found a new use in post-war America, as a means to distinguish individual potential in an increasingly meritocratic economy. The story of the intelligence test is one of intellectual exploration: of the human mind, of methodology and of the landscape moments where this new assessment tool could scale up quickly and facilitate massive movements of human capacity.

NEW IDEAS, NEW COMBINATIONS AND ADJACENT POSSIBLES

There were two key naturalistic phenomena (re)discovered in the 19th century that created fertile space for the eventual development of the intelligence test. First, Darwin's description of natural selection, "[as it] works solely by and for the good of each being, all corporeal and mental endowments will tend to progress towards perfection" (Chitty, 2007, p. 25). Second was the rediscovery of Mendel's rules of genetic inheritance, specifically heredity. Could science help build a better society and validate the extant social hierarchy based on merit and possibility?

As humans were genetically different (eye color, height, etc.), some reasoned the same could be said for character, for intelligence, for criminality or poverty (O'Brien, 2011). Darwin's second cousin, Francis Galton, applied natural selection and nature to explain all or almost all different outcomes between people (Chitty, 2007; Dudziak, 1986). This was "Social" Darwinism, which mixed scientific-social validation of a class-based society (inequality of situation and opportunity), combining naturalistic and constructed phenomena. This bricolage exposed a new adjacent possible: if heredity could explain society, might heredity build a wealthier, more harmonious population?

These views crystallized in the intellectual niche of eugenics, the pseudoscience of improving the "quality" of humanity (Chitty, 2007). In brief, this quality is a specific term that reflected the values and views of those in the eugenics niche. Quality was in part an issue of racial purity, but was usually seen from a middle or upper middle class Protestant perspective, borrowing elements from Malthusian and Darwinian theory (Dudziak, 1986; Zenderland, 1998). Importantly Galton was deeply passionate about creating data to support his hierarchical social theory, "whenever you can, count" (Herrnstein and Murray, 1994).

If ability could be traced through family trees, then could the same be said of the reverse? For many concerned with social improvement in the late 19th and early 20th centuries, a significant threat to public safety and social progress was the "Menace of the Feebleminded" (Samelson, 1987, p. 114). Public health and morals were perceived to be endangered by "promiscuity, adultery, incest, crime and alcoholism" (Dudziak, 1986, p. 845; Zenderland, 1998). This in turn highlighted the economic threat of the "feebleminded", who were either incapable of or uninterested in hard work, preferring crime and various other social ills. It was a cruel logic: your outcomes were baked in biologically, not systemic failures or any combination of nature, nurture, conditions and action.

INNOVATION(S)

The emerging belief that people's different circumstances were the result of fixed and determinate biological characteristics opened up a significant possibility for educators. Public education in North America and Western Europe was undergoing a fundamental pedagogical shift, from philosophy to psychology. Progressives argued for more technical and scientific influence in public policy, for new voices and authorities to be privileged in institutions and structures of legitimation and domination (Blanton, 2000; Cravens, 1987). Public education had largely become a norm in Western countries, and education officials increasingly sought to inform their curriculum and school design with these new voices and authorities (Chitty, 2007).

An association of American teachers established special education programs in 1902, an innovation to tailor education to the limitations or specific needs of a class of students, those who would be labeled "feebleminded" (Zenderland, 1998). To establish a physically and pedagogically separate educational space, educators needed a tool or method to identify these students effectively. Educators first used the emerging statistical study of human populations (a new technological process), especially the permanent census (Ramsden, 2003).

As measurement tools matured and the general faith in science grew, an experimental intellectual/laboratorial niche emerged around a two-part question: what differentiates us, and how can we measure that scientifically? Socio-economic failure was a confirmation of what the social Darwinists like Francis Galton believed were our moral and biological failings; generation after generation of poverty confirmed that these failings could be inherited. What if we could isolate those failings before the fact – find the scientific root of what they believed to be a natural phenomenon?

A DEEP DIVE: HOW THE INTELLIGENCE TEST WAS CREATED BY AN EMERGENT FIELD OF INQUIRY

French psychiatrist Jean-Etienne Dominique Esquirol suggested in the 1830s that "idiocy" was a condition rather than a disease (as some had previously thought or proposed) (Binet and Simon, 1916) (see Figure 3.1). Perhaps the brain itself contained the key to understanding the perceived difference in outcomes between the feebleminded and the more successful in society. The belief that the key to our different abilities (and socioeconomic outcomes) lay in our brains dated back to at least 1869, when Galton suggested that differences in mental ability were the core factor in explaining differences in outcomes (Galton, 1869: Reeve and Charles, 2008). Galton did not engage in any significant experiments, however.

A decade later, Leipzig University opened the first psychological laboratory, the beginning of a quarter century that saw both the number and technological sophistication of such labs grow (Spearman, 1904). Beginning in the late 1880s, experimental psychologists began empirical tests of intellectual ability; in particular, several experiments tested children

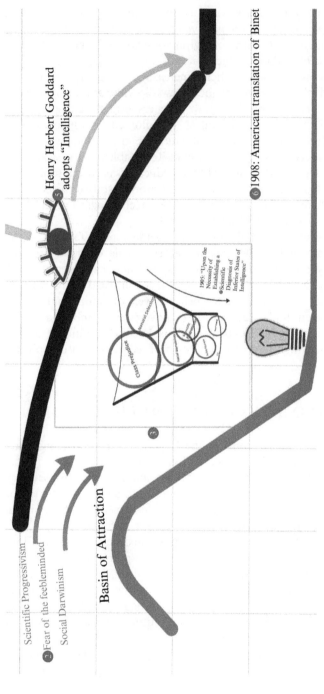

Scientific Progressivism

② Fear of the feebleminded
Social Darwinism

Basin of Attraction

Class Prejudice

Natural Selection

⑤ Henry Herbert Goddard
adopts "Intelligence"

1905: "Upon the
Necessity of
Establishing a
● Scientific
Diagnosis of
Inferior States of
Intelligence"

⑥ 1908: American translation of Binet

Figure 3.1   Deep Dive 1: ideas and need come together

(often in the thousands) and then compared the results with their teachers' impressions or expectations of the children's abilities (Spearman, 1904). Cross-comparisons of data sets proved initially difficult, as researchers debated the relative weight and possible correlation/causation of different tested abilities. On both sides of the Atlantic, decades of tests failed to consistently isolate a handful of identifiable characteristics that could reliably predict academic outcomes.

Experimental psychology became an avenue of inquiry into the human condition, although not without (somewhat predictable) push back from those uncomfortable with the measurement-obsessed clinical deconstruction of life. As one experimental psychologist, Charles Spearman, described these critics: "they protest that such means can never shed any real light upon the human soul, unlock the eternal antinomy of Free Will, or reveal the inward nature of Time and Space" (Spearman, 1904, p. 203).

At the beginning of the 20th century, Spearman felt his (comparatively young) discipline had not yet achieved its promise to transform everyday life: "the results of all good experimental work will live, but as yet most of them are like hieroglyphics awaiting their deciphering Rosetta stone" (Spearman, 1904, p. 204). In the same work, Spearman reported on a correlation he observed that could have a real world application: subjects who did well on one form of mental test generally performed well on all mental tests (Bartholomew et al., 2013). Spearman hypothesized that this was attributable to a "general mental ability" which he labeled g; "Spearman speculated that its [g] biological basis was some general aspect of how brains varied between people" (Bartholomew et al., 2013, p. 223).

Spearman criticized many of his colleagues for producing work of greater theoretical than practical value. This criticism could not be applied universally however, as Alfred Binet explicitly sought a useable test for school children that could reliably identify and measure g, this general mental ability. Working at first with very small numbers of children, and seeking out those already deemed bright and underachieving (strangely, selecting on the dependent variable), Binet repeatedly tested up to ten possible characteristics of intelligence (from the more obvious memory and faculty of comprehending, to the interesting muscular force and force of will) (Spearman, 1904). In 1905, Binet and his student Theodore Simon presented "Upon the necessity of establishing a scientific diagnosis of interior states of intelligence" in *L'Année Psychologique*, where they clearly outlined the rationale for this most recent test.

Reminiscent of Spearmen's praise for a practical eye, Binet and Simon explained that their test originated in the French Minister of Public Instruction's commission for the study of measures that could be used in the instruction of "defective children" (Binet and Simon, 1916). Such children were to be educated in the school system, albeit in special classes. As "to be a member of a special class can never be a mark of distinction, and such as do not merit it, must be spared the record", there needed to be a test that reliably identified those children in need of special education (Binet and Simon, 1916, p. 9). Importantly, this test needed to be "a work of administration, not a work of science" (Binet and Simon, 1916), suggesting it had to be easy to run and interpret. Between 1905 and 1911, Binet and Simon produced a scale of intelligence and key revisions to their tests, based on feedback from the increasing number of practical tests in Paris and other cities. These tests corrected earlier methodological problems, expanding to include "normal" children (Becker, 2003).

Binet devised the first seemingly reliable, replicable test of children's cognitive capabilities to distinguish the mentally incapable from those failing for environmental rather than genetic reasons (Chitty, 2007; Zenderland, 1998). Based on the assumption that the test was effective, those children whom the test deemed "feebleminded" could reliably be institutionalized (Blanton, 2000, p. 1016). Importantly, this conclusion was based firmly in the belief that this was for the best of the child and society generally, as odious as the passage of time might make it seem.

SCALING TOWARDS A TIPPING POINT AND MASS ADOPTION

In the years after Binet first introduced his test, psychologist Henry Herbert Goddard declared himself an advocate for the intelligence test and for intelligence as a naturalistic phenomenon. Goddard was a Director of Research at the Vineland Training School for Feeble-minded Girls and Boys in New Jersey, a niche that allowed him to experiment with different tests and their related hypotheses about the source of feeblemindedness years before he discovered Binet. Indeed, the quest for a test had been a singular concern for Goddard.

Although Binet's 1905 article arrived (physically) in the United States in 1906, the same year Vineland Research Laboratory opened, when Goddard ordered an exhaustive literature review on measuring intelligence, he found no mention of Binet's work.[1] Instead, "it was not until the Spring of 1908 when I made a visit to Europe in the interests of the work [of the Vineland Laboratory] that I learned of the tests", according to a Dr Decroly in Brussels, who had recently completed his own tests using the Binet–Simon method (Goddard, quoted in Binet and Simon, 1916, p. 5).

Goddard brought a (translated and revised) version back to the United States (Watson, 1953). When he received the revised Binet–Simon scale the next year, and after some hesitation ("It seemed impossible to grade intelligence in that way. It was too easy, too simple"), Goddard found the new scale "a surprise and a gratification", which met the school's needs (Goddard, quoted in Binet and Simon, 1916, p. 5).

He was able to convince American doctors working in institutions for the feebleminded to "redefine mental deficiency in terms of intelligence" (Zenderland, 1998, p. 104). Part of his success can likely be attributed to Goddard's extensive data and publication. Interestingly, in these early years as they collected data, Goddard used the absence of a complete translation of Binet's work as a shibboleth against critics – the idea of the test apparently being more attractive than the evidence of its application. This did not mean, however, that Goddard did not seek empirical validation. The Vineland Laboratory made multiple versions of Binet's work available, of which by 1916 they had distributed 22 000, as well as 88 000 blank exams to familiarize many with the test itself (Goddard, quoted in Binet and Simon, 1916, p. 6).

DISRUPTIONS, SOCIAL SHIFTS

Goddard's advocacy for intelligence testing and psychology's role in education successfully shifted the narrative of feeblemindedness in America to a question of intelligence (Zenderland, 1998). The intelligence test was (and is) an assessment tool – and it was unleashed on a country hungry for the ability to determine, behind the veil of scientific accuracy, everyone's potential.

Despite the popularity of institutionalization, some thought perhaps there was another way: sterilization. New medical techniques could make this a relatively safe procedure, and therefore with proper training, sterilized "feebleminded" people could "go out into the world and support themselves", without "the terrible danger of procreation" (Zenderland, 1998, pp. 181–2; Dudziak, 1986). The argument had come full circle; inheritance could explain outcomes, and eliminating the possibility of future inheritance could shift outcomes. Beginning with Indiana in 1907, eventually 28 states introduced compulsory sterilization laws (Dudziak, 1986).

Binet explicitly did not want his test to be used to rank people beyond separating those who fell below a certain floor and could benefit little from conventional education (Blanton, 2000). Once the process was available however, it was quickly seized on to differentiate people based on intelligence and race. Testing was quickly adopted by other groups who sought data to support their social vision – particularly those who believed racial stratification was good and preferable to integration.

A DEEP DIVE

The intelligence test's success in America relied on complementary activities and intentional cooperation of several well-placed individuals and emergent professional associations. The context in which these individuals functioned is equally important: American academia and bureaucracy during a time of crisis, the First World War (see Figure 3.2), for which the United States Army seemed to have been relatively poorly prepared when they joined the ongoing conflict in 1917. The Army decision-makers searched for tools (people and processes as well as technology) that could facilitate their war effort, from soup to nuts – they needed to recruit, dress, train and equip an Expeditionary Force for overseas service for a war already in progress.

The creation of a citizen army – soldiers picked from a workforce of industry, agriculture and white-collar work – created significant opportunities for the emergent profession of psychology. Over the late 19th and early 20th centuries, as Charles Spearman had hoped, psychology developed as a discipline of academic inquiry and an outward-looking consultative profession, in which the role of testing was introduced early. The American Psychological Association (APA) was founded in 1892;

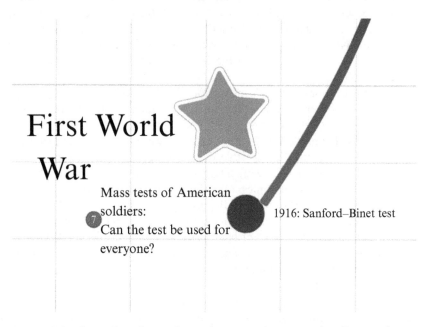

Figure 3.2   Deep Dive 2: windows of opportunity, networks align, scale up

they created the Committee on Physical and Mental Tests three years later (Watson, 1953).

The network of emerging American scholars who advanced the intelligence test is surprisingly easy to trace. G. Stanley Hall was president of Clark University, "the American Mecca for aspiring young psychologists" (Crosby and Hastorf, 2000, p. 138). He also worked at Johns Hopkins, held weekly clinics at the Bay View Hospital, and both taught and demonstrated for psychiatrists at the Worcester State Hospital (Watson, 1953). Included among his lecture topics was the emerging science surrounding testing. Among Hall's students were both Goddard and Lewis Terman, who identified Hall's Monday night seminars as the key to his interest in the possibility of mental testing (Watson, 1953; Crosby and Hastorf, 2000).

Terman and his student, Maude Merrill, spent three years revising the tests for standardization and validity; they also increased the age range of the test, and reduced the amount of coaching necessary to administer the test (Crosby and Hastorf, 2000). Terman shifted the test's focus away from simply providing a marker below which children were "feebleminded", and instead could be used to rank takers across a wide spectrum (Hegarty, 2007; Porter, 2009). The result, the Stanford–Binet test, facilitated the tests' passage through a key window of opportunity, thanks almost exclusively to Robert Yerkes, perhaps the key debater in the adoption of the intelligence test. Yerkes believed science could validate and inform a merit-based hierarchy of people based on their ability/potential contribution to the economy (Kevles, 1968), although some interrogation might be required around the "merit-based" element of Yerkes's thinking, as he became a prominent advocate for strict immigration reform and rallied against what he perceived as the racial denigration in America. Prior to the war, Yerkes established an internship program at the psychiatric institution for adults at the Boston Psychopathic Hospital (Watson, 1953) and furthered the cause of psychology as an applicable profession addressing America's current social problems.

As stated above, when America joined the Allies in 1917, it needed to raise a large army as soon as possible. Walter Dill Scott, an applied psychologist from the Carnegie Institute of Technology, approached military officials with a plan to create a test that would match civilian skills with military tasks (Keene, 1994). Army officials enthusiastically embraced Scott's project, only to grow increasingly frustrated as the process moved slowly, and their need for men grew more and more urgent (Keene, 1994).

The sequence of events that brought psychology into the American war effort was rapid and seemingly serendipitous, yet this partnership was the product of luck and intentionality multiplying across networks. Yerkes, like Scott, saw the war as an opportunity for intelligence tests to demonstrate their utility in evaluating human potential quickly and efficiently: "in common with the other and more exact sciences, psychology demonstrated its preparedness for wholly unexpected practical demands and responsibilities" (Yerkes, 1921, p. v).

A quick chronology highlights Yerkes's phenomenal systems entrepreneurial actions. President Woodrow Wilson addressed the Congress on 2 April 1917 to detail the German atrocities that, cumulatively, now demanded America's action. Both the Senate and the House had voted for war by 3 am on 6 April, and later that Good Friday Wilson signed the war resolution a little after 1 pm (Harries and Harries, 1997). That same day, the APA's experimental psychologists were gathered in Cambridge, Massachusetts, where Yerkes and his colleagues, including a Captain W.S. Bowen who taught military science and tactics at Harvard, formed a session "for discussion of the relations of psychology for national defense" (Yerkes, 1921, p. 7). As the APA president, Yerkes penned a letter to the organization on the 7th, wherein he said it was "desirable that psychologists of the country act unitedly in the interests of defense", and in a combination of patriotic spirit and practical considerations, "we should act at once as a professional group as well as individually" (1921, p. 7).

The attendees agreed to collect information about extant uses of psychology for military purposes, specifically in Canada, which had joined the war automatically in 1914 as a British colony. A quick trip to Montreal and Southern Ontario convinced Yerkes of "the urgent desirability of the application of psychological methods in the selection of recruits and in the study of incapacitated soldiers" (1921, p. 8). Whether this was the self-fulfilling confirmation of a committed believer or the dispassionate analysis of a scientifically objective observer is largely irrelevant – Yerkes had the proof he needed to defend the utility of the test.

On 14 April, Yerkes and his colleagues met with the Chairman of the National Research Council at a conference in Philadelphia; this encounter led to an invitation for Yerkes to attend the NRC's semi-annual meeting in Washington on the 19th. Through that meeting, and a special meeting of the APA two days later, members organized a committee specifically focused on military psychological work within the NRC (Yerkes, 1921; Keene, 1994). Yerkes's pitch was simple: mass testing could effectively distinguish the thousands of incoming recruits according to their intellectual capacity, and ultimately soldierly potential, to get "the right man to the right job" (Keene, 1994, p. 240).

Ideas traveled quickly through the linked scientific and military bureaucracy networks in Washington, DC. After the NRC received the report in early May, they referred it to their chairman of the Committee on Medicine and Hygiene, Dr Victor Vaughan, who liked the plan and submitted it to the Surgeon-General of the Army (Yerkes, 1921; Pinter, 1926). Unlike Scott and his comparison of civilian and military skill sets, Yerkes and the APA created a sample mass test for intelligence in advance, assuming the authority and availability associated with a finished product. The test deeply impressed the Army's General Staff, who approved a trial mass test (Keene, 1994; Kevles, 1968).

Throughout May 1917, Terman gathered fellow psychologists at Goddard's Vineland School to refine their testing process for the army (Keene, 1994). On reflection, Pinter celebrated this intensive work: "it is a splendid example of what co-operative research can do with the right motive or stimulus" (1926, p. 420). The Committee on Provision for the Feebleminded offered the psychologists $500 (later $700) to fund their work (Yerkes, 1921). The test had to be easy to implement quickly (the goal was to run the test within a week of a recruit's arrival in camp), and to clearly facilitate the army's personnel requirements of placing many men in the appropriate jobs *quickly*. Psychologists developed 400 practice exams, which the participant psychologists tested on marine officer cadets throughout June, and the military financed a second mass test of 4000 soldiers in July. These trials eventually informed the creation of two tests officially rolled out over the winter of 1917–18, labeled "Alpha" and "Beta", for which the Surgeon General created the Division of Psychology within the Medical Department (Yerkes, 1921).

At least one reflective officer doubted whether there was a certain degree of intelligence required to become cannon fodder, and it proved difficult for higher levels of command to ensure their juniors actually used test results, but such thoughts did not impede military psychologists' mission creep, eventually working in half a dozen military departments (Keene, 1994; Yerkes, 1921). Over the course of the war, 1.75 million of the United States' 4 million recruits took intelligence tests at one of four divisional cantonments' Psychological Testing buildings (both building and test were frequently introduced after significant opposition from individual commanders) (Keene, 1994).

Even in these early tests, we can clearly trace the social preferences of the master testers. Results really tested level of education more than capability, and given Yerkes's own racial assumptions against non-Caucasian Americans, there are serious questions about whether the tests represented any improvement over interviews and officers' observations (Blanton, 2000; Pinter, 1926; Watson, 1953). Nonetheless, tests on this massive scale lent significant weight and normalcy to intelligence as an idea and testing as a process. A year after the war ended, readers of *The Lancet* saw the following endorsement: "Intelligence, of course, is only one of the factors in military efficiency, but it is probably the most important single factor", and, thanks to the war, intelligence tests had given "clear indications of their future value in the work of human selection and vocational training" (*The Lancet*, 1919, p. 539).

Yerkes felt similarly laudatory, arguing in his official history of the Alpha and Beta tests that "the place of scientific tools in the Army personnel system was firmly established by the time of the Armistice . . . which have had an important effect upon the progress of comparable civilian work" (Yerkes, 1921, pp. 129–30). After the war, Goddard's Vineyard School began offering internships for consulting psychologists to train at what had become a center for Binet-based testing (Watson, 1953).

THE TEST SCALES OUT, FINDS NEW ADJACENT POSSIBLES

As the test was adopted widely in America's educational institutions, it heightened existing socio-economic divisions in America quite outside concerns for the feebleminded and special education. Perhaps this is unsurprising given the reaction to testing immigrants at Ellis Island before the war. The test offered the veneer of science to racist assumptions about hierarchy in American society. If Francis Galton had been focused primarily on class in his conception of Social Darwinism, in post-war America, race (which admittedly frequently had/has class implications ingrained) became the social structure supported by pseudo-science (see Figure 3.3). Differences in socio-economic outcomes and culture in America's increasingly multicultural society must have some scientific basis; surely Caucasians did better than others because they were better, genetically.

An instructive case is the mass IQ testing that Texas used to affirm a belief in a hierarchy of racial intelligence (Blanton, 2000). These tests essentially manufactured a difference between Caucasian, African and

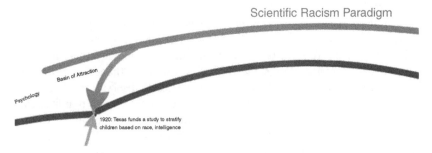

Figure 3.3   The test, schools and race in post-war America

Hispanic American children. Actual tests found that rural schools were less effective than urban ones, which the study's authors struggled with; they settled on the belief that those African and Hispanic students who did well on the test (and were largely urban) must be light-skinned (and therefore more European). The published results – reflective of the views of the testers – were exactly what the Texan administrators wanted, proof that white children performed inherently better than non-white children. That this subsequently justified less spending in predominantly non-white schools is a reminder of the policy paths chosen by those who believed in scientific racism (not to alleviate difference, but to reinforce it).

Unfortunately, the test did not just end as a tool to stratify (or justify existing stratifications of) races and classes. The test was used to justify the sterilization of those deemed feebleminded, an application that Lewis Terman strongly supported (Crosby and Hastorf, 2000). Not only did sterilization remove the feebleminded from the gene pool, thereby completing the hopes of Social Darwinists, but sterilization was also significantly cheaper than institutionalization for those feebleminded individuals capable of independent living (Dudziak, 1986; O'Brien, 2011). Improved medical techniques inspired sterilization laws, the first of which was passed in Indiana in 1907; in 1924 Virginia joined at least 15 other states in passing a law to restrict "the propagation of people it considered mentally defective and socially inadequate" (Dudziak, 1986, p. 848).

Advocates for this law brought a friendly challenge, using a test candidate whose mother had been deemed feebleminded, and who had become pregnant herself at 17 while living with her foster parents. Oliver Wendell Holmes Jr of the Supreme Court – son of the poet Oliver Wendell Holmes Sr who played a role in the establishment of the National Parks System – wrote the majority (8:1) opinion. The law was upheld, and celebrated, as it gave the candidate her freedom – if she could not propagate, she could be free of the institution (Dudziak, 1986). The intelligence test was a supposedly scientific means to determine who should and should not procreate, for the betterment of the individual and society as a whole.

The illogical and terrible ultimate conclusion of the link between eugenics and race was embodied in the genocidal policies of Nazi Germany. The test itself was never universally accepted as infallible (shockingly, given that the test was used to justify sterilization). As early as the 1920s some within psychology lampooned the tests, and especially the testers, for measuring something they could not consistently and effectively define – intelligence was a placeholder for many capacities and outcomes (Boring, 1961). The horrors of the Holocaust were significant enough to dislodge or at least disrupt many social facts: in this case the idea that science could inform the project to perfect the human species (see Figure 3.4). Yet the death knell

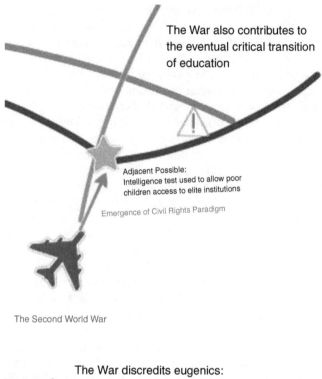

The War also contributes to the eventual critical transition of education

Adjacent Possible:
Intelligence test used to allow poor children access to elite institutions

Emergence of Civil Rights Paradigm

The Second World War

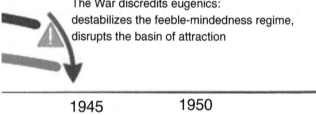

The War discredits eugenics: destabilizes the feeble-mindedness regime, disrupts the basin of attraction

1945   1950

Figure 3.4   Link between intelligence test and race hard to justify post-Holocaust

of eugenics did not end the perceived validity of testing, or the implicit assumptions about cognitive capacity, class and personal potential. Clyde Chitty argues that the link between fixed intelligence and class is reflected in the differentiation of academic and vocational education: "we need to *educate* the middle class but merely to *train* the working class" (2007, p. 1).

Although credible accusations of racism and classism remained, tests of intellectual capacity occasionally opened up educational opportunities for lower-income children beginning in the 1950s (Blanton, 2000).

Interestingly, intelligence tests have been used to demonstrate the exact structural factors the Texas testers worked so hard to racialize. The quality of the learning environment has a significant influence on IQ (Bradley et al., 1989), as the Texas testers inadvertently found when their results suggested rural students underperformed in comparison with urban children, but at least one study has found that "adjustments for economic and social differences in the lives of black and white children all but eliminate differences in IQ scores" between the two groups (Brooks-Gunn et al., 1996). From a systems perspective it is ironic that a test supposedly measuring biology, that many wanted to use to reframe the educational and economic system of the United States, actually captured the results of a problematic system and further deepened the basin of attraction of poverty.

Fatuously, there is an increasing recognition of the impression a person creates based on non-cognitive factors (particularly attractiveness) and a person's perceived intelligence. Simply put, there is a strong relationship between perceived attractiveness and perceived intelligence (Talamas et al., 2016). Beside the flippancy of such a correlation, it seems somehow appropriate that the concept devised to understand what flowed beneath – remember early testers found physical characteristics were inconsistent indicators of feeblemindedness – remains so difficult to effectively pin down outside of our wider social expectations. Indeed, Katharina Lochner (2016) points out that, in spite of tests used in everything from personality measurements to job performance, there remains no ultimately satisfying definition of intelligence for testers.

CONCLUSION

Drawing attention to the potential of children in low-income families is incredibly important, regardless of whether the intelligence test (or any modification thereof) is the assessment tool that facilitates that attention, for one simple and very appropriate reason. Regardless of the Kuhnian paradigm shift away from scientific racism and eugenics, one important element of inheritance does prove to be a consistently strong predictor of future outcomes: your parents' income (Brooks-Gunn et al., 1996). Nurture, not just nature.

The story of the intelligence test is not a celebratory one, but it was certainly an attempt to better serve the marginalized (in this case "serve" must be interpreted with the lens of the time), and build a more resilient society through scientific–social partnerships. It was the big ideas of scientific progressivism, and especially intelligence, that created the opportunity, the possibility of a test for ability (and inheritance, for sterilization based on the tests). Agents created and described this opening to the adjacent possible, created tests that could bring the current reality into line with that future, and debaters made the necessary connections (political, medical and institutional/educational) to bring the intelligence test from its niche in labs and small-scale schools to become a key element of the meritocracy in pre-war America. The history of social innovation offers us a glimpse of process, of agency and perspective: indeed, the entire lifecycle of the innovation process.

NOTE

1. I leave the reason for such an omission to the minds of the reader, as Spearman cited Binet's earlier work clearly and intelligently in his 1904 article, cited above.

REFERENCES

Bartholomew, D., Allerhand, M. and Deary, I.J. (2013). Measuring mental capacity: Thomson's Bonds model and Spearman's *g*-model compared, *Intelligence*, **41**, 222–33.

Becker, K. (2003). History of the Stanford–Binet Intelligence Scales: content and psychometrics. *Stanford–Binet Intelligence Scales, Fifth Edition Assessment Service Bulletin No.1*. Itasca, IL: Riverside Publishing.

Binet, A. and Simon, T. (1916). *The Development of Intelligence in Children (the Binet–Simon test)* (trans. Elizabeth Kite). Baltimore, MD: Williams & Wilkins.

Blanton, C.K. (2000). They cannot master abstractions, but they can often be made efficient workers: race and class in the intelligence testing of Mexican Americans and African Americans in Texas during the 1920s. *Social Science Quarterly*, **81**(4), 1014–26.

Boring, E. (1961). Intelligence as the tests test it. In J.J. Jenkins and D.G. Paterson (eds), *Studies in Individual Differences: The Search for Intelligence*. East Norwalk, CT: Appleton-Century-Crofts, pp. 210–14.

Bradley, R.H., Caldwell, B.M., Rock, S.L., Ramey, C.T., Barnard, K.E., Gray, C., Hammond, M.A., Mitchell, S., Gottfried A.W., Siegel, L. and Johnson, D.L. (1989). Home environment and cognitive development in the first three years of life: a collaborative study including six sites and three ethnic groups in North America. *Developmental Psychology*, **25**, 217–35.

Brooks-Gunn, J., Klebanov, P.K. and Duncan, G.J. (1996). Ethnic differences in children's intelligence test scores: role of economic deprivation, home environment, and maternal characteristics. *Child Development*, **67**(2), 396–408.

Chitty, C. (2007). *Eugenics, Race and Intelligence in Education*. London: Continuum.

Cravens, H. (1987). Applied science and public policy: the Ohio Bureau of Juvenile Research and the problem of juvenile delinquency, 1913–1930. In M. Sokal (ed.), *Psychological Testing and American Society, 1890–1920*. New Brunswick, NJ: Rutgers University Press, pp. 158–94.

Crosby, J.R. and Hastorf, A.H. (2000). Lewis Terman: scientist of mental measurement and product of his time. In G. Kimble and M. Wertheimer (eds), *Portraits of Pioneers in Psychology* (Vol. 4). Washington, DC: American Psychologists Association, pp. 131–47.

Dudziak, M. (1986). Oliver Wendell Holmes as a eugenics reformer: rhetoric in the writing of constitutional law. *Iowa Law Review*, **71**, 833–67.

Galton, Francis (1869). *Hereditary Genius: An Enquiry into its Laws and Consequences*. London: Macmillan & Co.

Harries, M. and Harries, S. (1997). *The Last Days of Innocence: America at War, 1917–1918*. New York: Random House.

Hegarty, P. (2007). From genius inverts to gendered intelligence: Lewis Terman and the power of the norm. *History of Psychology*, **10**(2), 132–55.

Herrnstein, R. and Murray, C. (1994). *The Bell Curve: Intelligence and Class Structure in American Life*. New York: Free Press.

Keene, J.D. (1994). Intelligence and morale in the army of a democracy: the genesis of military psychology during the First World War. *Military Psychology*, **6**(4), 235–53.

Kevles, D. (1968). Testing the army's intelligence: psychologists and the military in World War I. *The Journal of American History*, **55**(3), 565–81.

Lochner, K. (2016). *Successful Emotions: How Emotions Drive Cognitive Performance*. Hamburg: Springer.

O'Brien, G. (2011). Eugenics, genetics, and the minority group model of disabilities: implications for social work advocacy. *Social Work*, **56**(4), 347–54.

Pinter, R. (1926). Intelligence tests. *Psychological Bulletin*, **23**(7), 366–81.

Porter, T. (2009). Measurement and meritocracy: an intellectual history of IQ. *Modern Intellectual History*, **6**(3), 637–44.

Ramsden, E. (2003). Social demography and eugenics in the interwar United States. *Population and Development Review*, **29**(4), 547–93.

Reeve, C.L. and Charles, J.E. (2008). Survey of opinions on the primacy of *g* and social consequences of ability testing: a comparison of expert and non-expert views. *Intelligence*, **36**(6), 681–8.

Samelson, F. (1987). Was early mental testing: (a) racist inspired, (b) objective science, (c) a technology for democracy, (d) the origin of the multiple choice exams, (e) none of the above? (Mark the RIGHT answer). In M. Sokal (ed.), *Psychological Testing and American Society, 1980–1930*. New Brunswick, NJ: Rutgers University Press, pp. 113–27.

Spearman, C. (1904). General intelligence: objectively determined and measured. *The American Journal of Psychology*, **15**, 201–92.

Talamas, S.N., Mavor, K.I. and Perrett, D.I. (2016). The influence of intelligence on the endorsement of the intelligence–attractiveness halo. *Personality and Individual Differences*, **95**, 162–7.

The Lancet (1919). Intelligence test, *The Lancet*, 9 September, p. 539.

Watson, R. (1953). A brief history of clinical psychology. *Psychological Bulletin*, **50**(5), 321–46.

Yerkes, R.M. (ed.) (1921). *Psychological Examining in the United States Army. Memoirs of the National Academy of Science* (Vol. 15). Washington, DC: Surgeon General's Office & Division of Psychology.

Zenderland, L. (1998). *Measuring Minds: Henry Herbert Goddard and the Origins of American Intelligence Testing*. Cambridge: Cambridge University Press.

4. Synthesis: agency and opportunity

Per Olsson

INTRODUCTION

The large-scale, systemic change that is the focus of this book is driven by purposeful action on the part of deeply committed change agents. These actors exert agency at the level of individual, organizational and network interactions and, within the scope of this book, their agency involves changing the system conditions that created social, economic and/ or ecological problems in the first place. As Westley et al. (2013) describe, this type of transformative agency is challenging and changing: (1) roles and routines; (2) power; (3) relations among groups and networks; (4) resource flows; and (5) meaning and values (and culture) across different opportunities and scales.

In the context of global challenges – such as those focused upon in Sustainable Development Goals for instance – there is an increased sense of urgency about the need for large-scale systemic change. But the focus on systemic transformation has led to the emergence of a body of social change and social innovation literature that focuses on complex systems and non-linear change, and often discusses agency in terms of entrepreneurship (Westley et al., 2013). Within these discussions, scholars have identified different types of entrepreneurship, including: social entrepreneurs, policy entrepreneurs, institutional entrepreneurs (Kingdon, 1984; Maguire et al., 2004; Moore and Westley, 2011) and others such as empathetic entrepreneurs and moral entrepreneurs (Chiles et al., 2010; Antadze and McGowan, 2016). Maguire et al. define institutional entrepreneurship as the "activities of actors who have an interest in particular institutional arrangements and who leverage resources to create new institutions or to transform existing ones" (2004, p. 657). Policy entrepreneurs are "advocates who are willing to invest their resources – time, energy, reputation, money – to promote a position in return for anticipated future gain in the form of material, purposive, or solidary benefits" (Kingdon, 1984, p. 188). A social entrepreneur is "the inventor of a novel norm, idea, or product" (Moore and Westley, 2011, p. 5). Within this chapter, these different entrepreneurship lenses will be used to identify and analyze strategies associated with different elements of social innovation processes across history.

The concept of entrepreneurship brings into sharp focus the idea of strategy. Agents seeking broad, systemic change will need strategies to challenge the status quo, develop novel ideas, and navigate the process to ensure the new idea or innovation moves towards impact. But in large-scale systemic change, entrepreneurs will also need to involve strategies that challenge the larger institutional context and underlying normative paradigms, if an innovation is to have any transformative impact. For example, Westley et al. capture these two important aspects of social innovations by using a quote from Edwin Land: "Every innovation has two parts: the first is the invention of the thing itself; the second is the preparation of expectations so that when the invention arrives it seems both surprising and familiar – something long awaited" (2015, p. 5).

The case studies reviewed in this chapter also show that in addition to the capacities required for the invention of alternative solutions and preparation of social and cultural expectations, there may also be a need to understand how to effectively "break down" and let go of the existing dominant system, the dynamics of its interactions and, ultimately, its undesired pathways. There are roles to play for the different types of entrepreneurship that scholars have identified as important for social change. More specifically, different types of entrepreneurship can play different roles in different phases of transformative/large-scale changes (Olsson et al., 2006; Moore and Westley, 2011). This is particularly important for changing large-scale, complex systems that involve multiple levels, scales and sectors. Sometimes the breakdown can happen through strategic agency but it may also be due to a crisis such as war or a natural disaster.

As stated by McGowan et al. (Chapter 1) and Moore (Chapter 12), social innovation and change happen at different levels and scales; the multi-level perspective helps us understand and organize the phenomena of transformative change in society. Transition management scholars have developed an elaborate and detailed model for understanding cross-scale interactions in socio-technological systems, which involves niches at a micro scale, regimes at a meso scale, and landscapes at a macro scale (see, for example, Rotmans et al., 2001; Geels and Schot, 2007; Loorbach and Rotmans, 2010). They define landscapes as cultural values, social trends, environmental change, economic discourses. Regimes are defined as dominant rule-sets, social networks and organizations, prevailing infrastructures. Niches are defined as small, safe spaces in which new practices can develop, protected from harsh selection criteria and the resistance of prevailing regimes. In this chapter, this framework is used to understand the role of agency in the dynamics within each scale, as well as in cross-scale interactions, for example, the mechanisms by which agents working within niches can cause change at the regime and landscape scales, and vice versa.

Agency needs to be visionary but also navigate opportunities. In the past, scholars have described the importance of single windows of opportunity (Kingdon, 1984), a moment in time when change is possible because problems, solutions and politics briefly align. Crisis, or anticipated crisis and fear of it, has often been described as an important part of opening windows; it can be part of triggering the initiation of a new idea or opening up for the scaling of an idea (Westley et al., 2011). Thus crisis can be part of the initiation and first testing of a social innovation and may contribute to its impact. For example, an environmental crisis can lead to environmental issues rising to the top of the political agenda, and motivating politicians to act (Olsson et al., 2004). However, the notion that a social innovation will only succeed at a particular moment in time and that if it misses that precise moment, transformation will not occur, is far too limiting. As the cases show, social innovation does not just occur at a specific moment or during a "temporal window". It can also emerge, develop, meet resistance, and possibly become institutionalized across a range of opportunity contexts, each of which can look very different. Dorado describes an opportunity context as "the likelihood that an organizational field will permit actors to identify and introduce novel institutional combinations and facilitate the mobilization of resources required to make it enduring" (2005, p. 391). Dorado argues there are at least three kinds of opportunity contexts: opaque, hazy, and transparent (see Chapter 1).

FRAMING QUESTIONS

In this chapter I draw on themes related to agency from the literature – a multiplicity of entrepreneurship forms, cross-scale interactions and opportunity contexts – as lenses to investigate some of the cases in this book. I specifically concentrate on a set of framing questions to explore the cases and analyze the role of agency and opportunity in these complex systems. First, what are the triggers for agents to take action and begin early niche development? Did specific drivers (e.g. a broader social, economic or ecological change that affects values and meaning-making) serve as triggers? What are the strategies that ensure an agent can build momentum for an idea? Next, I will explore the actions and strategies that agents adopt to target the regime and landscape levels, and explore how the regime and landscape, in turn, shape agency. Then I will examine the opportunities and pivotal moments that emerged and how actions and strategies either created or seized those opportunities in different contexts. The final concluding section provides emerging insights from these cases of social innovation history about agency and opportunity for transformative change.

TRIGGERS FOR ACTION AND EARLY NICHE DEVELOPMENT

In the cases in this book, the early development of a social innovation often starts with a response by individuals and small groups to a crisis or anticipated crisis. These crises are associated with broader societal developments driven by certain paradigms and discourses that have negative effects on parts of society. Early development also involves struggles to establish an organizational platform that enables the (re)combination and incubation of ideas, experiments with and tests these ideas, generates leading examples, and mobilizes resources.

The development of option pricing and the derivatives market was tightly linked to a larger movement toward a neoclassical economic paradigm and the discourse of market liberalism, which in turn grew out of a fear of Keynesianism. The Keynesian economic paradigm had become widely popular after World War II and dominated global economics in the 1950s and 1960s. But concerns were raised that the Keynesian discourse put nations on a path towards becoming totalitarian states, which infringed on people's freedom. There was also a growing concern that the international monetary systems such as the Rival Blocs, and the following Bretton Woods systems, did not provide economic stability. This instability and discomfort with the current pathway led early pro-market proponents such as Friedrich Hayek and his predecessor and mentor Ludwig von Mises to start challenging the Keynesian paradigm. For example, in the 1930s, Hayek participated in a series of debates with Keynes about macroeconomics at several locales including the London School of Economics and Cambridge University.

A key moment in the early development of the neoliberal economics movement was when Hayek convened the Mont Pelerin meeting in Switzerland in 1947 and, together with prominent thinkers in the field such as Frank Knight, Karl Popper, Ludwig von Mises, George Stigler and Milton Friedman, founded the organization known as the Mont Pelerin Society. The idea behind the Mont Pelerin meeting was to adopt similar strategies to push a market-oriented agenda, as the Fabian Society had done to advance the principles of democratic socialism in the UK. Hayek included pro-market philosophers and economists at the meeting, showing early signs of network-building, a point the literature has shown can be essential for the distributed agency that social innovations require (Westley et al., 2006). The strategy that has been documented about the Mont Pelerin meeting was to organize and mobilize a diverse and fragmented set of pro-market thinkers in order to identify common interests and agree on some basic liberal principles. In the case of birth control, Margaret Sanger used similar network strategies to mobilize a fragmented movement but also to create new links to groups outside the movement.

Hayek's initiative in calling the meeting helped achieve two things that were important for challenging the Keynesian paradigm and institutions and would eventually pave the way for neoliberalism: (1) the spawning of a series of think tanks and more organized forms for collaboratively exploring these ideas (Antony Fisher in particular would go on to found a series of conservative think tanks including the Institute of Economic Affairs in 1955) and (2) helping set a research agenda for advancing the research in this field.

The Mont Pelerin meeting became the seed for establishing the Chicago School of Economics, which to a large extent adopted the research agenda developed at that meeting. The Chicago School, with Milton Friedman as a key figure, provided a platform for supporting research on neoclassical economics that helped challenge the Keynesian paradigm and discourse.

In the case of residential schools, the idea was triggered by concern about the negative effects of Western civilization on Native Peoples and the marginalization of Indigenous groups, which included loss of culture, identity and ways of living. This caused people like Chief Augustine Shingwauk, who was instrumental in developing the idea of teaching in wigwams, to act. Together with his brother and missionary E.F. Wilson, Shingwauk raised enough money to open up the Shingwauk Industrial Home at Garden River in 1873. The deliberate agency of Chief Shingwauk and others was focused upon creating schools for their people so that they could adapt to new ways of living. The vision was to develop an education system that was based on Indigenous values and meaning, but also included lessons so that Indigenous youth would have the skills to navigate and thrive in a society dominated by settlers. It was an effort to maintain traditional life and identity in the new context in which the Indigenous people found themselves.

In the case of birth control, in the late 19th century the existing regime had stifled a growing movement in the US, led by women such as Victoria Woodhull, advocating women's rights, liberal views on sex, and increased use of contraceptives. The regime instead cemented the conservative Christian worldview of morality and vice. The renewed grip by the regime resulted in the Comstock Act, which, together with the miserable living conditions of working class women, became the trigger and major target for a counter movement. This was led by women's rights activists and by 1910 women such as Margaret Sanger, Emma Goldman and Mary Dennett started campaigning against the Act. Sanger was a leader of this movement and had the reputation of being a troublemaker. She used disobedience and illegal measures to challenge the law – a specific kind of disruptive agency that is not present in all of the cases. Sanger's work included publishing *The Woman Rebel* and distributing the "Family Limitation" pamphlet in 1914, and working with Otto Bobsein to popularize the term "birth control", so it became part of mainstream discourse. Sanger started an illegal clinic in 1916, which received significant attention.

While Sanger was unsuccessful at changing the law in 1914, her very public persistent struggle cultivated a following, and some of her followers were ready to carry the message and the movement forward. For example, Dennett started the National Birth Control League in 1915, when Sanger was in Europe to avoid prosecution. But this was just one of many actions, and the movement continued challenging the Act in numerous ways, until it began to find "cracks" in the legislation. For example, several filmmakers, such as Lois Weber, were engaged in the sexual education and birth control movements and used film to communicate to the masses, because films had the legal protection of free speech. However, the Supreme Court changed this in 1915 and filmmakers had to find new creative ways of communicating.

From 1916 to 1919 Sanger went on lecture tours and published the periodical *Birth Control Review*; she gave speeches to raise awareness and support the formation of various Birth Control Leagues at the state level. In 1921, Sanger and others established the American Birth Control League at the First American Birth Control Conference in New York City. They adopted a statement of principles and aims as its platform and program of work (American Birth Control League, 1921). The conference was an important moment, signaling changes in Sanger's strategy and the way she exercised agency. Having initially focused on gathering a fragmented movement, she now began forging links to new people and a broader set of actors who worked in the same field, as is evident in this quote from Sanger's opening speech:

> The idea in calling this Conference was to bring together not our old friends, the advocates of Birth Control, whose worth we know and whose courage has stood the test of opposition; but rather to bring together new people, with other ideas, the people who have been working in social agencies and in other groups for the same results as we, namely a better nation and the banishment of disease, misery, poverty, delinquency and crime. (American Birth Control League, 1921, pp. 14–15)

The event ended with the arrest of Sanger and conference committee member Mary Wilson on the last day of the conference. During transformation, the dominant system often resists and hits back – responding with police raids, campaigns and new legislation. But despite the heavy-handed efforts to enforce the regime's "morals", many people were willing to challenge the system even when they faced prosecution for doing so, such as Sanger's sister Ethel Byrne and Fania Mindell (who were arrested and prosecuted along with Sanger in 1916). Although social movements and protest do not automatically lead to systems change, resistance and conventional tools of protest and disruption are a clear part of some cases of social innovation. This type of disruptive protest movement involves distributed and networked agency, which is predicated on public fearlessness and a willingness by the agents to be arrested for what they believe in.

The networking in the birth control case probably helped to capture and navigate the adjacent possible that opened up when a clause in the Act was expanded to enable contraception (condoms) to be prescribed by physicians to prevent disease, but not for birth control. This issue had been addressed and championed by sex education advocates like Prince Morrow (who had started the American Society for Sanitary and Moral Prophylaxis in 1905) and supported by philanthropists such as John D. Rockefeller. The legal change created conditions which allowed Sanger to open her first legal birth control clinic, and to start implementing her ideas and conducting research to generate data on progress.

Having the capacity to establish early organizational platforms in niches such as the American Birth Control League and the Clinical Research Bureau was important; it helped provide a safe space for people to explore and experiment with alternative solutions, generate new knowledge, build new networks, bricolage and incubate new ideas, and capture the adjacent possible. The Chicago School of Economics and other academic institutions formed a part of a new academic environment, with emerging networks of neoclassical economics scholars. This allowed Myron Scholes, Fischer Black and Merton to meet and develop their option-pricing model, which was a bricolage of pre-existing ideas in economics. These types of niche organizational platforms, often defined by common principles and aims, provide transformative spaces to start building an alternative system based on meanings and values fundamentally different from the prevailing, dominant ones. A system that is wired on different relationships, principles and meanings, which uses the language of multi-level perspective, results in a new proto regime.

AGENCY TARGETING THE REGIME AND LANDSCAPE LEVELS

The ability of actors to "work the system", including working on the individual components of a system and the links between them, at several scales, has been shown to be an important part of achieving transformative change. So far in this chapter, I have focused on the creation of change at the niche level; I now turn to focus on the agency and capacity to work across scales. Cross-scale work is needed in the multi-level perspective in order to influence and change the regime and landscape levels, which includes institutions as well as socially constructed meaning and values. I have identified three aspects of the social innovation process in which agency working across scales matters: (1) building up a new system – the role of the early niche organizational platforms in increasing capacity that will eventually change the regime and the landscape levels; (2) breakdown or dismantling of the old system; and (3) competing normative paradigms and co-optation.

As shown earlier, strategies for addressing the landscape and regime levels are important in order to develop and maintain the niche in the face of constant pressure from the regime level (Antadze and McGowan, 2016). However, establishing early organizational platforms as part of the niche development also appears to be of strategic importance in creating substantial changes at the landscape and regime levels. The Clinical Research Bureau (CRB) conducted research studies to generate data on contraceptive use, which was used to support the evidence and learning about the social innovation and to build capacity and create a readiness for scaling up into the regime and scaling deep into landscape level meanings and values. Having a steady supply of quality contraceptives was an important part of the work at the Bureau and although it was now legal to manufacture contraceptives, the industry still feared legal repercussions. Sanger had to use her networks, J. Noah Slee, Herbert Simonds and the Holland-Rantos Company, to mobilize the resources needed to secure both the niche and the legal changes within the regime. The creation of the Bureau started to apply pressure and change the system around it. The case shows the role of distributed agency and its ability to work on different parts and scales of the system to remove barriers and keep momentum.

Similarly, in the case of option pricing, the Mont Pelerin Society, the Chicago School and new economic departments around the world provided platforms for developing a new economic paradigm (what would become a landscape shift). This work paved the way for economists to develop models and formulas such as the Black–Scholes–Merton model that supported the emergence of a market-liberal discourse as well. At the same time the early successes of the Black–Scholes–Merton model built support for the new paradigm and led to the creation of new institutions. Hence, the relationship between the Black–Scholes–Merton model and the neoliberal paradigm was a symbiotic one. The platforms were also created at a key moment in time to meet the growing demand for risk-mitigation options contracts to create stability in an uncertain and changing economic environment. The change that was building was not necessarily a linear set of cause–effect factors, but was the result of distributed agency working across different scales and in different parts of the system.

The platform provided by the Chicago School of Economics was also instrumental in creating the International Monetary Market as part of the Chicago Mercantile Exchange and the Chicago Board Option Exchange. It was the academic platform for the Chicago Boys, who, together with the Pinochet regime, were instrumental in implementing market liberalism in Chile. These initiatives became leading examples and played a major role in the spread and adoption of neoclassical economics and market liberalism around the world. For example, the lessons from Chile were important to the Reagan and Thatcher administrations in adopting and implementing market-based economies in the United States and the United Kingdom.

As mentioned in the introduction, a crisis can break down a dominant system and create an opening up of resources for change, but strategic agency can also have the same effect. In our cases, strategic agency seems to involve engaging at the landscape level to target normative paradigms and meanings and values, and at the regime level to target the policies, laws and institutional forms that enact and reflect those norms and values. In the case of birth control, Sanger and her peers established the National Committee on Federal Legislation for Birth Control in 1929 and started a campaign to make birth control a socially acceptable choice (an attempt to shift landscape-level norms) and to make it legal (regime level). The former involved educating congressmen's constituents and the latter involved targeting legislators to create an amendment to the existing law that would allow physicians to distribute contraceptives and educational material on birth control. At the regime level there was a change in the cost of raising children and in unemployment in the 1930s and 1940s; at the landscape level, there was an increased demand for easily acquired, affordable and effective birth control. Also, the manufacturers' advertising campaigns began to change individual consumer attitudes to birth control – a different kind of agency, which contributed to Sanger's ability to navigate the regime level. At the regime level there were also several things happening after 1929, including the legal case about trademark infringement, *Youngs Rubber Corporation, Inc.* v. *C.I. Less & Co.*, where it was ruled that birth control could be advertised, distributed and sold (although in a limited manner). Further, in 1937 the powerful American Medical Association approved the use of contraception in certain circumstances. These are just some of the examples of small achievements by various agents that, bit by bit, contributed to eroding the dominant system.

In the case of option pricing, the Keynesian and the Bretton Woods system was weakened by the fact that it did not deliver economic stability. This failure shook the landscape-level norms and values that were attached to this system, and the instability, rather than any agent-based strategy, resulted in a crisis-driven collapse of that system. Then, Milton Friedman's ideas appealed to the Nixon administration, which led to the Nixon shocks in 1971 and the abandonment of the Bretton Woods system.

The regime actors that interacted and partnered on the residential schools – such as religious and government officials – did not result in an overthrowing of the regime. The residential schools started out as other social innovations, with reactions to a problem, the mobilization of resources, and the establishment of a niche organization that could test the idea in practice and generate new knowledge and interactions. But this testing period was cut short when agents strategically chose to interact with the regime, and then instead of the regime beginning to break down, the socially innovative initiative lost focus. Although there was Indigenous representation in formulating the new treaties that included Indigenous education, the treaties were interpreted very differently by the settler regime and the Indigenous community. The interpretations were based on two very different normative paradigms: assimilation with Western Christian culture versus education and a preservation of traditional Indigenous culture. The assimilation proponents saw it as a chance to convert young Indigenous children into Christian citizens, which was very different from the view of the Indigenous groups. The former were much more powerful and over time the assimilation regime grew stronger and began to forcibly remove children from their parents to attend off-reserve schools: a violent enforcement, rather than an empowering and innovative initiative.

Within social innovation processes, the expected positive outcomes can sometimes be derailed by unanticipated negative consequences. The residential school case is an example of co-optation where individual agency from a niche, wanting change, sought to interact with the regime, and ultimately this was detrimental. It is possible that the actors began exerting agency to interact with the regime too early, that is, without having the protection of a niche or safe space for testing and learning.

Similarly, in the case of birth control, in the late 19th century medical and technological advances in abortion and spermicide, campaigns for equal rights of women, and contraceptive ad campaigns based on commercial interests, were all niche activities and part of a growing movement. However, the American Medical Association put in place a restriction on abortions nationwide, and Anthony Comstock and his organization institutionalized the ban on birth control to include contraceptives. This was not so much co-optation, but again, an exertion of power to enforce the regime approach. Subsequently, a second wave of niche development was triggered for birth control, led by Sanger and others, which found more success. The difference in the two cases (residential schools and birth control) was that there were no agents or entrepreneurs that carried forward the intent and vision of Indigenous education, challenging the regime's tendency to co-opt, control and violently enforce. Therefore, a new education system that was built on the proactive adaptation discourse instead of the assimilationist one did not emerge. The interaction and battle between the different values in both the residential schools and birth control cases shows that multiple actors (some of whom are for or against the social innovation) have agency, and the agents represent a set of conflicting values and struggles as the conflict plays out.

AGENCY AND ACTIONS FOR ENGAGING WITH KEY MOMENTS AND OPPORTUNITIES

In the case of birth control, the Comstock Law created an opaque opportunity context for Sanger and others. I have described the plethora of strategies that Sanger used during this time. An opportunity arose when Sanger opened the first birth control clinic in the USA, which resulted in a police raid and arrests. The following trial drew media attention and created public interest in birth control. In this way, the agency exercised by Sanger created turbulence that provoked the dominating system to react. This in turn was strategically used to draw public attention and move the idea forward.

In the case of birth control, the work by Prince Morrow provided an opening of the regime by advocating contraceptives for health reasons (disease prevention) rather than for birth control. This adjacent possible provided an opportunity for Sanger to open up her first legal clinic where she could pursue her work. Despite the momentum, it seems that this was the moment that things started to shift towards a hazy opportunity context. One sign of that was the confusion on the part of the contraceptives manufacturers and their fear of repercussions in this changing context.

For residential schools, the assimilation and the adaptation of meaning and values created two different landscape attractors. The opportunities that emerged were co-opted by the existing regime and used to strengthen it. What seemed to be an opportunity for Shingwauk and others actually became an opportunity for the assimilation proponents to push their version of education. Opportunity context might change because of a crisis that creates change at the landscape level, as in the case of residential schools where World War II triggered both a change in the normative paradigm and an increased skepticism towards the schools (see Westley et al., 2016). However, the support from former soldiers and the public did not create an opaque opportunity context, nor serve as a punctuated moment of crisis that really shifted the system.

As described, for the option pricing and Black–Scholes–Merton model, the failure of the Bretton Woods system to provide economic stability opened up opportunities for new ideas. The rapid spread of the model was also due to the fact that the Chicago Board Options Exchange and Chicago's International Monetary Market provided markets that allowed for derivative exchanges. The Black–Scholes–Merton model was *also* helped by technological advances in computing power, which provided the capacity to carry out complicated calculations to make the model work. This also radically changed the role of the *quants* (mathematical analysts). Other examples of technological breakthroughs are the railroad in the National Parks case or rubber technology in the case of birth control. In all of these instances, the agency to take specific actions when these opportunities either opened, or shifted from opaque to hazy or transparent, was critical to the social innovation process.

CONCLUSION

Change agents have a key role to play in social innovation processes (Seyfang and Haxeltine, 2012) and understanding agency is key to understanding large-scale, transformative change (Westley et al., 2013). However, as shown in this volume, such change might take several hundreds of years and span several generations, which challenges some of the current approaches to studying transformative agency that focus on much shorter timescales. By applying a lens that combines insights from the literature on multiplicity of entrepreneurship forms, cross-scale interactions, and opportunity contexts to social innovation histories, this chapter has generated some key insights on transformative agency and identified possible areas for future research.

First, the study supports the notion that change agents play different roles in different phases and at different scales of social innovation

processes. In some instances, social entrepreneurs and niche actors established early platforms for developing alternative approaches. The institutional entrepreneurs in the case of option pricing targeted the regime level
for abandoning the Bretton Woods system. The moral entrepreneurs in the
case of National Parks targeted landscape-level and change discourses in
order to open up the possibility for changes at the regime level that allowed
the niche ideas to be institutionalized. However, there is an important
relationship between the different types of entrepreneurship and how
those interactions affect large-scale, transformative change. As pointed
out by Moore (Chapter 12, this volume), cross-scale interactions are key
in this regard. Scholars interested in the role of agency in large-scale,
transformative change need to focus more on distributed agency (Riddell,
2013) and incorporate concepts such as system entrepreneurship (Moore
and Westley, 2011). Based on the cases analyzed here, I define system
entrepreneurship as the accumulated, collected quality of individual, often
intergenerational, entrepreneurship interacting over long time periods.
System entrepreneurship as an organizing concept can help us analyze and
understand the combined strategies of all different forms of entrepreneurship and cross-scale interactions that are crucial for achieving large-scale,
transformative change.

Secondly, the study supports the notion that different opportunity
contexts require different strategies (Dorado, 2005). For example, in an
opaque opportunity context, such as in the case of birth control and the
early stages of that movement, change agents prepared for system change
by building awareness and targeting deeper meanings and values, mobilizing the movement, and challenging the dominant system, sometimes by
illegal methods. Then the institutional landscape changed slightly, which
created a more hazy opportunity context that allowed for the setting up of
legal clinics. Even though the institutions changed in favor of Sanger, she
still had to deal with the legacy of the Comstock Act and use new strategies to take advantage of cracks in the regime. This example also reveals
that the ability to change strategies when the opportunity context changes
is crucial. As pointed out by Westley et al. (2013), this ability is an important part of transformative agency and the capacity to achieve large-scale
change.

The cases of this book show that large-scale, transformative change can
take a long time, sometimes hundreds of years. At the same time, researchers and practitioners working on major global challenges, such as climate
change, push for large-scale change within a couple of decades. Hopefully
the insights on the role of agency and opportunity presented here can help
increase the pace of social change and contribute to achieving important
transformations.

REFERENCES

American Birth Control League (1921). Birth control: what it is, how it works, what it will do. *The Proceedings of the First American Birth Control Conference*, 11–12 November 1921. New York: The Birth Control Review.

Antadze, N. and McGowan, K.A. (2016). Moral entrepreneurship: thinking and acting at the landscape level to foster sustainability transitions. *Environmental Innovation and Societal Transitions*, in press.

Chiles, T.H., Tuggle, C.S., McMullen, J.S., Bierman, L. and Greening, D.W. (2010). Dynamic creation: extending the radical Austrian approach to entrepreneurship. *Organization Studies*, **31**(1), 7–46.

Dorado, S. (2005). Institutional entrepreneurship, partaking, and convening. *Organization Studies*, **26**(3), 385–414.

Geels, F.W. and Schot, J. (2007). Typology of sociotechnical transition pathways. *Research Policy*, **36**, 399–417.

Kingdon, J.W. (1984). *Agendas, Alternatives, and Public Policies*. Boston, MA: Little, Brown & Co.

Loorbach, D. and Rotmans, J. (2010). The practice of transition management: examples and lessons from four distinct cases. *Futures*, **42**, 237–46.

Maguire, S., Hardy, C. and Lawrence, T.B. (2004). Institutional entrepreneurship in emerging fields: HIV/AIDS treatment advocacy in Canada. *Academy of Management Journal*, **47**(5), 657–79.

Moore, M. and Westley, F. (2011). Surmountable chasms: networks and social innovation for resilient systems. *Ecology and Society*, **16**(1), 5.

Olsson, P., Folke, C. and Hahn, T. (2004). Social-ecological transformation for eco-system management: the development of adaptive comanagement of a wetland landscape in southern Sweden. *Ecology and Society*, **9**(4), 2.

Olsson, P., Gunderson, L.H., Carpenter, S.R., Ryan, P., Lebel, L., Folke, C. and Holling, C.S. (2006). Shooting the rapids: navigating transitions to adaptive governance of social-ecological systems. *Ecology and Society*, **11**(1), 18.

Riddell, D. (2013). Bring on the r/evolution: integral theory and the challenges of social transformation and sustainability. *Journal of Integral Theory and Practice*, **8**(3/4), 126–45.

Rotmans, J., Kemp, R. and Van Asselt, M. (2001). More evolution than revolution: transition management in public policy. *Foresight*, **3**, 15–31.

Seyfang, G. and Haxeltine, A. (2012). Growing grassroots innovations: exploring the role of community-based initiatives in governing sustainable energy transitions. *Environment and Planning C: Politics and Space*, **30**(3), 381–400.

Westley, F., Patton, M. and Zimmerman, B. (2006). *Getting to Maybe: How the World is Changed*. Toronto: Random House Canada.

Westley, F., Tjörnbo, O., Schultz, L., Olsson, P., Folke, C., Crona, B. and Bodin, Ö. (2013). A theory of transformative agency in linked social-ecological systems. *Ecology and Society*, **18**(3), 27.

Westley, F., Laban, S., Rose, C., McGowan, K., Robinson, K., Tjörnbo, O. and Tovey, M. (2015). *The University of Waterloo social innovation lab guide*. Available at https://uwaterloo.ca/waterloo-institute-for-social-innovation-and-resilience/projects/social-innovation-lab-guide.

Westley, F.R., K.A. McGowan, N. Antadze, J. Blacklock and O. Tjörnbo (2016). How game changers catalyzed, disrupted, and incentivized social innovation:

three historical cases of nature conservation, assimilation, and women's rights. *Ecology and Society*, **21**(4), 13.

Westley, F., Olsson, P., Folke, C., Homer-Dixon, T., Vredenburg, H., Loorbach, D., Thompson, J., Nilsson, M., Lambin, E., Sendzimir, J., Banerjee, B., Galaz, V. and van der Leeuw, S. (2011). Tipping toward sustainability: emerging pathways of transformation. *AMBIO*, **40**, 762–80.

5. The legalization of birth control in North America

Nino Antadze and Jaclyn Blacklock

Mrs Morel was alone, but she was used to it. Her son and her little girl slept upstairs; so, it seemed, her home was there behind her, fixed and stable. But she felt wretched with the coming child. . . . She could not afford to have this third. She did not want it. . . . This coming child was too much for her. If it were not for William and Annie, she was sick of it, the struggle with poverty and ugliness and meanness.

(Lawrence, 1913 [1991], p. 5)

INTRODUCTION

From the perspective of the 21st century, birth control is assumed to be the result of technological and medical breakthroughs. Yet family planning has always been exercised, albeit with different means and varying success; examples are many and historical sources abound (Riddle, 1999). McLaren sheds light on changing attitudes towards fertility control in his discussion of St Augustine. In the 4th century AD, before converting to Christianity, (the future) St Augustine led a rather loose life. For 15 years he lived with two concubines in succession, yet fathered only one child. In an age when childbearing was a constant employment of women, such a low fertility could be attributed to "Augustine's and his partners' employing those 'execrable' methods 'against nature' which he was later to lead Christians in condemning" (McLaren, 1990, p. 1).

As in the case of St Augustine, attitudes towards exercising different means of fertility control have changed repeatedly over time. These changes were not determined by economic or social conditions, medical breakthroughs, gender relations or cultural and religious contexts, but rather grew out of the web connecting all these elements.

This case considers the evolution of the constructed social phenomena surrounding the legality of birth control use and dissemination from the 1700s through to the present time. It will describe how this social innovation emerged through persistent efforts that rode the waves of changing social conditions and concerns, technological advances and legal rulings that each served to open up windows of opportunity for social entrepreneurs to pursue an adjacent possible – those new realities that are now, but were not previously, acceptable due to a change in present conditions. This particular case suggests that an adjacent possible can be instrumental in gaining momentum towards ultimately achieving a social innovation in one of two ways: either by building capacity for the social innovation or by weakening the capacity of the competition to resist the innovation.

The rivalry between those who fought for the innovation and those who fought against is at the core of this case. The ability to capitalize on a window of opportunity is strongly associated with the strength of the coalition, the group's organization, their financial and social resources and their relative power and reputation. Incremental attempts to pursue an adjacent possible most often succeeded when windows of opportunity were discovered and explored. Otherwise, no matter how organized, attempts to create change tended to be met with resistance, hostility and legal action.

THE CRUSADE AGAINST PUBLIC VICE

In the early 1800s, abortion – a radical form of birth control – was legal under the common law as long as the abortion was conducted before the mother could feel the fetus move (the quickening). In addition, other contraceptives, primarily spermicide, were commonly prepared and used in the home to prevent unplanned pregnancies (Riddle, 1999). By the early 1830s, the process of vulcanized rubber vastly improved condom and diaphragm technology – moving much of birth control out of the realm of wise women and into mass commercialization. Then the marketplace

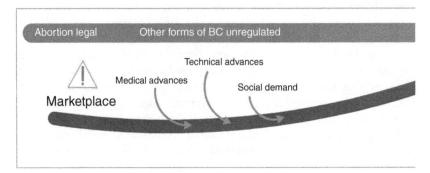

Figure 5.1   The birth control market before the Comstock Act

capitalized on the demand for birth control (Tone, 2000). Technological and medical advances in the mid-1800s contributed to the commercialization of abortions and allowed for the domestic manufacturing of condoms and rubber cervical caps, which increased the general public's use of birth control practices.

However, this increasing use of birth control spurred concerns, particularly with regard to abortions. In 1857, the American Medical Association began a crusade against abortion and petitioned for criminalization (Tone, 2000). By the end of the century, every American state had restricted abortion (Tone, 1996). However, the demand for other forms of birth control was booming. By the 1870s, many forms of regulated birth control could be purchased from mail-order houses, wholesale drug-supply houses and pharmacies (Tone, 1996). Yet public concerns lingered about the difference between birth control and abortion. Was birth control an early form of abortion? Religious supporters, particularly those of the Catholic faith, questioned the right of an individual to "play God": preventing a pregnancy was to go against the will of God (Tone, 1996).

Technical and medical advances opened a window of opportunity to commercialize birth control and a receptive marketplace indicated that the timing was right to do so (Tone, 1996). Inversely, public concerns around

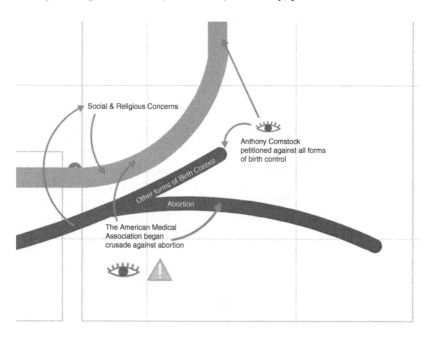

Figure 5.2   Agents seek to change the law

the morality and right of an individual to "play God" provided support for the American Medical Association to oppose open access to birth control (Tone, 1996). At this point, the coalition against birth control (led by the American Medical Association) was well organized, powerful and well-regarded by the public. Their stance on birth control, particularly abortion, may have helped define birth control, of all kinds, as immoral (Tone, 1996).

A leader in the war against immorality and public vice was Anthony Comstock. Raised at his family's farm in Connecticut, Comstock was a deeply religious man who condemned all the vices of Earthly temptation – theater, sex, alcohol; he became a "one-man crusade to eradicate sexual vice" (Tone, 2000, p. 439). Comstock had a strong conviction about right and wrong, and about the need for the collective supervision of public morals. This passion fueled his dramatic crusade against the "ways of evil" (Horowitz, 2000).

After the Civil War, Comstock started to work as a clerk in New York City. In his first attempt to banish immorality from public life, in 1868 he sued a seller of erotic material. This effort made him popular with the like-minded public. Most importantly, it earned him financial support from New York's YMCA. Assured in the truth of his mission and encouraged by the support of the YMCA, Comstock shifted his gaze from anonymous sellers to well-known celebrities (Horowitz, 2000).

Comstock targeted Victoria Woodhull, who was outspoken about women's sexuality and free love. With her sister, and the financial backing of the Vanderbilts, Woodhull published *Woodhull & Claflin's Weekly*, a newspaper where traditional structures of religion, capitalism and family were discussed and often questioned. In 1872, Comstock had Woodhull arrested for sending obscene literature through the mail. The obscene literature was Woodhull's weekly detailing the affair of a Brooklyn pastor. In June 1873, the judge acquitted Woodhull, as the existing law did not cover newspapers (Horowitz, 2000).

Although he lost the battle against Woodhull, Comstock continued his crusade against public vice; that year he founded the New York Society for the Suppression of Vice (NYSSV) (Tone, 2000). In winter 1873, Comstock lobbied for a law that would grant the Post Office the power to confiscate immoral material. The federal act for the "Suppression of Trade in, and Circulation of, Obscene Literature and Articles of Immoral Use" was adopted in 1873 (Horowitz, 2000). Under this law contraceptives were considered to be "obscene" and their advertising forbidden (Jütte, 2008). The federal law was expansive and inclusive, outlawing any: "book, pamphlet, paper, writing, advertisement, circular, print, picture, drawing, or other representation, figure, or image on or of paper or other material, or any cast, instrument, or other article of an immoral nature, or any drug

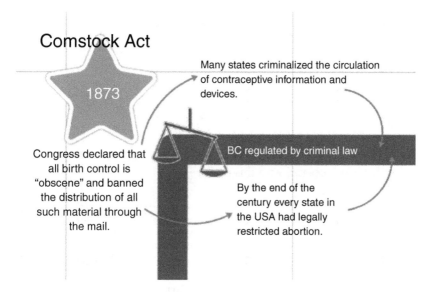

Figure 5.3   The Comstock Act and its ripples

or medicine or any article whatever for the prevention of contraception" (Tone, 1996, p. 488). The intention was for this law to inspire equal anti-obscenity state laws; the division of powers in the United States was such that the federal government outlawed interstate mailing, shipping and importation of such materials, but could not necessarily ban their sale within each state (Bailey, 2010, p. 104).

This call-and-answer style legislation was incredibly effective in the main (although language – and therefore outcome – varied significantly across geographic political boundaries). Although some states had such laws on the books before Congress passed the anti-obscenity Act, in the decades following 1873 the rest essentially followed suit (Bailey, 2010). The Act was popularly known as the Comstock Act, for its dogged and enthusiastic lobbyist and defender (Horowitz, 2000).

For the rest of his life, Comstock would serve as a special agent of the US Post Office and the NYSSV's secretary. Both posts reflected his deep commitment to ridding America of obscenity; the former post gave him access to the mail (a primary distribution channel and one of the exchanges the federal government could police) and the latter gave him a platform, especially when his organization's members were deputized to arrest those who broke both federal and New York state law (Tone, 2000). He even inserted himself into investigations – NYSSV arrested 105 people between 1873 and 1898 – and prosecutions against those selling obscene materials (Tone, 2000).

The Comstock Act and state-based mirror acts affected many. Before the Comstock Act, one-third of all advertisements in the New York-based *Sporting Times* and *Theatrical News* were related to abortion and contraceptives (Jütte, 2008). A typical advertisement would look like this:

> Best protectors against disease and accident. French rubber goods $6.00/dozen; rubber $4.00/dozen. Sample 30 cents. Trade supplied. Ladies protectors $3.00. (Jütte, 2008, p. 131)

The obituary of Comstock, published in the *New York Times* on 22 September 1915, opened with this passage:

> Anthony Comstock, Secretary for the Society for the Suppression of Vice, known world over through the controversies that have followed his crusade against books, pictures and plays that he deemed indecent, died last night at the age of seventy-one years after an illness of ten days which developed into pneumonia. (*New York Times*, 1915)

The Comstock Act was an important turning point that would base the conversation about sexual representation in society on middle-class Christian attitudes towards the body and sexuality, effectively silencing it (Horowitz, 2000; Schoen, 2005). The passage of the Comstock Act marked a tipping point, or discrete moment, where a change occurred that ultimately disrupted the entire system, effectively changing the constructed social phenomena that governed norms, values and the law. While black market entrepreneurs continued to defy Comstock and his namesake Act, overturning the Comstock Act would require a social innovation with an impact great enough to create a new institutionalized reality regarding birth control.

REDEFINING PUBLIC VICE: THE BIRTH CONTROL MOVEMENT

Driven by his passion to expel public vice, Comstock managed to silence Woodhull and other like-minded individuals. However, his victory was not long-lived; not only did many black market entrepreneurs continue to thumb their noses at his efforts using state loopholes (Tone, 2000; Bailey, 2010), but the Act itself created a target. Beginning in 1910, a campaign to overturn the Comstock Act was launched by social entrepreneurs Emma Goldman, Mary Ware Dennett and Margaret Sanger (Parry, 2011). This marked the beginning of the birth control movement spearheaded by Margaret Sanger (Tone, 1996).

Margaret Sanger was one of the most influential social reformers of her time. Commenting on the work of Sanger, Reed concludes: "through these achievements she had a greater impact on the world than any other American woman" (1978, p. 67). Comstock was driven by his inner convictions about right or wrong, vice and virtue; Sanger's long and persistent fight was ignited by her personal experiences and beliefs about the role and rights of women in society. Sanger insisted that women's sexual liberation and economic autonomy depended on the availability of safe, inexpensive and effective birth control and she wasn't afraid to defy the law to get her point across (Tone, 1996).

Margaret Sanger was born Margaret Higgins in 1879, the sixth child in an Irish-Catholic family living in a factory town in New York state. Margaret's mother had 11 children, suffered from tuberculosis and died in her forties. The loss of her mother remained a painful memory for Margaret. In her autobiography she explained that the contrast between her mother dying so young and her father living to be 84 had a profound and lasting impact on her and planted the seed of future action (Reed, 1978).

Sanger's emergence as a radical activist and social reformer was influenced by several events in the early 1910s. After attending a nursing school and getting married, Sanger moved to New York City, where she got involved in active socialist and anarchist circles. She was particularly active during the radical labor movement and participated in textile workers' strikes in Massachusetts and New Jersey in 1912 and 1913. This experience brought to Margaret's attention the poverty, desperation and misery of the workers and their families (especially the children). She concluded that unless family sizes could be controlled, workers could never provide decent support to their families. An even more important revelation for Sanger was that male leaders of the labor movement were completely unaware of and/or indifferent to women's everyday struggles (Reed, 1978).

A second instance that influenced Sanger and her future work was when she witnessed the tragic death of one of her patients, Sadie Sachs, from a self-induced abortion. Abortions, self-induced or performed by a "five-dollar abortionist" (Sanger, 1938), were common when pregnancy was a constant condition of poor and working-class women (Schoen, 2005). Sanger witnessed how women, after begging doctors to tell them how to avoid further pregnancies only to be left without answers, relied on dangerous and often fatal remedies such as self-induced abortion (Reed, 1978, pp. 81–2). Sanger recalls the impact of this traumatic experience: "no matter what it might cost, I was finished with palliatives and superficial cures; I was resolved to seek out the root of evil, to do something to change the destiny of mothers whose miseries were as vast as the sky" (Sanger, 1938, p. 92).

At the same time, Sanger experienced the Comstock Act's power first hand. In 1912 she authored articles on syphilis in the socialist daily, *The Call*. The content of the article was considered to be obscene and the Post Office decided to refuse to distribute the daily, based on regulations under the Comstock Act. Similarly in 1914, Sanger started to publish the periodical with the catchy title *The Woman Rebel* and even more revolutionary anarchist slogan "No Gods, No Masters!" As *The Woman Rebel* gained popularity, Sanger illegally published a pamphlet titled "Family Limitation" with detailed information about contraception. However, in 1914, to avoid prosecution she left the US for Europe, only to return upon the death of Anthony Comstock (Reed, 1978).

When Sanger returned to America, she opened the first birth control clinic in that country with her sister Ethel Byrne and colleague Fania Mindell. The clinic was located in Brooklyn, New York and nine days after the grand opening, police raided it and arrested the three founders – an outcome Sanger anticipated and provoked (Parry, 2011). As anticipated, a great deal of media attention surrounded the trial and heightened public curiosity about birth control (Parry, 2011). As Reed explains, Sanger was good "at capturing the public imagination, a master of the dramatic, and a skillful exploiter of the media and of uncommonly silly laws" (1978, p. 103).

With the distribution of print material on contraception strictly regulated by the Comstock Act, sexual education promoters desperately needed another medium through which to communicate with the masses. Film offered that avenue and many sexual education promoters turned to film and spurred a genre of "sex hygiene" films that were created as educational pieces but disguised as entertainment (Parry, 2011). However, the legal forces quickly caught on to this and in 1915 the Supreme Court denied film the protection of free speech (Parry, 2011). This had the inverse effect of encouraging filmmakers to be more creative – rather than silent – in how they got their messages across.

Lois Weber, a well-respected director in Hollywood at the time, was very creative and successful in her effort to create a film promoting birth control (Parry, 2011). Weber's film, *Where are My Children?*, used a double narrative to demonize abortion on the one hand, and on the other hand to promote birth control as a humane way for poor families to take care of the children they already had (Parry, 2011). Despite the underlying message that birth control was not immoral, Sanger wished the film's narrative was more forthright about the necessity of birth control (Parry, 2011). However, later films that were more direct in addressing the birth control issue, including Sanger's film *Birth Control* and Weber's second film *The Hand that Rocks the Cradle*, were banned, so never got mass showings (Parry, 2011).

While film offered a new medium for social entrepreneurs, the agenda to promote birth control, at this time, failed miserably. Without a clear window of opportunity and an organized and powerful social enterprise to support the agenda, Sanger's attempts to challenge the Comstock Act were met with great resistance. She was run out of the country due to the illegal publication of a birth control pamphlet, she was arrested and criminally charged after opening an illegal birth control clinic and her films experienced extreme censorship due to her outright disregard for film regulations. While Sanger certainly stirred things up, she also created a reputation for herself as a troublemaker.

Early in the movement for birth control and women's sexual liberation, syphilis and gonorrhoea had become significant social problems for both sexes. This was accentuated during the First World War, when sexually transmitted diseases among the troops soared. Prince Morrow, a New York physician, set out to tackle the issue by initiating a sex education campaign. He began to talk about sex and related issues in public forums. Suddenly the use of condoms seemed important for the sexual health of both partners, not just for birth control (Morrow, 1904).

This campaign opened a window of opportunity to petition for the legal use of one form of birth control: condoms. Until 1918, section 207 of the Criminal Code, which made birth control illegal, contained a clause that allowed for the distribution of birth control that was used for public good. However, physicians who provided information on birth control risked prosecution. In 1918, the New York Court of Appeals expanded this exception by allowing physicians to prescribe contraception for the sure prevention of disease (Parry, 2011, p. 119). This exception allowed for the creation of an adjacent possible whereby physician-run clinics could legally prescribe birth control for the prevention of disease.

In 1923 Sanger capitalized on this loophole in the law and opened the first legal, physician-run birth control clinic in the United States (Parry, 2011). This clinic was called the Clinical Research Bureau and the primary activities of the clinic included dispensing contraceptives and collecting data on their use (Parry, 2011). Finally, Sanger had the beginnings of a social enterprise. However, without an existing market for safe and effective birth control, supply proved to be an issue (Parry, 2011).

Most American manufacturers still feared the legal repercussions of manufacturing birth control products. Sanger's second husband, J. Noah H. Slee, financed the Holland-Rantos Company, which, with the involvement of an engineer and plastic manufacturer Herbert Simonds, manufactured diaphragms and lactic acid jelly for Sanger's clinics (Tone, 1996). As Reed points out, "the availability of reliable contraceptives in the United States by the late 1920s was made possible by J. Noah Slee and Herbert

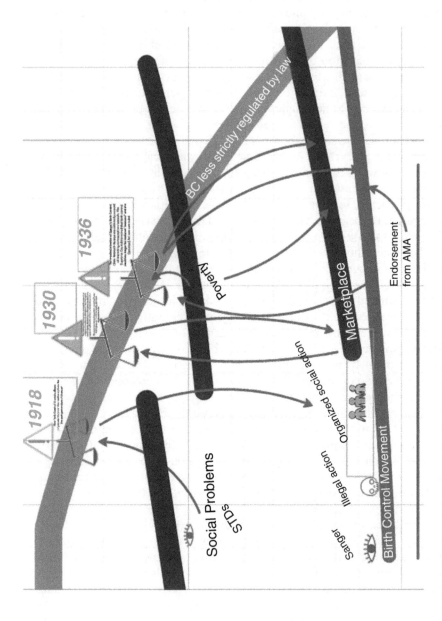

Figure 5.4 The fight(s) against the Comstock Act: from niche to landscape

Simonds, two staunch capitalists who sought the favor of Margaret Sanger more than profit" (1978, p. 115). For the first time, Sanger's pro-birth control coalition was gaining momentum and compiling resources.

In 1929, Sanger established the National Committee on Federal Legislation for Birth Control (NCFL) in New York City (Murphree and Gower, 2008). In this initiative Sanger and her colleagues used communication objectives, strategies and tactics to implement a widespread public relations campaign to make birth control both legal and socially acceptable (Murphree and Gower, 2008). The Committee's task was twofold. The first objective was to persuade legislators to create an amendment allowing physicians to disseminate contraceptive and educational information about birth control. The second was to conduct a widespread ongoing campaign to educate the Congressmen's constituents, urging them to voice their opinions and mobilizing them into pressure groups in case of "legislative emergency" (Murphree and Gower, 2008).

In 1930, the case *Youngs Rubber Corporation, Inc.* v. *C.I. Less & Co., Inc., et al.*, where makers of Trojan condoms successfully sued a rival company for trademark infringement, forced the court to decide whether the contraceptive business was legal and thus legitimately entitled to trademark protection. The court ruled that as long as birth control had "other lawful purposes", it could be legally advertised, distributed and sold (Tone, 1996). Now, birth control for any lawful purpose, not just the prevention of disease, could be advertised and sold in the open market. Still, birth control could not be advertised or sold as birth control. However, social issues such as poverty were becoming prominent, in addition to sexual health concerns. At a time when the cost of raising children was increasing, poverty as a result of family size was of great concern.

In the 1930s and 1940s, the cost of raising children was rising. An unprecedented and increasing proportion of the population was officially unemployed. Controlling fertility assumed added urgency. With public birth control clinics few in number and privately prescribed diaphragms financially and medically out of reach for most women, access to easily acquired, affordable and effective birth control became a widely shared goal. Millions of women turned to the contraceptive market (Tone, 1996). Access in this period was very much tied to class and political geography (Tone, 2000; Schoen, 2005); women who lived in states with more explicit individual laws were 25 to 30 percent less likely than their interstate sisters to have used contraceptives before 1965 (Bailey, 2010).

Manufacturers of contraception campaigned for more women to use birth control, but also ensured that the majority of them used female-controlled, commercially acquired contraceptives (Tone, 1996). The commercial market, through persuasive advertising, helped to change individual consumer attitudes. Birth control advertising in the 1930s implicitly asked the obvious: Could a woman in the "modern age" afford not to buy the newest contraception? (Tone, 1996).

The United States did not act in a vacuum: the Anglo-American world and beyond has stories of birth control campaigners pushing for adjacent possibles. The first Canadian birth control clinic opened in 1932 in Hamilton, Ontario, with Dr Elizabeth Bagshaw as clinical director (Tone, 1996). While the clinic gained acceptance over time, it operated illegally until 1969 (Tone, 1996). The Parents' Information Bureau in Canada was opened in 1935 by A.R. Kaufman, Chair of Kaufman Rubber Company in Kitchener, an industrial Ontario town similar to Hamilton (Tone, 1996). Kaufman realized that during the great depression, many of his employees struggled with poverty because of their large families (Tone, 1996). However, Dorothea Palmer, one of the Parents' Information Bureau nurses, was arrested for distributing birth control devices. She was eventually acquitted under the "public good" clause of Canada's Criminal Code (Tone, 1996).

At this point, Sanger's clinics were expanding and as public attitudes began to favor the idea of birth control, they served more and more people. However, the supply of affordable and effective birth control in North America was still minimal. In 1936 the medical director of Sanger's Birth Control Clinic Research Bureau in NYC was criminally accused of importing contraceptive materials from Japan. In this case, known as *US* v. *One Package of Japanese Pessaries*, the Supreme Court determined that birth control could no longer be declared obscene. This allowed physicians in every state to legally send and receive contraceptive devices and information through the mail for the first time since the Comstock Act was passed in 1873 (Tone, 1996). While this declaration marks a significant turning point in the birth control movement, contraception for the purpose of controlling pregnancies was still not legal.

In 1937, the American Medical Association finally endorsed the use of contraception for certain circumstances, such as preventing sexually transmitted diseases (Tone, 1996). By 1938 many conversations arose surrounding birth control and related issues. At this time at least four hundred firms, in addition to Holland-Rantos, were competing in the lucrative birth control market (Tone, 1996).

In 1938, the Federal Food, Drug, and Cosmetic Act enlarged the Food and Drug Administration's regulatory powers, authorizing the government agency to hold medical devices to some of the same standards as drugs (Tone, 1996). However, because devices used for the purposes of birth control were still not legal, they could not be FDA regulated and many people became sick and even died from the use of unsafe contraception (including Lysol) (Tone, 1996). Condoms, on the other hand, could be considered a medical device for the prevention of venereal disease. As a result, in 1938 and 1939 the FDA destroyed 75 batches of defective condoms (Tone, 1996).

While many women were buying birth control, to use it was still taboo in the public eye. Department stores distributed contraception under the guise of "feminine hygiene" in personal hygiene departments that were staffed primarily by women. Contraceptive manufacturers promoted the creation of personal hygiene departments by emphasizing to store owners and managers the revenues they would generate. Women could also buy at home through catalogues that were written in a "legally censored" manner (Tone, 1996). However, many commercial products (because they were not legally birth control products) remained ineffective and/or unsafe (Tone, 1996).

Meanwhile, the Sanger crusade to become organized, resourceful and powerful in the quest to legitimize birth control contributed to the creation of many social enterprises. The Clinical Research Bureau was renamed several times between 1923 and 1942 to reflect present circumstances and changing public attitudes (Parry, 2011). It became the Birth Control Clinical Research Bureau in 1928 and in 1939 it joined with the American Birth Control League to form the Birth Control Federation of America, which in 1942 changed its name to Planned Parenthood Federation of America (Parry, 2011). The Birth Control Clinical Research Bureau, which continued to function as the largest contraceptive clinic in the country, changed its name to the Margaret Sanger Research Bureau in 1940, in honor of its founder (Parry, 2011).

The birth control pill became available in Canada in 1960. Although it was illegally prescribed for contraception, doctors could prescribe it for therapeutic reasons such as "menstrual regulation" (Parry, 2011). Condoms could generally be bought at drug stores although they were kept out of sight. In 1961 a Toronto pharmacist was charged, convicted and fined for selling condoms (Parry, 2011). Barbara and George Cadbury established the Planned Parenthood Association of Toronto for the purpose of changing the law (Parry, 2011).

Margaret Sanger died in 1966. At the time of her death, contraceptives for married couples were legal in almost all states, the Pill was widely marketed, and national branches of the International Planned Parenthood Federation flourished in the US and beyond (Parry, 2011).

In Canada, on 1 July 1969, Parliament decriminalized contraception by passing amendments to Section 251 of the Criminal Code. The same legislation also decriminalized abortions under extremely restricted conditions (Parry, 2011).

In 1988, the Supreme Court of Canada ruled that Canada's abortion law was unconstitutional (Parry, 2011). It was found to infringe upon a woman's right to "life, liberty and security of person" under the Charter of Rights and Freedoms (Parry, 2011). This decision decriminalized abortions in Canada, making it a medical procedure governed by national health policy rather than criminal law (Parry, 2011).

Today, in both Canada and the US the use of birth control is widespread and conversations about "safe sex" and planned pregnancies are commonplace in homes and schools across the nations. Condoms are readily available in pharmacies and other stores that sell health-related products, and the Pill is available with a prescription from a doctor. In addition, "Plan B", the first product approved by Health Canada to be packaged and marketed specifically as Emergency Contraception in Canada became available with a doctor's prescription in 1999. Presently Plan B is available from pharmacies over-the-counter, without a medical consultation.

A NEW SOCIAL PHENOMENON

In North America, the widely accepted idea that birth control is not "obscene" or "immoral" is an example of a constructed social phenomenon that has had broad impact and implications at the landscape level.

The decriminalization of contraception in Canada on 1 July 1969 by Parliament marked a major institutional shift that significantly changed the rules, norms and procedures for providing and using contraception in Canada, a feat that might not have been possible without the culmination of new ideas, adjacent possibles and innovations.

With freedom of choice came the sexual liberation of women. This brought us one step closer to gender equality and helped families to financially plan and prepare for the upbringing of children. The social benefits included families having the chance to stave off poverty by limiting the number of mouths they had to feed, and young women getting the opportunity to pursue desires outside of motherhood. Without the burden of unplanned or multiple pregnancies, birth control affords young women a greater opportunity to pursue post-secondary education and paid employment.

REFERENCES

Bailey, M. (2010). Momma's got the Pill: how Anthony Comstock and *Griswold vs. Connecticut* shaped US childbearing. *American Economic Review*, **100**(1), 90–129.
Birth Control (1917). Documentary film produced and written by Margaret Sanger, USA: B.S. Moss Motion Picture Corporation.

Hand that Rocks the Cradle (1917). Film produced and directed by Lois Weber and Phillips Smalley, USA: Universal Film Manufacturing Company.

Horowitz, H.L. (2000). Victoria Woodhull, Anthony Comstock, and conflict over sex in the United States in the 1870s. *The Journal of American History*, **87**(2), 403–34.

Jütte, R. (2008). *Contraception. A History*, trans. V. Russell. Cambridge: Polity.

Lawrence, D.H. (1913 [1991]). *Sons and Lovers*. New York: Alfred A. Knopf.

McLaren, A. (1990). *A History of Contraception: From Antiquity to the Present Day*. Cambridge, MA: Basil Blackwell.

Morrow, P. (1904). *Social Diseases and Marriage: Social Prophylaxis*. New York: Lea Bros.

Murphree, V. and Gower, K.K. (2008). Mission accomplished: Margaret Sanger and the National Committee on Federal Legislation for Birth Control, 1929–1937. *American Journalism*, **25**(2), 7–32.

New York Times (1915). Anthony Comstock dies in his crusade. *New York Times*, 22 September, p. 6.

Parry, M. (2011). "Pictures with a purpose": the birth control debate on the big screen. *Journal of Women's History*, **23**(4), 108–30.

Reed, J. (1978). *From Private Vice to Public Virtue: the Birth Control Movement and American Society since 1830*. New York: Basic Books.

Riddle, J. (1999). *Eve's Herbs: A History of Contraception and Abortion in the West*, revised edn. Cambridge, MA: Harvard University Press.

Sanger, M.H. (1938). *An Autobiography*. New York: W.W. Norton.

Schoen, J. (2005). *Choice & Coercion: Birth Control, Sterilization, and Abortion in Public Health and Welfare*. Chapel Hill, NC: University of North Carolina Press.

Tone, A. (1996). Contraceptive consumers: gender and the political economy of birth control in the 1930s. *Journal of Social History*, **29**(3), 485–506.

Tone, A. (2000). Black market birth control: contraceptive entrepreneurship and criminality in the gilded age. *The Journal of American History*, **87**(2), 435–59.

United States v. *One Package of Japanese Pessaries* (1936), 86 F.2d 737 (2d Cir.)

Youngs Rubber Corporation, Inc. v. *C.I. Lee & Co., Inc., et al.* (1930), 45 F.2d 103 (2d Cir.) Circuit Court of Appeals, 347.

Where Are My Children? (1916). Film produced and directed by Lois Weber and Phillips Smalley, USA: Lois Weber Productions, Universal Film Manufacturing Company.

6. The duty to consult and accommodate in Canada

Erin Alexiuk

INTRODUCTION

The question underlying Aboriginal[1] and non-Aboriginal relations in Canada may be summed up by Michael Asch, "What, beyond the fact that we have the numbers and the power to insist on it, authorizes our [Non-Aboriginal Canadians] being here to stay?" (2014, p. 3). The answer is not static: as a social phenomenon, land ownership in Canada has had three major phases since the Seven Years War: (1) shared authority by multiple sovereign Aboriginal nations; (2) dominance by the Crown/Canadian government; and (3) recognition of Aboriginal title and the legal duty to consult and accommodate. This last social phenomenon has created space for an emergent social innovation, one that builds on the past: the duty to consult and accommodate.

The social fact/phenomenon surrounding authority and ownership over land has shifted significantly over the past two hundred and fifty years, with remarkable political, economic and cultural consequences. Therefore, this chapter tracks the social fact over time, beginning with the Seven Years War (1756–63) (see Figure 6.1). At first, competing European sovereignties held military alliances (of convenience) with Aboriginal Peoples, implicitly or explicitly recognizing the latter as sovereign nations, even if under the Crown. Over time, unilateral assertions of British sovereignty were buttressed by the additional, powerful social facts dearly held by most Canadian colonists and government officials: the superiority of Enlightenment science, Christian beliefs and European culture. These social facts, which privileged the new Canadian state, justified and drove assimilation policies that saw Aboriginal land rights as usufructuary (and not a matter of ownership), and Aboriginal cultures, traditions and ways of life as backward and in need of state intervention. Programs like the Residential School system (see Chapter 10) were born into and very much part of this intellectual environment.

However, these social facts – powerful as they may be – were not immutable. In 1973, the *Calder* decision disrupted the path of assimilation policy.

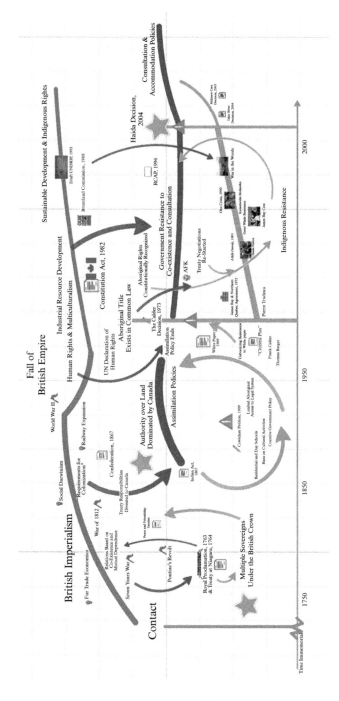

Figure 6.1   The duty to consult and accommodate as an emergent social innovation: a historical perspective from the Seven Years War until the present

89

This decision, that sovereignty did not necessarily flow from the Crown, but could also flow from original occupancy, created a huge window of opportunity towards an adjacent possible. Eventually this led to a critical tipping point, the *Haida* decision, which committed the Crown to pursuing a reconciliatory relationship with Aboriginal Peoples and restricted government authority over lands through a legal duty to consult and accommodate. Although structures of colonialism persist, subsequent court rulings and the rise of consultation and accommodation practices – emergent social innovations – demonstrate the power of social phenomena around land.

1750–1800: NEGOTIATING PEACE AND SETTLEMENT AFTER THE SEVEN YEARS WAR

The mid-18th century was a chaotic time in North America as British and French forces fought across the globe. Both sides sought out Aboriginal Nations as allies and respected their own, if not their enemies', Aboriginal allies' sovereignty with treaties and presents. White explains, "precisely because so many interests were at stake in a region where no single group exercised significant control, the road to conflict became more and more slippery" (2011, p. 227). This chaos culminated in the Seven Years War, wherein the British defeated the French in 1760.

Once dominant, the British acted in accordance with the Enlightenment belief that civilized society should not bend to the "savage" inhabitants of their newly acquired colonies. This social fact – the superiority of British society to Aboriginal ones encountered in North America – justified the British's end to symbolic present-giving and to the new paternalistic policies that "infantilized" Aboriginal Peoples (White, 2011, p. 256). In response, Aboriginal nations near the Great Lakes quickly mounted a military offensive. Pontiac's Revolt in 1763, named after Chief Pontiac of the Ottawa nation, was successful in both uniting several Aboriginal nations and capturing all but three British outposts in the Great Lakes region (White, 2011). This significant show of strength forced the British to explore treaties, negotiations and gifts, as the French had often done. This was a strategic choice, not an emergent social phenomenon or new social arrangement (White, 2011; Miller, 2009).

At the resulting peace conference at Niagara in 1764, Aboriginal and colonial representatives affirmed the Royal Proclamation of 1763. The Proclamation included guidelines for sharing lands and resources, and prohibitions on the sale of Aboriginal land outside of the Crown treaty process (Borrows, 1998; Godlewska and Webber, 2007). As the following excerpts show, the Royal Proclamation formalized a system of authority over lands that acknowledged multiple Aboriginal sovereigns within the Crown colonies of North America:

> the several Nations or Tribes of Indians with whom We are connected, and who live under Our Protection, should not be molested or disturbed in the Possession of such Parts of Our Dominions and Territories as, not having been ceded to or purchased by Us, are reserved to them, or any of them, as their Hunting Grounds . . . We do hereby strictly forbid, on Pain of Our Displeasure, all Our loving Subjects from making any Purchases or Settlements whatever, or taking Possession of any of the Lands above reserved, without Our especial Leave and Licence for that Purpose first obtained . . . if, at any Time, any of the said Indians should be inclined to dispose of the said Lands, that same shall be purchased only for Us, in Our Name, at some public Meeting or Assembly of the said Indians. (As quoted in INAC, 2016)

Although left with few options, 2000 chiefs made the journey to Niagara (Borrows, 1998; 2005; White, 2011). Numerous exchanges of presents, oral promises and wampum belts (a common diplomatic tool used by Aboriginal Peoples, particularly in Eastern Canada) marked the event. Among these was a Two Row Wampum belt that represented a relationship between Aboriginal Peoples and the British Empire built on peace, friendship, respect and a promise of non-interference in each other's internal affairs (Borrows, 1998; 2005) (see Figure 6.2).

Some British bureaucrats and many Aboriginal Peoples working to forge productive relationships understood that the events at Niagara in 1764 did not imply Aboriginal Peoples' loss of sovereignty. A year later, Superintendent of Indian Affairs William Johnson (husband of a Mohawk woman, and a highly regarded British negotiator) invoked the symbolism of the Two Row Wampum when he evaluated a report that implied Aboriginal Peoples had been mistreated: "These people had subscribed to a Treaty with me at Niagara in August last . . . they can not be brought under our laws, for some Centuries" (as quoted in Borrows, 1998, p. 164). As Yirush explains, "[Aboriginal Peoples] saw themselves as both subjects and allies of the Crown . . . a conditional subjection in which they ceded some of their original rights in return for being treated as coequal polities in the empire, with autonomy over their own affairs" (2012, p. 146).

A SOCIAL PHENOMENON AND ASSIMILATION

1800–1900: New Conditions, New Social Facts, New Laws

The early 1800s saw a steep erosion of the relationships affirmed at Niagara in 1764. The end of the Napoleonic Wars and the War of 1812

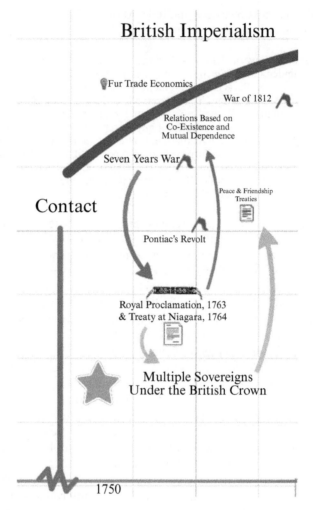

*Figure 6.2   Negotiating peace and settlement after the Seven Years War
(1750–1800)*

were coupled with dramatic emigration to British North America (Miller,
2009). Miller explains that in 1812, the Aboriginal population had
dropped to 10 percent of the settler population in Upper Canada and
"between 1821 and 1851, British North America's population increased
from 750000 to 2.3 million" (2009, p.94), compounded by decreased
access to traditional food sources and staggering losses due to smallpox
and other imported diseases. In the absence of a significant military

agenda after the War of 1812, and a growing settler state in North America, expensive payments and presents promised in treaties were no longer a strategic necessity (Miller, 2009).

While fiscal drivers influenced declining interest in treaty promises, a growing British imperial ethos gained traction and strength as a social fact. Britain pursued assimilation across its colonies to bring non-Europeans into their political and economic systems, Christian beliefs and the settled, agricultural lifestyles perceived to be necessary for progress (Miller, 2009; Chamberline, 1998). This powerful set of social phenomena drove Canadian policy and practice (see Figure 6.3).

Colonists increasingly regarded Aboriginal Peoples as hindrances to economic progress, and conflicts became the norm (Miller, 2009). Near Sault Ste Marie, mining tickets were awarded for exploration along the northern coast of Lake Huron, leading to a years-long conflict that led to the Superior and Robinson Huron treaties of 1850. Reflecting on the treaty negotiation and the shift away from traditional relations between the British Crown and Aboriginal nations, Garden River Chief Shinguakonse said:

> When your white children came into this country, they did not come shouting the war cry and seeking to wrest this land from us . . . Time wore on and you have become a great people, whilst we have melted away like snow beneath an April sun; our strength is wasted, our countless warriors dead, our forest laid low, you have hunted us from every place as with a wand, you have swept away all our pleasant land. (As quoted in Miller, 2009, p. 117)

Canada's Confederation in 1867 marked a continuance of assimilation policies. Progress-oriented policy makers continued to foster cultural shifts among Aboriginal Peoples toward the European ideal, supported by popular theories (social facts) such as Social Darwinism (Smith, 1999; Yazzie, 2000). Exerting its now substantial power over a declining Aboriginal population, Canada introduced the Indian Act in 1876, which identified Aboriginal Peoples as wards of the Crown, created/reduced reserve lands, and established Indian agents to implement the Act. This was a policy embodiment of the social phenomenon of imperialism.

Cairns (2000) explains that although assimilation policy is now viewed as arrogant, ignorant and ineffective, Canada's fiscally prudent approach to colonizing Canada was then touted as superior to the military approach in the US. Miller explains, "in the 1870s, when the United States was spending $20 million a year on Indian wars, Ottawa's entire budget was only $19 million" (2000, p. 210). Railway construction and westward expansion characterized early Canadian government priorities; treaties continued to formally extinguish Aboriginal titles and facilitate economic

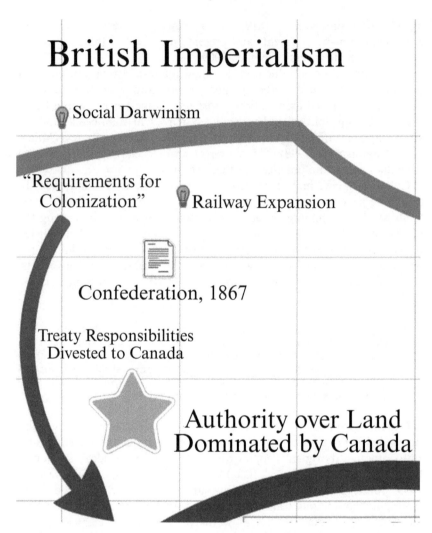

British Imperialism

Social Darwinism

"Requirements for Colonization"   Railway Expansion

Confederation, 1867

Treaty Responsibilities
Divested to Canada

Authority over Land
Dominated by Canada

Figure 6.3   New conditions, new social facts, new laws

and railroad expansion to the north and west (Godlewska and Webber, 2007; Miller, 2009). Desperation grew on the Prairies as the buffalo herd died out and broken promises mounted. In 1885, the Metis led a major military action against Canada, now known as the North-West Rebellion/ Second Riel Rebellion/ Second Riel War. Unlike Pontiac's revolt, this rebellion encouraged Canada to take a hard-line, coercive approach to Aboriginal policy which included: prohibitions on ceremonies such as the

Potlatch and Sun Dance, coercive methods for voluntary (and for a time, involuntary) enfranchisement and compulsory attendance at residential schools (Miller, 2004).

Contemporaneous with the Rebellion was the *St Catherine's Milling* decision. An early provincial–federal conflict over when Crown land became provincial (within a province) or federal (within a territory), the case hinged on whether the Saulteaux Tribe of Ojibwa peoples had previously held title and transferred it to the Crown when they signed Treaty 3 (the North-West Angle Treaty) in 1873 (McNeil, 1999). The decision, ultimately heard by the Privy Council, concluded that all sovereignty and control over land flowed from the Crown by way of the Royal Proclamation 1763 and prior occupation only supported usufructuary rights (McNeil, 1999; *St Catherine's Milling and Lumber Co.* v. *R.*, 1887). This decision codified the social phenomenon the Canadian government used in their interactions with Aboriginal peoples: Aboriginal rights and title were limited and all flowed from the Crown.

1900–1930: A Glimpse of the Adjacent Possible

Despite the deep basin of attraction created by ideological, cultural, political and economic elements of assimilation policy, Aboriginal Peoples resisted colonial policy and asserted self-determination (see Figure 6.4).

In the early 1900s, Aboriginal leaders on the west coast advanced a new strategy to address authority over Aboriginal title lands that had not been ceded to the Crown. A delegation of chiefs (including Squamish Chief Joe Capilano (Kayapalanexw) and Cowichan Chief Charlie Tsulpi'multw) traveled to London to meet King Edward and the Canadian High Commissioner, with a petition:

> In other parts of Canada the Indian title has been extinguished, reserving sufficient land for the use of the Indians, but in British Columbia the Indian title has never been extinguished, nor has sufficient land been allotted to our people for their maintenance . . . We have appealed to the Dominion government, which is made up of men elected by the white people who are living on our lands, and of course, can get no redress from that quarter . . . We are but poor ignorant Indians and know nothing of the white man's law; but we are persuaded that your majesty will not suffer us to be trodden upon, or taken advantage of. (As quoted in UBCIC, 2014)

Perceiving some success, the delegation spread word that the British Crown supported their cause, spurring several more petitions by Aboriginal nations throughout British Columbia (Foster and Berger, 2008).

This increase in Aboriginal activism and political involvement drew the

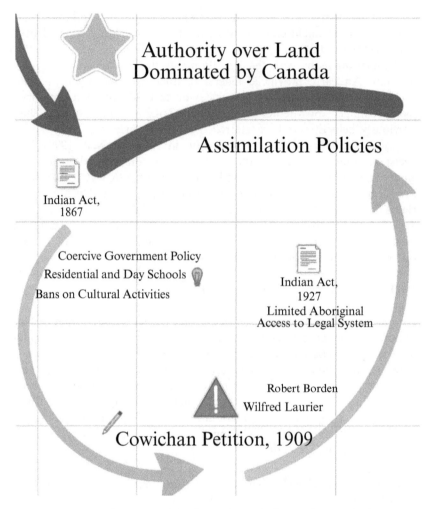

Figure 6.4   Legal petitions for Aboriginal title deepen basin of attraction

attention of the legal profession and, in particular, that of lawyers John Murray McShane Clark and Arthur O'Meara (Foster, 2007). The addition of lawyers as allies and advocates for Aboriginal title introduced novel discourse to the discussion. The resulting bricolage of Aboriginal understandings of land authority and British legal interpretations of title resulted in the Cowichan Petition, the first petition to express Aboriginal title in British legal terms. Specifically, the Cowichan Petition outlines Cowichan rights and title "since time immemorial" with respect to the Royal Proclamation:

The lands belonging to and claimed by the said Cowichan Tribe as aforesaid were never ceded to or purchased by the Crown nor was the Indian title otherwise extinguished. These lands were not within the limits of the territory at the date of the said proclamation, namely, 7th October 1763 . . . the said Cowichan Tribe as well as all Indians in North America have always regarded the said Proclamation of their great Father King George III as the Charter of their rights. (As quoted in Foster and Berger, 2008, p. 262)

Several other west coast nations followed suit with legal petitions to London, using the Cowichan Petition as a template (Foster and Berger, 2008). In response, the federal government sought a legal opinion on Aboriginal title in British Columbia. Tom McInnes wrote a critical response for Canada that argued the federal government had an obligation to settle the Aboriginal title question through the courts. He asserted Aboriginal title was clearly not extinguished in several parts of the province and therefore Aboriginal Peoples likely retained some authority over lands in British Columbia (Foster, 2007; Foster and Berger, 2008).

Prime Minister Laurier appeared to take McInnes's arguments seriously. Uneasy with the direction Ottawa seemed to be taking, British Columbia Premier Richard McBride wrote a letter to Prime Minister Laurier in 1910:

[A court decision favoring Aboriginal title] . . . would affect the title to all the land on the mainland . . . and would have a most disastrous effect on our financial standing and would jeopardize the very large sums of money already invested in this province by English and other investors. I think you will agree with me that this is too serious a matter to be submitted to the determination of any court, however competent from a legal point of view . . . the considerations involved in this are political considerations and not legal questions. (Quoted in Foster and Berger, 2008, p. 71)

Premier McBride was steadfast in his reluctance to allow any Aboriginal claims in the courts. This position was made possible through the Crown's "sovereign immunity from suit", which prohibited anyone from suing the Crown without its prior permission (Foster, 2007, p. 70). Several negotiations took place between the federal and BC government in attempts to sway Premier McBride. In early 1911, Laurier is quoted as saying:

It is our duty to have the matter inquired into. The Government of British Columbia may be right or wrong in their assertion that the Indians have no claim whatever. Courts of Law are for just that purpose – where a man asserts a claim and it is denied by another. But we do not know if we can force a Government into Court. If we can find a way I may say we may surely do so. (As quoted in Foster and Berger, 2008, p. 258)

Following through on his words, in a substantial demonstration of political will in favor of Aboriginal Peoples, Order-in-Council 1081 was passed in May 1911 and the federal government ordered the land question in British Columbia to court for legal review (Foster and Berger, 2008). Could that have set the stage for a landscape scale shift in Canadian Aboriginal policy?

Six months later, before the scheduled court date, the Laurier government fell. Robert Borden's conservative government took power and the window of opportunity for a change in Aboriginal policy quickly shut. Borden's top priority was economic expansion and accordingly he supported Premier McBride's position that settling Aboriginal title was a political matter, not a legal one (Cairns, 2000; Foster, 2007). Prime Minister Borden initiated the Royal Commission on Indian Affairs in British Columbia in 1912 (now known as the McKenna–McBride commission) which, after four years of hearings, recommended the establishment of smaller reserves on less valuable lands (Foster, 2007).

When the federal government implemented the McKenna–McBride commission recommendations in 1927, the *Indian Act* was also amended to prohibit raising funds to argue Aboriginal title claims in court, and a parliamentary joint committee released a decision stating that all Aboriginal title was extinguished in British Columbia (Foster, 2007; Miller, 2004).

These developments contributed to the deep path dependency of colonial policy and a deep basin of attraction that would keep the assimilationist regime in place for another 50 years. Chief Peter Kelly of the Haida Nation aptly predicted the situation that would persist in the interim:

> The Indians have no voice in the affairs of this country. They have not a solitary way of bringing anything before the Parliament of this country, except as we have done last year by petition, and it is a might hard thing. If we press for that we are called agitators, simply agitators, trouble makers, when we try to get what we consider to be our rights. . .it has taken us between forty and fifty years to get where we are today. And, perhaps, if we are turned down now. . .it might be another century before a new generation will rise up and begin to press this claim. (As quoted by Foster, 2007, p. 84)

A SHIFTING POLITICAL AND LEGAL LANDSCAPE

1945–70: Aboriginal Rights and the Unifying Impact of Trudeau's White Paper

The end of the Second World War marked the beginning of the fall of the British Empire and the end of colonialism – naming Canada, Australia and New Zealand as (post) colonial countries – despite the ongoing colonial experience of the original inhabitants (Yazzie, 2000). In Canada,

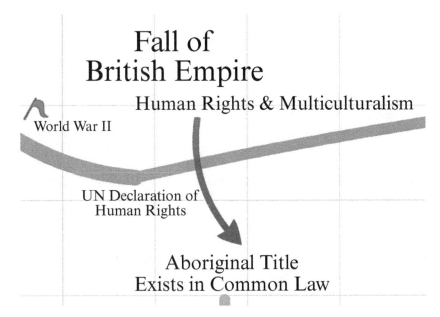

Figure 6.5   Political and legal landscapes shifts following World War II

returning Aboriginal soldiers resisted paternalistic policies and inequities (Shewell, 2012). Similarly, non-Aboriginal Canadians became acutely aware of discriminatory, assimilationist policies after fighting side-by-side with Aboriginal soldiers (Shewell, 2012). These realizations – emerging social phenomena about Aboriginal Peoples among Canadians broadly – undermined the social facts that had supported assimilation policies (see Figure 6.5).

The Canadian government's 1951 Indian Act amendments lifted the prohibitions on traditional ceremonies and obtaining legal counsel for land claims, although the law remained heavily assimilationist (Cairns, 2000; Shewell, 2012). The growing disparity between law and shifting social facts meant that government policy towards Aboriginal Peoples continued to draw criticism, both nationally and internationally (Shewell, 2012). In response, Prime Minister John Diefenbaker began a three-year study on the socio-economic status of Indigenous Peoples in Canada led by H.B. Hawthorn, a known assimilation critic and Aboriginal rights supporter (Cairns, 2000; Shewell, 2012). The resulting Hawthorn Report concluded that assimilationist policies since Confederation had resulted in Aboriginal Peoples' structural poverty (Hawthorn, 1966).

However, the civil rights movement in the US and new federal policy on multiculturalism focused discussion regarding social problems in

Aboriginal communities on racial prejudice, rather than the denial of Aboriginal title and rights. In 1969, the Trudeau government released its *White Paper*, an official policy statement on the federal government's approach to Indigenous Peoples (DIAND, 1969). The *White Paper* proposed the end of the *Indian Act*, effective termination of treaties, elimination of Indian status, and no recognition of Aboriginal rights (Godlewska and Webber, 2007; DIAND, 1969). The *White Paper* stated that "the separate legal status of Indians and the policies which have flowed from it have kept the Indian people apart from and behind other Canadians" (DIAND, 1969, p. 6) and that to argue against elimination of Indian status "is to argue for discrimination, isolation and separation" (DIAND, 1969, p. 8).

The *White Paper* had the unexpected outcome of fostering unprecedented unity in opposition among Aboriginal Peoples across Canada. Networks like the National Indian Brotherhood (NIB), precursor to the present-day Assembly of First Nations (AFN), grew and sought the national stage. In addition, the Indian Chiefs of Alberta united with other groups to publish their *'Red Paper'*, *Citizen Plus*, which, building on the *Hawthorn Report*, outlined special status for Aboriginal Peoples living in Canada as defined by treaties, not by colonial law or policy (Dickason, 2006; Godlewska and Webber, 2007). Indian Association of Alberta leader Harold Cardinal's book, *The Unjust Society*, referred to the *White Paper* as a tool for "cultural genocide" and condemned the government's perceived disrespect for history:

> The treaties are important to us, because we entered into these negotiations with faith, with hope for a better life with honour . . . Did the white man enter into them with something less in mind? . . . The Indians entered into the treaty negotiations as honourable men who came to deal as equals with the queen's representatives. Our leaders of that time thought they were dealing with an equally honourable people. (As quoted in Miller, 2009, p. 249)

Aboriginal Peoples' fierce and sustained resistance prompted Trudeau's government to reject the *White Paper* in 1971 and at the same time Trudeau announced the end of assimilation policy (Cairns, 2000; Miller, 2009; Shewell, 2012). The policy vacuum left by Trudeau's denouncement of assimilation would see shifting legal, political and resource development contexts as well as increased funding for Aboriginal political organization (Cairns, 2000).

DEEP DIVE: THE 1973 CALDER DECISION

Shortly after the *White Paper* was rejected, the Nisga'a nation's title case, known as *Calder* v. *British Columbia (Attorney General)*, was brought to the Supreme Court of Canada (SCC). Specifically, the Nisga'a declared "the aboriginal title . . . of the Plaintiffs to their ancient tribal territory . . . has never been lawfully extinguished" (*Calder* v. *British Columbia (Attorney General)*, 1973, p. 313). The *Calder* case was the first to seek judicial ruling on Aboriginal title in decades and therefore contained the possibility of a new social phenomenon around land ownership.

Institutional Entrepreneurs

When he was young, Frank Calder was instructed by his adoptive father, Nisga'a Chief Arthur Calder, to use his abilities as a leader to gain title over Nisga'a lands (Harper, 2013). Calder heeded this calling by serving in the BC legislature as an NDP MLA, the first Aboriginal with status to do so, and by serving as president of the Nisga'a Tribal Council (Foster et al., 2007; Miller, 2009). An institutional entrepreneur par excellence, he was the driving force behind the Nisga'a title case, acting as a knowledge broker between the legal team and the Nisga'a nation, coordinating resources, and keeping motivation to continue funding the court battles (the lower court cases were funded entirely by the Nisga'a people) (Harper, 2013). Fulfilling these roles in the community along with his responsibilities in the legislature, Frank played the role of institutional entrepreneur well. However, he could not achieve success alone. Another notable institutional entrepreneur was Thomas Berger, a young lawyer well versed in Aboriginal title issues and fellow NDP MLA in BC. Berger would go on to author the Mackenzie Valley Pipeline Inquiry (the *Berger Commission*) in 1977, as well as two other royal commissions, and become well-known for his activism on behalf of Aboriginal communities in Canada (Harper, 2013). Together, Calder and Berger largely built the case for Aboriginal title in the Nass Valley.

The Nisga'a lost at both the BC Supreme Court and the BC Court of Appeal; when Calder returned to the Nisga'a Tribal Council for funding to bring the case to the SCC, many of the Nisga'a refused. There was considerable fear among the Nisga'a and other Aboriginal nations that confronting the federal government would result in retaliation, such as reductions in already meager funding (Harper, 2013). Berger recalls other Aboriginal nations in BC cautioning the Nisga'a against pursuing their title case, saying, "Don't do this. You'll lose and then the federal government will say forget about it, we're through" (Foster et al., 2007, p. 40). In addition, many concurred with the lower courts, that Aboriginal title had been extinguished on two prior occasions: once when the Vancouver Island colony joined British Columbia, and again when British Columbia joined Canada (Harper, 2013). These social facts were deeply engrained; Canada's West Coast was built on these assumptions. A new social phenomenon would require an unusual alliance of institutions and institutional entrepreneurs. Calder found funding from an unlikely source, the Anglican Church, through the connection with an Anglican Archdeacon who had worked in Nisga'a territory and sympathized with Calder's mission (Harper, 2013). This is a clear example of Calder's insight and ability as an institutional entrepreneur to seize opportunities to effect system change from even the unlikeliest of sources; in this case he engaged a powerful stranger, the Anglican Church, to help fund the Nisga'a appeal to the SCC.

The case opened with chief attorney for the Crown, Douglas McKay Brown, arguing that the Nisga'a had brought their case to the SCC to exploit its nuisance value and should be dismissed (Harper, 2013). As the Nisga'a legal counsel, Berger cited the Douglas Treaties as evidence of the negotiating capacity of Aboriginal Peoples and invoked the Royal Proclamation of 1763 as the foundation for the continued existence of Aboriginal title on unoccupied lands (Harper, 2013). The proceedings lasted five days and, just over a year later, the SCC ruled that the Nisga'a did indeed historically hold title but gave a split decision (3:3) on whether Aboriginal title had been extinguished (*Calder* v. *British Columbia (Attorney General)*, 1973; Godlewska and Webber, 2007; McNeil, 1997).

The split decision was largely viewed as a loss in legal terms. However, upon reading the ruling and subsequently meeting with Calder and other Aboriginal leaders, Prime Minister Pierre Trudeau is quoted as saying, "perhaps you have more legal rights than we thought you had when we did the white paper" (Anonymous, 1973). Still looking for policy to fill the vacuum left by the *White Paper*, Trudeau took the split decision to parliament and argued that Aboriginal title should be recognized, a motion that led to the reopening of the comprehensive land claims process that had been halted since 1923 (Foster et al., 2007; Harper, 2013).

A new social phenomenon, and attendant social fact, was recognized within the Canadian court system: prior occupation could be the source of Aboriginal title. Change came quickly after the ruling, with the first treaty signed since 1923: the *James Bay and Northern Quebec Agreement* (see Figure 6.6).

1980–2000: BUILDING POLITICAL CAPACITY

Aboriginal Activism and a Royal Commission Shift Political Priorities and Discourse

Recognizing the window of opportunity afforded by repatriation, the NIB, the Union of BC Indian Chiefs, and other Aboriginal leaders and activists led a successful campaign to have Aboriginal and treaty rights included in the

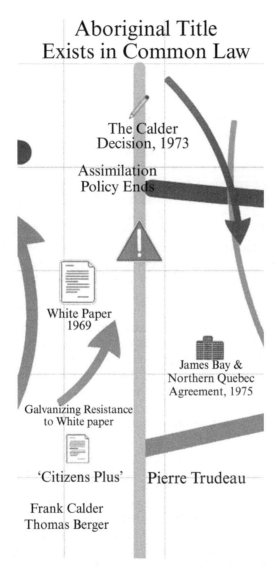

Aboriginal Title
Exists in Common Law

The Calder
Decision, 1973

Assimilation
Policy Ends

White Paper
1969

James Bay &
Northern Quebec
Agreement, 1975

Galvanizing Resistance
to White paper

'Citizens Plus'   Pierre Trudeau

Frank Calder
Thomas Berger

Figure 6.6   1973 Calder decision = emergence of a new social phenomenon regarding Aboriginal title

Constitution (Shewell, 2012; Dickason, 2006; Godlewska and Webber, 2007). Often solely referred to as section 35 (or s. 35), the *Constitution Act, 1982* states, "The existing aboriginal and treaty rights of the aboriginal peoples of Canada are hereby recognized and affirmed". Although s. 35 did not guarantee, define or include the right to self-government, it added considerable leverage for a growing body of Indigenous leaders, thinkers, and advocates working towards change (Godlewska and Webber, 2007; Shewell, 2012).

However, by the end of the 1980s, a relative policy vacuum and increasingly disruptive protests prompted Prime Minister Mulroney to initiate a Royal Commission on Aboriginal Peoples (RCAP). Co-chaired by George Erasmus, former National Chief of the AFN and president of the Dene Nation, and Rene Dussault, former Quebec Deputy Minister of Justice, RCAP evoked the symbolism of the Two Row Wampum belt exchanged at the Treaty at Niagara, stating that "the co-operative relationships that generally characterized the first contact between Aboriginal and non-Aboriginal people must be restored" (RCAP, 1996a: v.1, ch.1, s.1.1). The report critiqued assimilationist policies of past governments, specifically citing misguided interpretations of progress: "the false assumptions and abuses of power that have pervaded Canada's treatment of Aboriginal people are inconsistent with the morality of an enlightened nation" (RCAP, 1996a: v.1, ch.1, s.1.2). In order to address these past wrongs, the RCAP commissioners called for a "sharp break with past policies" and proposed drafting a new Royal Proclamation to "begin the cycle of renewal", grounded in "principles of mutual recognition, respect, responsibility and sharing in the relationship between original peoples and those who came later" (RCAP, 1996b). RCAP represented a major (if not final) repudiation of the path created by one set of social phenomena, and the recognition of a new path, based on a rediscovery and reimaging of previous ones.

The Supreme Court of Canada Institutionalizes Aboriginal Rights and Title

The late 1990s was a dramatic time at the SCC with several major decisions on Aboriginal rights and title released. For example, the *Sparrow* decision represented the first time an obligation to consult Aboriginal Peoples arose in the Supreme Court in the context of s. 35 rights, introducing the burden of proof to the Crown: "The government is required to bear the burden of justifying any legislation that has some negative effect on any aboriginal right protected under s. 35(1)" (Morellato, 2008; *R. v. Sparrow*, 1990, p. 1078). The 1996 *Van der Peet* decision described Aboriginal rights as arising from Aboriginal Peoples' prior occupation on the land, therefore clarifying that s. 35 rights apply in both proven and unproven rights and title cases (*R v. Van der Peet*, 1996). The *Van der Peet* decision also asserted that the Crown must take Aboriginal rights and title seriously, stating that "any ambiguity as to the scope and definition of s. 35(1) must be resolved in the favour of aboriginal peoples" (*R v. Van der Peet*, 1996, p. 508).

The *Delgamuukw and Gisdayway*[2] decision is regarded as the most significant ruling on Aboriginal title since *Calder*. Notably, the decision defined the nature and content of Aboriginal title, clarifying that Aboriginal title is a *sui generis* property right, unique within the law and understood only with reference to both the Canadian legal system and Aboriginal legal systems. The decision also marked the first instance in which oral histories were admissible as evidence in the Canadian court system, indicating a shift in the value attributed to Aboriginal knowledge systems and a distinct awareness of the social justice issues inherent in disallowing oral histories in the courts (*Delgamuukw* v. *BC*, 1997). Finally, the decision established a process for determining whether Aboriginal title had been extinguished and, if not, outlined a process to determine whether or not infringement was justified (Morellato, 2008). Of particular importance to the natural resource industry, the *Delgamuukw and Gisdayway* decision identified a requirement to accommodate Aboriginal title rights in addition to Aboriginal rights and treaty rights, placing substantial responsibility on the Crown to identify, justify and accommodate any potential infringements on title lands or resources (McNeil, 2007; Morellato, 2008). Thus, the Supreme Court of Canada introduced the foundations of consultation and accommodation and clarified that "the purpose of s. 35(1) is to reconcile the prior presence of aboriginal peoples in North America with the assertion of Crown sovereignty" (*Delgamuukw* v. *BC*, 1997, para. 141).

DEEP DIVE INTO SOCIAL INNOVATION: *HAIDA NATION* V. *BRITISH COLUMBIA* (MINISTRY OF FORESTS)

In 2004, the Haida brought their title case to the Supreme Court of Canada. At the heart of the case was a tree farm license to harvest timber on Haida Gwaii (T.F.L. 39), which was transferred by the Province without consulting the Haida Nation. Chief Justice McLachlin described the issue being brought forth by the Haida to the Supreme Court:

> The government holds legal title to the land. Exercising that legal title, it has granted Weyerhaeuser the right to harvest the forests in Block 6 of the land. But the Haida people also claim title to the land – title which they are in the process of trying to prove – and object to the harvesting of the forests on Block 6 as proposed in T.F.L. 39. (*Haida Nation* v. *BC*, 2004, para. 6)

For the Haida, the case was about asserting power as decision makers on Haida Gwaii lands that had been occupied since time immemorial and had never been surrendered. Justice McLachlin described the Haida's argument in her ruling:

> The Haida argue that absent consultation and accommodation, they will win their title but find themselves deprived of forests that are vital to their economy and their culture . . . The Haida's claim to title to Haida Gwaii is strong . . . But it is also complex and will take many years to prove. In the mean-time, the Haida argue, their heritage will be irretrievably despoiled. (*Haida Nation v. BC*, 2004, para. 7)

For the Province and the Crown, although consultation had been brought up in previous rulings, this case was the first to seriously threaten their unilateral authority over lands. A ruling in favor of the Haida Nation would introduce a system shock potentially larger than *Calder*. In her ruling on the decision, Chief Justice McLachlin emphasized the importance of the case: "The stakes are huge" (*Haida Nation v. BC*, 2004, para. 7). Then president of the Council of the Haida Nation (CHN), Guujaaw, wrote, "It is our contention that all tenures issued unilaterally by the province are unlawful" (as quoted in Gill, 2009, p. 201). Both the government and the forest industry were uneasy. To date, the industry had relied upon government processes to shelter their interests, but a decision in favor of the Haida would reduce the province's authority on Haida Gwaii and question the legitimacy of conventional decision-making processes.

In this latest iteration of the paradox between Aboriginal and Crown interpretations of authority over lands, both the Haida and Crown attorneys demonstrated remarkable consistency with their predecessors. For example, in an interview with the New York Times, Guujaaw explained: "We're a few thousand people with no resources except a stubborn belief that we are the owners of this land just as our parents and grandparents believed . . . If they fly the Canadian flag over the land, they think they have the right to spoil it. For us, that is unacceptable" (Krauss, 2004).

This was a clash of social phenomena: the Haida articulated their authority on Haida Gwaii in a manner similar to the early petitions to the British Crown. With similar consistency, British Columbia and Canada's position reflected the deep basin of attraction created by colonialism (*Spruce Roots*, 2004). Despite significant legal decisions acknowledging the pre-existing nature of Aboriginal title and rights (as affirmed in the *Delgamuukw and Gisdayway* decision), the government was determined to argue against its fiduciary duties to Aboriginal Peoples and to retain singular authority over Haida Gwaii.

The network of alliances within and across the communities of Haida Gwaii played a key role *in Haida v. BC* (2004) and demonstrated that even the most heavily resource-dependent communities recognized that reconciliation and coexistence with Aboriginal Peoples were important and in the best interest of community-building. As Gill explains, this "came less from any dewy-eyed conversion to the aboriginal cause, than their conclusion that the fate of the forests of Haida Gwaii was in better hands with the Haida than with distant offshore companies in collusion with dishonest off-island governments" (2009, p. 195). One forestry worker exclaimed, "Let's do this thing right and start working with them right away" (as quoted in Gill, 2009, p. 195). The village of Port Clements, whose residents are primarily not of Haida ancestry and rely heavily on Haida Gwaii's forestry industry, joined the SCC case with intervener status and, in a rare act of solidarity, argued in favor of the Haida's position (*Spruce Roots*, 2004).

Having Terri-Lynn Davidson, a Haida lawyer, argue the case for the Haida Nation was a key SCC precedent. Co-counsel for the Haida Nation, Louise Mandell, spoke of the tone this set for the case:

> It was very much done from a Haida perspective and not from an aboriginal law, non-aboriginal perspective . . . She did quite an unusual thing when she referred to the Haida in the personal sense, as in 'I', and 'we,' and 'our'. To see the way in which an aboriginal person speaking about their own rights and their own territory and their own people would try and get the court to see it from their perspective. (As quoted in Gill, 2009, p. 200)

Having Davidson working inside the courts and Guujaaw and other Haida leaders working the politics outside sent a consistent message to the media about the strength, determination and cultural continuity of the Haida Nation.

In her ruling, Chief Justice McLachlin may have also indirectly raised questions regarding the legitimacy of Crown assertions of sovereignty in Canada. She wrote, "put simply, Canada's Aboriginal peoples were here when Europeans came, and were never conquered" (*Haida Nation v. BC*, 2004, para. 25) and also commented directly on the role of treaties: "treaties serve to reconcile pre-existing Aboriginal sovereignty with assumed Crown sovereignty, and to define Aboriginal rights guaranteed by s. 35 of the *Constitution Act, 1982*" (*Haida Nation v. BC*, 2004, para. 20). Asch (2014) interprets the novel presence of the qualifier "assumed" to describe Crown sovereignty as an indirect invitation to question its legitimacy and, as a result of the possibility for co-existing sovereigns within Canada, to finally acknowledge Aboriginal self-determination and self-governance as s. 35 rights. Although Asch (2014) admits his interpretation is likely a liberal one, the language within the ruling represented a significant departure from previous cases and effectively entrenched a process of reconciliation between Aboriginal and non-Aboriginal Peoples, including reconciling authority over lands, in Canadian law.

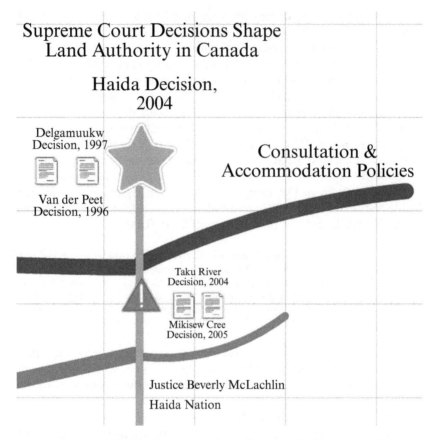

Figure 6.7 2004 Haida *decision outlines the Crown's duty to consult and accommodate*

Essentially, the SCC read into the law the window of opportunity and necessary remedy for a new social phenomenon: the duty to consult and accommodate, an innovative process intended to address the question of how to reconcile Crown and Aboriginal jurisdiction (see Figure 6.7). The SCC decision also clarified that the legal duty to consult and accommodate was determined to arise "when the Crown has knowledge, real or constructive, of the potential existence of the Aboriginal right or title and contemplates conduct that might adversely affect it" (*Haida Nation* v. *BC*, 2004, para. 35) and must be fulfilled so as "to effect reconciliation between the Crown and the Aboriginal people" (*Haida Nation* v. *BC*, 2004, para. 45). The legal doctrine laid out by the *Haida* decision was expanded through the *Taku River* decision, also in 2004, which explained that the legal duty to consult could be fulfilled through the environmental assessment process, and a year later in the *Mikisew Cree* decision, when the court ruled that the legal duty to consult also applies when the Crown has knowledge of potential infringements on Treaty rights (Newman, 2009).

The trilogy of cases – *Haida, Taku River* and *Mikisew Cree* – represents a re-emergence of the Aboriginal interpretations of the Royal Proclamation and Treaty of Niagara, especially in regard to multiple sovereignties over lands, co-existence, reconciliation and long-term relationships. Like so many innovations, the duty to consult and accommodate was a bricolage of history and modern concerns.

2005–14: RAMIFICATIONS OF *HAIDA*

Scaling Up and Out: The Rise of Consultation Policies at Multiple Scales and Across Sectors

Today, consultation and accommodation are constitutionally protected rights intended to effect reconciliation between the Crown and Aboriginal peoples. Although the *Haida* decision clearly states that the Crown is solely responsible for fulfilling the duty to consult and accommodate, the corporate sector is heavily involved in developing consultation policies – an ongoing cross-sector innovation space. Newman explains that the legal duty to consult opened a new arena for competition, stating, "a well-developed consultation policy will, in some instances, be a competitive advantage" (2009, p. 76). For example, in June 2016, the Federal Court of Appeal ruled that Canada had failed to fulfill its constitutional duty to consult and accommodate First Nations significantly affected by Enbridge's proposed Northern Gateway Pipelines Project; the multi-billion dollar pipeline project was recently rejected by the Trudeau government (*Gitxaala Nation v. Canada*, 2016; Tasker, 2016). The emergence of these types of risks and opportunities for competitive advantage has given rise to consultation departments and outreach protocols within resource development companies and professional associations such as the Mining Association of Canada (MAC) and the Prospectors and Developers Association of Canada (PDAC) (MAC, 2014; Newman, 2009; PDAC, 2014). By disrupting the flow of financial resources within the corporate resource sector, the duty to consult and accommodate shifted power relationships between corporations and Aboriginal Peoples in Canada.

Politically, the AFN has invoked the duty to consult and accommodate with respect to policy and legislation that may affect Aboriginal title and rights, ensuring that the duty is applied at the policy level (Newman, 2009).

Provincial, regional and Treaty organizations as well as individual nations have also developed consultation policies that outline preferred methods of Crown engagement. Although the government has no obligation to follow Aboriginal consultation protocols that fall outside the law, it is becoming accepted practice to follow these guidelines, when available, to ease the consultation process and build positive working relationships with Aboriginal Peoples (Newman, 2009). Changes to the distribution of power after the *Haida* decision, with respect to increased Aboriginal authority over traditional lands, available funds to pursue necessary traditional land use and occupancy studies, and reduced government control over resource development decisions, demonstrate the durability and impact of the *Haida* decision between multiple actors and across the scales of government.

ONGOING EFFORTS IN RELATIONSHIP-BUILDING

Advances in Aboriginal rights and title within the Canadian court system continue to play out in the SCC. June 2014 saw yet another landmark ruling on Aboriginal title when Justice McLachlin ruled in favor of the Tsilhqot'in nation, granting Aboriginal title for the first time in Canadian history and laying out a test for determining Aboriginal title (*Tsilhqot'in Nation* v. *BC*, 2014). Notably, Aboriginal title considerations now require a culturally sensitive approach based on a dual perspective, namely the "laws, practices, size, technological ability and the character of the land claimed" by the Aboriginal group and the common law (*Tsilhqot'in Nation* v. *BC*, 2014, para. 41). This decision deepens the landscape shift legitimating the procedural requirements for developing a relationship between Aboriginal and non-Aboriginal Peoples based on shared land authority in Canada.

In 2008, Prime Minister Stephen Harper read a formal apology to residential school survivors for the harms perpetuated through assimilation policy. Notably, the apology stated, "you have been working on recovering from this experience for a long time and in a very real sense, we are now joining you on this journey" (as quoted in Regan, 2010, p. 1). However, many felt that the apology was insufficient, "too little, too late" (Regan, 2010, p. 2). Of more long-term impact was the establishment of Canada's Truth and Reconciliation Commission (TRC), mandated to gather testimonies and histories of the residential school system. Notable outcomes following the TRC's (2015) conclusion include Canada's shift to becoming a full supporter of the United Nations Declaration on the Rights of Indigenous Peoples (UNGA, 2008) and the launch of a National Inquiry into Missing and Murdered Indigenous Women and Girls (NIMMIWG, 2016).

While continuing advances are made at the highest levels of law and policy, Aboriginal activism remains strongly rooted on the ground. One example of this continued activism and advocacy for recognition of the original treaties is the ongoing Idle No More movement. Idle No More gained international media attention in the winter of 2012 when a surge of public gatherings, blockades, educational campaigns and marches by Aboriginal Peoples once again brought attention to the need for national conversations regarding Aboriginal rights, title, and treaty relationships. This surge in activity drew attention to the need for further progress on meaningful consultation at the policy scale, particularly with respect to environmental policies affecting resource development on Aboriginal lands.

CONCLUSION

This historical narrative tracks the evolution of authority over lands in Canada using a social innovation lens to demonstrate how the *Haida* decision (2004) led to fundamental changes in Canadian law and policy with respect to Aboriginal Peoples. Through a string of decisions, the Supreme Court of Canada successfully disrupted assimilation policy and established a novel legal doctrine which commits the Crown to pursuing a reconciliatory relationship with Aboriginal Peoples and which restricts government authority over lands in Canada through a legal duty to consult and accommodate.

As the characteristics of land authority continue to change in Canada, the starting conditions explored through this case will continue to be prophetic, since paternalistic, colonial policies are still embedded in Canadian political and legal structures and work still needs to be done to fully institutionalize collaborative relationships between Aboriginal and non-Aboriginal Peoples (see for example, Godlewska et al., 2013; McCarthy et al., 2010; Morellato, 2008). For example, in 2014 the UN Special Rapporteur on the rights of Indigenous Peoples, James Anaya, released the report of his findings in Canada. He stated that although a strong legal framework and supportive policies are in place to protect Aboriginal rights, the government still adopts adversarial positions with respect to negotiating treaties and land claims, the gap in well-being between Aboriginal and non-Aboriginal peoples has not significantly improved, and the government continues to be perceived as distrustful by the Aboriginal population (Anaya, 2014). Issues around resource development, treaty promises and distrust remain intractable problem domains, ripe for further social innovation.

NOTES

1. A note on terminology: Throughout this discussion, Aboriginal Peoples is used as the term appears in section 35 of the *Constitution Act, 1982* (and includes First Nations, Metis and Inuit Peoples). While this language, alongside non-Aboriginal, invokes a collective identity imposed by the Canadian government, it is applied here to emphasize a shared experience of colonization in Canada and to remain consistent with current constitutional and legal discourse.
2. The contributions of both the Gitxsan and Wet'suwet'en Nations are recognized here by using the full title, *Delgamuukw and Gisdayway v. British Columbia*.

REFERENCES

Anaya, J. (2014). *Report of the Special Rapporteur on the Rights of Indigenous Peoples: The Situation of Indigenous Peoples in Canada.* New York: United Nations General Assembly.

Anonymous (1973). Indians have more land rights than he thought, Trudeau says. *The Globe and Mail*, 8 February, p. 8.

Asch, M. (2014). *On Being Here to Stay: Treaties and Aboriginal Rights in Canada.* Toronto: University of Toronto Press.

Borrows, J. (1998). Wampum at Niagara: The Royal Proclamation, Canadian legal history, and self-government. In M. Asch (ed.), *Aboriginal and Treaty Rights in Canada: Essays on Law, Equality and Respect to Difference.* Vancouver: UBC Press, pp. 155–72.

Borrows, J. (2005). Creating an Indigenous legal community. *McGill Law Journal*, **50**, 153–75.

Cairns, A. (2000). *Citizens Plus: Aboriginal Peoples and the Canadian State.* Vancouver: UBC Press.

Calder et al. v. Attorney-General of British Columbia, [1973] S.C.R. 313.

Chamberline, J.E. (1998). Culture and anarchy in Indian country. In M. Asch (ed.), *Aboriginal and Treaty Rights in Canada: Essays on Law, Equality and Respect to Difference.* Vancouver: UBC Press, pp. 3–37.

Delgamuukw v. British Columbia [1997] 3 S.C.R. 1010.

Department of Indian Affairs and Northern Development (DIAND) (1969). *Statement of the Government of Canada on Indian Policy, 1969.* Ottawa: Department of Indian Affairs and Northern Development.

Dickason, O.P. (2006). *A Concise History of Canada's First Nations.* New York: Oxford University Press.

Foster, E.B.H., Raven, H. and Webber, A.J. (2007). *Let Right be Done: Aboriginal Title, the Calder Case, and the Future of Indigenous Rights Law and Society.* Vancouver: UBC Press.

Foster, H. (2007). We are not O'Meara's children: law, lawyers, and the first campaign for Aboriginal title in British Columbia. In E.B.H. Foster, H. Raven and A.J. Webber (eds), *Let Right be Done: Aboriginal Title, the Calder Case, and the Future of Indigenous Rights Law and Society.* Vancouver: UBC Press, pp. 61–84.

Foster, H. and Berger, B.L. (2008). From humble prayers to legal demands: the Cowichan petition of 1909 and the British Columbia Indian land question. In

H. Foster, B.L. Berger and A.R. Buck (eds), *The Grand Experiment: Law and Legal Culture in British Settler Societies*. Vancouver: UBC Press, pp. 240–67.

Gill, Ian (2009). *All That We Say is Ours: Guujaaw and the Reawakening of the Haida Nation*. Vancouver: Douglas & McIntyre.

Gitxaala Nation v. *Canada*, 2016 FCA 73.

Godlewska, C. and Webber, J. (2007). The Calder decision, Aboriginal title, treaties, and the Nisga'a. In E.B.H. Foster, H. Raven and A.J. Webber (eds), *Let Right be Done: Aboriginal Title, the Calder Case, and the Future of Indigenous Rights Law and Society*. Vancouver: UBC Press, pp. 1–33.

Godlewska, A., Schaefli, L.M. and Chaput, P.J. (2013). First nations assimilation through neoliberal educational reform. *The Canadian Geographer/Le Géographe Canadien*, **57**(3), 271–9.

Haida Nation v. *British Columbia (Minister of Forests)*, 2004 SCC 73, [2004] 3 S.C.R. 511.

Harper, J. (2013). *He Moved a Mountain: The Life of Frank Calder and the Nisga'a Land Claims Accord*. Vancouver: Ronsdale Press.

Hawthorn, H.B. (1966). *A Survey of the Contemporary Indians in Canada: A Report on Economic, Political, Educational Needs and Policies*. Ottawa: Department of Indian Affairs and Northern Development.

Indigenous and Northern Affairs Canada (INAC) (2016). *250th Anniversary of the Royal Proclamation of 1763*. Accessed 17 December 2016 at https://www.aadnc-aandc.gc.ca/eng/1370355181092/1370355203645.

Krauss, C. (2004). Natives' land battles bring a shift in Canada economy. *New York Times*, 5 December. Accessed 22 July 2014 at http://www.nytimes.com/2004/12/05/international/americas/05canada.html?_r=0.

McCarthy, D.D., Whitelaw, G.S. and Tsuji, L.J.S. (2010). The Victor Diamond Mine environmental assessment and the Mushkegowuk Territory First Nations: critical systems thinking and social justice. *Canadian Journal of Native Studies*, **30**, 83–116.

McNeil, K. (1997). The meaning of Aboriginal title. In M. Asch (ed.) (1998), *Aboriginal and Treaty Rights in Canada: Essays on Law, Equality and Respect to Difference*. Vancouver: UBC Press, pp. 135–54.

McNeil, K. (1999). Social Darwinism and Judicial conceptions of Indian title in Canada in the 1880s. *Journal of the West*, **38**(1), 68–76.

McNeil, K. (2007). Judicial approaches to self-government since Calder: searching for doctrinal coherence. In E.B.H. Foster, H. Raven and A.J. Webber (eds), *Let Right be Done: Aboriginal Title, the Calder Case, and the Future of Indigenous Rights Law and Society*. Vancouver: UBC Press, pp. 129–52.

Mikisew Cree First Nation v. *Canada (Minister of Canadian Heritage)*, 2005 SCC 69, [2005] 3 S.C.R. 388.

Miller, J.R. (2000). *Skyscrapers Hide the Heavens: A History of Indian–White Relations in Canada*, 3rd edn. Toronto: University of Toronto Press.

Miller, J.R. (2004). *Reflections on Native–Newcomer Relations: Selected Essays*. Toronto: University of Toronto Press.

Miller, J.R. (2009). *Compact, Contract, Covenant: Aboriginal Treaty-making in Canada*. Toronto: University of Toronto Press.

Mining Association of Canada (MAC) (2014). Aboriginal and community outreach. Accessed 20 July 2014 at http://www.mining.ca/towards-sustainable-mining/protocols-frameworks/aboriginal-and-community-outreach.

Morellato, M. (2008). The Crown's constitutional duty to consult and accommodate

Aboriginal and treaty rights. Research Paper prepared for the National Centre for First Nations Governance. Ottawa.

National Inquiry into Missing and Murdered Indigenous Women and Girls (NIMMIWG) (2016). Accessed 17 December 2016 at http://www.mmiwg-ffada. ca//.

Newman, D.G. (2009). *The Duty to Consult: New Relationships with Aboriginal Peoples*. Saskatoon: Purich Publications.

Prospectors & Developers Association of Canada (PDAC) (2014). *Aboriginal Affairs*. Accessed 20 July 2014 at http://www.pdac.ca/programs/aboriginal-affairs.

R. v. *Sparrow* [1990] 1 S.C.R. 1075.

R. v. *Van der Peet* [1996] 2 S.C.R. 507.

Regan, P. (2010). *Unsettling the Settler Within: Indian Residential Schools, Truth Telling, and Reconciliation in Canada*. Vancouver: UBC Press.

Royal Commission on Aboriginal Peoples (RCAP) (1996a). *Volume 1: Looking Forward, Looking Back*. Ottawa: Minister of Supply and Services.

Royal Commission on Aboriginal Peoples (RCAP) (1996b). *People to People, Nation to Nation: Highlights from the Report of the Royal Commission on Aboriginal Peoples*. Ottawa: Minister of Supply and Services.

Shewell, H. (2012). Dreaming in Liberal white: Canadian Indian policy, 1913–1983. In K. Burnett and G. Read (eds), *Aboriginal History: A Reader*. Don Mills, ON: Oxford University Press, pp. 170–80.

Smith, L.T. (1999). *Decolonizing Methodologies: Research and Indigenous Peoples*. New York: Zed Books.

Spruce Roots (2004). A summary of intervenor arguments. *Spruce Roots Magazine*. Accessed 20 July 2014 at http://www.spruceroots.org/July%202004/Arguments. html.

St Catherine's Milling and Lumber Co. v. *R*, 1887 13 S.C.R. 577.

Taku River Tlingit First Nation v. *British* Columbia (Project Assessment Director), 2004 SCC 74, [2004] 3 S.C.R. 550.

Tasker, J.P. (2016). Trudeau cabinet approves Trans Mountain, Line 3 pipelines, rejects Northern Gateway. *CBC News*, 29 November. Accessed 17 December 2016 at http://www.cbc.ca/news/politics/federal-cabinet-trudeau-pipeline-deci sions-1.3872828.

The Constitution Act, 1982, Schedule B to the Canada Act 1982 (UK), 1982, c 11.

Truth and Reconciliation Canada (TRC) (2015). Honouring the truth, reconciling for the future: Summary of the final report of the Truth and Reconciliation Commission of Canada. Winnipeg: Truth and Reconciliation Commission of Canada.

Tsilhqot'in Nation v. *British Columbia*, 2014 SCC 44.

Union of British Columbia Indian Chiefs (UBCIC) (2014). Historical perspective on Aboriginal title in BC. Accessed 11 October 2014 at http://www.ubcic.bc.ca/ Resources/landquestion.htm#axzz4TCkVu1xn.

United Nations General Assembly (UNGA) (2008). United Nations Declaration on the Rights of Indigenous Peoples. Resolution adopted by the General Assembly. Accessed 17 December 2016 at http://www.un.org/esa/socdev/unpfii/ documents/DRIPS_en.pdf.

White, R. (2011). *The Middle Ground: Indians, Empires, and Republics in the Great Lakes Region, 1650–1815*, 20th Anniversary edn. New York: Cambridge University Press.

Yazzie, R. (2000). Indigenous peoples and postcolonial colonialism. In

M. Battiste (ed.), *Reclaiming Indigenous Voice and Vision*. Vancouver: UBC Press, pp. 39–49.

Yirush, C. (2012). "Chief princes and owners of all": Native American appeals to the Crown in the early-modern British Atlantic. In S. Belmessous (ed.), *Native Claims: Indigenous Law Against Empire, 1500–1920*. New York: Oxford University Press, pp. 129–51.

7.   The Internet: a dynamic history

Ola Tjörnbo

The Internet is undoubtedly one of the most important social innovations to have emerged since the end of the Second World War, even if it is not yet clear what the full scope of its impact will be. From the rise of online retail, to the demise of traditional news media and the impact of the Wikileaks revelations, there is virtually no sphere of life that is unaffected by the Internet today. The Internet is actually not a single unified entity but rather a combination of technological inventions, rules and institutions. The technological components are perhaps the most widely recognized and include day-to-day services like email, the World Wide Web (WWW) and message boards, but the social constructs underpinning the Internet are at least as critical to its identity if not more so. Unlike the communication systems that came before the Internet, which were heavily centralized networks controlled by a handful of powerful actors, the Internet is radically decentralized. It puts many of the same tools used by multinational media companies, for the production and dissemination of information, into the hands of ordinary citizens.

In part, the Internet was designed to favor this kind of decentralized approach. The earliest technology that went into creating the Internet, packet switching, was intended to be a robust decentralized network. Nonetheless, it was by no means inevitable that the modern Internet should look as it does. As the Internet has grown in prominence, there have been many attempts to control it, to establish standards and to give prior-itized access to those who own the infrastructure it relies on. The fact that these attempts have so far failed, though they are ongoing, is in no small part due to the conscious efforts of some of the Internet's earliest pio-neers, who were building not only a technological edifice, but also a vision of a future where information is shared openly by all. Even the modern Internet, dominated as it is by giants like Google, Facebook and Amazon, continues to espouse many of the values that were established at its incep-tion by its founding fathers. This is an example of what we have come to term "prophetic starting conditions", referring to the fact that decisions made early on in the life cycle of a social innovation can have tremendous consequences for the way that the innovation develops and comes to influence the system it transforms. These choices drive the innovation towards a particular stable configuration of institutions, resource flow, behaviors and norms instead of another adjacent possible.

Of course, the pure vision of the free, global information commons has not quite come to pass. The modern Internet is a compromise between the ideals of equality of access and the demands of commercial interests, which have undoubtedly been key in popularizing the Web. Moreover, like all social innovations, it will never be complete, but will rather continue to grow and evolve, adapting to changes in the environment, as technology, ideology and patterns of behavior change over time. But in recounting the history of the Internet, it is impossible to ignore the long-term influence of certain key actors, values and ideas that have played a profound role in its realization. In this chapter I will give an overview of the story of the Internet as social innovation, focusing especially on two key moments, the adoption of TCP/IP protocols as the international standard for communication in computer networks, and the creation of the World Wide Web.

THE PHENOMENON: PACKET SWITCHING

The technological invention that laid the foundation for the Internet is called packet switching. Essentially, packet switching is a strategy for transmitting information over communication networks. Instead of sending a message out wholesale, you break it up into smaller chunks that are able to follow different routes to their destination before being reassembled in the right order by the receiving party. Imagine that instead of putting a letter in an envelope, addressing it and then depositing it in the mail and having it taken to a central clearing house, where it is moved on until it eventually reaches its ultimate destination, you were to cut that same letter into pieces. Each piece would then be numbered to show which order they all go in and put into its own envelope. These envelopes are then handed to the nearest available postman. Instead of taking them to a clearing house the postman would simply pass them on to the next postman they happened to encounter who was closer to the final destination of the letter than they were. Each piece of the letter could be given to a different postman so that each made its own separate way to the end destination, not necessarily arriving at the same time, where the recipient would open them and be able to reassemble them in the right order. It might seem inefficient, but transmitting information in this way actually has two key advantages. First, it means that information can be sent as it is ready. Rather than waiting until the whole letter has been written you could send pieces of it as they are completed and moreover, postmen can transmit letters between each other continually, rather than only making deliveries in bulk, say once a day. Second, in the first example, where a letter is sent out in its own envelope, each node in the network is essential. If the clearing house disappears, or the postman tasked with delivering your letter to its destination doesn't show up to work, the information isn't delivered; it might even be lost. But in the second example, where the letter is cut into pieces, if any node in the network is missing a postman simply hands the packet off to someone different and it still reaches its destination, and even if a piece of the whole message is lost you might be able to make sense of the communication with the remaining pieces.

These advantages are what attracted two different researchers to the idea of packet switching and led to this technology being invented in two different places at roughly the same time. Packet switching takes the metaphor above much further. It relies on breaking larger communications into very small pieces that can be transmitted along communication networks in milliseconds, leading to a much more efficient use of resources. In the 1960s, in the middle of the Cold War, Paul Baran was working in the US on the problem of survivable communications. In other words, how could you build a communication network that would survive a hostile attack? His solution was packet switching, since a packet switching network could continue to function even if nodes were destroyed. A few years later in the UK, Don Davies, a mathematician at the National Physics Laboratory (NPL) was working on a different problem. At the time the laboratory had only a few computers that were shared by all the researchers at the lab. If the computer you needed was in use, you had to wait until it finished whatever calculation it was working on before it could start on yours, even if your calculation was simple and quick while the one being worked on would take hours. Once again, the solution was packet switching, since this would allow the computer to work on several problems at the same time and deliver results as they became ready, meaning that small, fast calculations would be performed quickly without having to wait for bigger jobs to be finished.

Although packet switching might seem like a modest idea it was radical in its implications since packet switching networks were so different from the prevailing communication technology. Telegraphs and telephone networks rely heavily on large, centralized processing hubs to direct communication where it needs to go, whereas packet switching networks are made up of decentralized systems of small independent nodes. As such, packet switching as a technology was suited to the kind of decentralized, open access system that the Internet would become. In our terminology, it had an "elective affinity" for such a communication system, and it laid the foundations for the invention of the Internet. However, the technology alone did not determine the form that this new system of communication would take.

FROM IDEA TO INNOVATION: STARTING CONDITIONS

While the technology was promising, the idea of a packet switching network is clearly a long way from the modern incarnation of the Internet and needed significant investment before it could be realized as a working innovation. Had this investment been made by the British Government, the Internet might be seen today as a British invention and would probably have been a very different beast. However, Don Davies was not able to move forward with his idea as quickly as he would have liked, in part because in the UK the state-owned Post Office had a monopoly on telecommunications and he couldn't be seen to be stepping on their toes: "Davies was in a delicate position . . . post office had national monopoly on telecommunications . . . he was a government employee" (Gillies and Cailliau, 2000, p. 30). The Post Office was inherently skeptical of the new technology and had a vested interest in the existing centralized telecommunications network so that although the NPL did build a packet-switching network, it remained small and tightly controlled. The real pioneers of the technology were the researchers at the Advanced Research Projects Agency (ARPA) in the US.

ARPA was a research agency created by Eisenhower in 1958 in response to the 1957 launch of the Sputnik satellite, to help the US stay ahead of the USSR in the technology race (Abbate, 1999). Research at ARPA was well funded, and researchers were afforded a great deal of independence to pursue projects even without obvious defense applications (Abbate, 1999). In addition, ARPA was the home of several visionaries in the field of computer networking, most notably J.C.R. Licklider, Director of the Information Processing Techniques Office and author of a 1963 memorandum describing an "intergalactic computer network" (Leiner et al., 2003). Although Licklider left ARPA before the creation of its packet switching network, he convinced his successors Bob Taylor and Lawrence Roberts of the importance of computer networking. Packet switching seemed to provide the answer to how such a network could be created and by 1967 Roberts had published his plan for ARPANET, ARPA's own packet switching network. ARPA had connections with several different university campuses in the US and early nodes connected to ARPANET included the Stanford Research Institute (SRI) and the Network Measurement Centre at UCLA, which formed the first permanent ARPANET connection in 1969. Suddenly, some of the most prestigious research institutions in the US were joined by a packet switching network.

The fact that ARPANET was the first and would come to be the biggest packet switching network would have important ramifications for the development of the Internet. ARPANET was funded by ARPA and composed of leading research institutes and universities. The men who built it had no ties to leaders in the telecommunications networks of the time, but rather saw ARPANET primarily as a research project. In fact, Vint Cerf, who would later become known as one of the "fathers of the Internet" was a student at UCLA when he first began working on ARPANET. ARPANET was promoted widely and expanded quickly. By 1971 the network included 23 university and government hosts. By 1981 the number stood at 213 with a new host joining approximately every 20 days (Stewart, 2015).

But it was not only the freedom afforded by ARPA and the universities in which it grew up that lent ARPANET its particular character. It was also the philosophies of the men behind it. In part, these philosophies were technical; for example Bob Khan arrived at ARPA in 1972 and introduced the concept of "open architecture" computing (Leiner et al., 2003). Simply put, this principle encouraged the growth of ARPANET through the integration of smaller packet switching networks, each of which could be designed according to its own specifications and with its own interface. However, there was also social philosophy underpinning some of these ideas, grounded in the anti-authoritarian movements of the time. For example, Vint Cerf (2002) would later write: "The Internet is for everyone – but it won't be if Governments restrict access to it, so we must dedicate ourselves to keeping the network unrestricted, unfettered and unregulated. We must have the freedom to speak and the freedom to hear."

In its origins then, the Internet continued to be influenced by the idealistic notions of a global, open access information network, articulated by men such as Licklider, and while the Internet as we know it was still several decades away in the 1970s, we perhaps see glimpses of it in these descriptions. But the idea of an open, global network was not the only vision that existed at the time; as early as the 1970s there was a struggle for control over the network.

DEEP DIVE 1: THE BIRTH OF TCP/IP

By the early 1970s, ARPANET was not the only game in town. The three biggest packet switching networks were ARPANET, the NPL and Cyclades, a French research network sponsored by the French Government. In 1972, leaders from each of these networks met and formed the International Network Working Group. They agreed that in order to realize the full potential of computer networking, international standards would have to be developed that allowed these separate networks to communicate with each other. Vint Cerf of ARPANET, Donald Davies of the NPL and Louis Pouzin and Hubert Zimmerman of Cyclades shared a commitment to an open global computer network.

However, as data networking expanded, it attracted the attention of large telecommunications firms, particularly many of the European nationalized carriers, who planned to create their own data networks. Accustomed to centralized modes of operation, these networks wanted to establish new transmission protocols as the standard for their networks. This set of protocols, known as X.25, would be under the control of the nationalized carriers and would not make it easy to connect to diverse networks. From the perspective of the telecommunications companies, it seemed logical that there would be one national data network whose integrity and reliability were ensured by the companies themselves. They could not see the need for multiple private networks except in a very few instances (Abbate, 1999).

Similarly, private firms such as IBM had their own protocols that they kept secret and non-compatible with competitors. This discouraged anyone who used IBM products from buying rival products since they could not be networked. In 1975, Canada was planning to build its own data network, and IBM wanted its System Network Architecture to be used. Canada instead insisted on using X.25 (Drezner, 2004).

Keen to realize their vision for computer networking, Cerf, Davies, Pouzin and others created a proposal for a global networking standard and submitted it to the international organization that seemed at the time to have the clearest jurisdiction over matters related to computer networking, the International Telegraph and Telephone Consultative Committee (CCITT), which had already helped to establish global standards for those older technologies. The CCITT was staffed largely by telecommunications engineers, comfortable with the model of switchboards and centralized steering of network communications. The Network Working Group proposed something radically different, as Pouzin put it: "The essence of datagram is connectionless. That means you have no relationship established between sender and receiver" (Russell, 2014, p. 177).

For CCITT, the proposal looked unworkable and the Committee was put under pressure by large telecom interests and in particular by France's nationalized telecommunications industry. Pouzin complained that the CCITT members "do not object to packet switching, as long as it looks just like circuit switching" (Russell, 2013). As a result, Cyclades suffered funding cuts from 1975 until Pouzin left the organization in 1978.

However, that was not the end of the dream of a global computer networking standard. The British tried an alternative approach to forging consensus by reaching out not to the CCITT, but to the International Standards Organization (ISO) in 1977. The ISO had already developed protocols for other aspects of computing and was not as dominated by telecommunications interests and staff. Gradually, a project got underway to develop the global protocol standards that would become OSI.

Meanwhile, Cerf, also frustrated by the failure with the CCITT, took up a full-time position at ARPA where he worked on a project to design protocols for ARPA's own network, TCP/IP. ARPANET had a history of spawning additional networks (former ARPA employees had gone on to found SATNET and TELNET among others), while maintaining good relationships with those still at ARPA. True to the vision of the Network Working Group, TCP/IP was designed to be easily accessible and compatible with a wide range of networks, and it was made available outside ARPA.

Throughout the 1980s, work on TCP/IP and OSI ran in parallel. OSI was a big, collaborative, international effort that had the support of European and US governments as well as major businesses such as IBM, but, as can be expected of such a process, negotiations between the parties quickly became arduous and subject to fierce lobbying. The first chairman of the OSI recalls it as follows: "Can you imagine trying to get the representatives from ten major and competing computer corporations, and ten telephone companies and PTTs [state-owned telecom monopolies], and the technical experts from ten different nations to come to any agreement within the foreseeable future?" (Russell, 2013).

John Day, a member of the IBM delegation to the OSI project, described in his memoir the fierce disputes and political maneuvering that occurred within the OSI process, "fighting over who would get a piece of the pie. . . . IBM played them like a violin. It was truly magical to watch" (Russell, 2013).

Nonetheless, the OSI project gathered steam and, with powerful supporters, it seemed destined to become the global standard in computer networking.

Work also continued on TCP/IP, and an increasing number of networks began to use them. The ARPANET community, which was by far the biggest data network at the time, championed TCP/IP and had the backing of the US government's American National Standards Institute and National Bureau of Standards, in part because the US lacked a national telecommunications monopoly. In 1983 ARPANET officially made the switch from the existing protocols to using TCP/IP exclusively, a grueling process that led engineers at ARPA to wear t-shirts with the logo "I survived the TCP/IP switch", but once it was completed, ARPANET and all the networks joined to it were fully converted.

OSI, on the other hand, still wasn't ready and was taking a painfully long time to complete. However, the US government was still requiring that all of its agencies switch over to OSI by 1990 and in 1985 the National Research Council recommended a switch away from TCP/IP. But the networking standards of ARPANET continued to flourish, computer networks were proliferating rapidly, TCP/IP was available and accessible and the number of networks using it grew by the day. In 1989, Brian Carpenter, an advocate of the OSI project, gave a speech where he asked, "Is OSI too late?" and received a standing ovation (Russell, 2013).

OSI was never officially abandoned. It still survives today, but a compromise was found whereby TCP/IP was incorporated into the OSI design, which meant, mostly, that those already using the Internet went on as before and were not forced to undergo another transition. It wasn't only that TCP/IP was on the scene first, but it was seen as a simpler, more flexible and elegant technology. Perhaps most importantly, it was free, whereas ISO required users to pay a fee for each copy of the protocols they ran. Computer engineers already involved in networking turned against it and by the mid-1990s it was clear that OSI would never take off, despite the best efforts of those in power to ensure that it did. At CERN, a heavy emphasis was laid on OSI protocols but a small team led by Ben Segal investigated the viability of TCP/IP for use strictly confined to CERN's internal network. By 1989 TCP/IP was established at CERN and Tim Berners-Lee was ready to make TCP/IP the backbone of the World Wide Web.

THE CULTURE OF THE INTERNET AND THE IETF

To understand why TCP/IP triumphed over OSI one has to understand the culture of the community that was being created around this new technology. Although packet switching had originally been conceived as a way of sharing computer resources, it quickly became clear that this was not the primary way the technology was being utilized. Instead, ARPANET was soon primarily used to facilitate collaboration between users and its most widely used application was email. Email was created in 1971 and gave ARPANET researchers the means to send messages to individual users through their machines; it became a wildly successful new communications tool. The most popular mailing list was a Science Fiction discussion group, an early indication that one of the prime uses for the Internet would be social interaction (Castells, 2000). Similarly, in 1978, Ward Christensen and Randy Suess developed the first Bulletin Board System (BBS). Operating like a physical bulletin board, it allowed users with connected computers to post messages that all other networked computers could see. BBSs became another hugely popular application for computer networking and a way to build virtual communities, since all members of the network could participate in collaborative conversations (Abbate, 1999).

As we have already seen, at ARPA there was a heavy emphasis on freedom and openness. New nodes were welcome to join the network and new, experimental additions were constantly being made to the Internet in order to expand its range of functionality.

This process was managed through the use of Request For Comment (RFC) messages. RFCs were invented by Steve Croker in 1969 as a way to solicit opinions about the technical development of ARPANET (Stewart, 2015). These requests were written in an open way to encourage discussion about how best to move the technical and social organization of the Internet forward and epitomize the open, non-hierarchical spirit of ARPANET. Alongside the RFCs, governance of the emerging Internet (defined as the network of computers that used TCP/IP to communicate) was handled by the Internet Engineering Task Force (IETF). As the network grew it became more and more vital to have agreed technical standards and protocols to ensure that it remained inclusive and open. The IETF started in January 1986 with a small handful of researchers from the government research centers that had grown out of ARPANET; later it was opened up to non-government centers. In fact, the IETF was soon open to everyone. Traditional international standards organizations such as the ISO typically have high barriers to entry for new members and make decisions in a careful and highly bureaucratic manner. By contrast, the IETF had two core values, still expressed in its mission statement today:

1. "Any interested person can participate in the work, know what is being decided, and make his or her voice heard on the issue" (Alvestrand, 2004).
2. "We reject kings, presidents and voting. We believe in rough consensus and running code" (Clark, 1992).

Even today, the IETF remains open to anyone who wants to attend its meetings. Participants are encouraged to dress and interact in a casual manner, and much of the actual work is done by informal "working groups" that are run by volunteers and that also have an open membership policy (see Hoffman, 2012 for more details).

From its inception, the governance structures of the Internet were designed to reflect the values from the early days at ARPANET. This was a social innovation developed without input from the dominant players of the telecommunications era, primarily by academics and researchers with a disdain for bureaucracy and an idealistic belief in the emancipatory potential of a free universal network of information. Moreover, they focused on creating technology that could be shown to work, rather than controlling the network. The foundations they laid would directly shape the structures of signification and legitimation that govern the Internet today, but before that could happen, it needed to be made accessible to the public.

THE INNOVATION: THE WORLD WIDE WEB AS AN EXAMPLE OF BRICOLAGE

In the early days, ensuring that computers continued to be able to talk to each other and that the Internet could accommodate technological innovations that increased its functionality were primary goals of Internet governance. But as the Internet expanded in size, a new challenge arose. As more and more computers joined the network, each carrying its own information, there needed to be new ways for users to access that information. Early on you had to know the name and address of the computer you were trying to access in order to get the information it held, much like needing a phone number or a mail address, which made much information inaccessible to the majority of users. It was not the Internet we have today, and it was not the vision of the hypertext movement.

The idea of hypertext has its origins in the work of Vannevar Bush, who in 1945 published an article called "As we may think", which was further developed by Ted Nelson and Douglas Engelbart who would both be very influential in the development of computing and networking technology. Tim Berners-Lee, a physicist from Oxford University with a longstanding interest in computing, was particularly influenced by Nelson's work on Xanadu, a hypertext project conceived in 1965 but not made available until 2014. Berners-Lee would later describe hypertext in the following way:

> Hypertext was "nonsequential" text, in which a reader was not constrained to read in any particular order, but could follow links and delve into the original document from a short quotation. . . . For example, if you were reading this book in hypertext, you would be able to follow a link from my reference to Xanadu to further details of that project. (Berners-Lee and Fischetti, 1999, p. 5)

Anyone who has used the modern Internet will instantly recognize the approach to managing organization, since it is exactly the way the Internet is used today. Links between documents allow users to follow information trails without needing to know where a particular document is located. They allow open access to information.

Although it remained primarily a theoretical way to manage information, by the 1980s hypertext had acquired a dedicated following and attracted the attention of Berners-Lee (1999). He was also inspired by the notion of creating a common repository of human information. In fact Berners-Lee says that he conceived of the World Wide Web as such a repository: "There would be a single, global information-space" (Berners-Lee and Fischetti, 1999, p. 4). Berners-Lee's vision would begin to be realized in the late 1980s while he was working at CERN. CERN was then, as now, one of the largest physics research centers in Europe, with over 10 000 employees who needed to share information frequently. Berners-Lee had worked there as an independent contractor for a stint in the early 1980s while creating his first hypertext system, ENQUIRE, to organize CERN employee contact details. But during his second tenure at CERN conditions were ripe for the creation of something bigger. In 1989 CERN adopted TCP/IP protocols, which were the only standards that worked for all three computer systems used at the laboratory, and in 1990 it became connected to ARPANET, thereby becoming the largest Internet node in Europe (Stewart, 2015). Almost immediately upon joining CERN in 1984, Berners-Lee began working to start a hypertext project. He was helped in his efforts by Robert Cailliau, who had independently wanted to begin a hypertext project at CERN. Cailliau was adept at managing the politics of CERN and instrumental in getting the hypertext project up and running, leaving Berners-Lee to concentrate on the technical aspects.

The World Wide Web (WWW), as Tim Berners-Lee conceived it, is the means by which the principles of hypertext are adapted to organize information on the Web. Hypertext was the means by which the Web would be navigated, allowing users to move smoothly between different types of content. For the hypertext community this was something new. They had envisaged links between whole and fixed pieces of information but Berners-Lee envisaged information as an interaction and from the beginning he hoped that people would read, publish and edit information as they went. In fact, the Web would only be useful if people were prepared to upload content to servers where it could be accessed.

The WWW is really three inventions packaged into one product. The first is HTTP (Hypertext Transfer Protocols), a set of protocols that allow different computers to communicate, and crucially, to determine which types of files both can read. If both computers are able to use C language for example, they can communicate; if there is no language in common both can use the second Berners-Lee invention, HTML (Hypertext Markup Language), a very simple programming language that relies only on the ability of all devices to produce plain text files. Finally, Berners-Lee devised the URI (Universal Resource Indicator), now called URL, which was a way of indicating where files were located. Together, these three inventions allowed all connected computers to share files or to access servers, machines dedicated to hosting World Wide Web content. The first server was set up on Berners-Lee's own NeXT computer at CERN and hosted, among other items, the content at info.cern.ch, which included instructions on how to set up the World Wide Web, the necessary programs and a master list of known servers, with hypertext links to access them. Like the design for TCP/IP, the design for the World Wide Web emphasized flexibility, simplicity and robustness.

The modern Internet is the very essence of bricolage. When you take the three inventions that make up the World Wide Web and combine them with TCP/IP, email and a host of other technologies, we have most of the infrastructure of the modern Internet. On their own, none of these could have created the global phenomenon that has changed the world, but the WWW was the final piece in the puzzle needed to help the Internet explode. There was just one challenge remaining: to distribute the technology worldwide.

DEEP DIVE 2: THE ADOPTION OF WWW AS A GLOBAL INTERNET STANDARD

The task facing Tim Berners-Lee in the early 1990s seems monumental in retrospect. The Internet was no longer the small research community of the 1970s and 1980s. When ARPANET was launched, computers were enormous machines, often taking up whole rooms and maintained by technicians. Researchers did not interact with them directly but rather made occasional pilgrimages to the rooms where they were housed when they wanted to execute a program. However, in 1975 the first personal computer was created, the MITS Altair 8800. The dominant name in computing at the time was IBM, but IBM failed to anticipate the demand for personal computers from individuals and schools all over the country and so did not launch its own PC until 1981. In the intervening period a number of smaller companies had entered the market including Intel and Microsoft. IBM's PC was built using products from all of these companies, which was a break from the standard IBM model of designing and building its products from scratch, based on proprietary technologies; it opened the door to other companies like Compaq who could also make modular PCs (Moschovitis et al., 1999, pp. 96–8). In 1985 there were 2000 computers linked to the Internet; by 1989 the number had grown to 159 000. By then there was a healthy commercial market for computers able to run

TCP/IP. The military began to take more of an interest in the network and was initially appalled at the lack of security and the open access policies. Ultimately they split it into two: the military's own MILNET and ARPANET. Finally, the National Science Foundation (NSF) constructed its network NSFNET, which was connected to ARPANET. ARPA eventually made the decision to step away from running the network and in 1990 handed responsibility over to the NSF; ARPANET was decommissioned. A struggle for ownership of Internet technology continued between those who wanted to promote proprietary technologies they could control and charge a fee for, and those who wanted computer networking to remain open and free. This battle took place alongside the burgeoning computer industry. For example, Unix was an operating system, meaning software that allowed computer users to interface with computer resources, which had been developed by Bell Laboratories (a division of telecommunications firm AT&T), thanks to generous government subsidies. Along with Unix, inventors Ken Thompson and Dennis Ritchie developed the C operating language that allowed the software to be ported onto any computer. Unix was designed to be a simple and highly adaptable system and its popularity went hand in hand with the emergence of smaller computers to replace the old large mainframes (Moschovitis et al., 1999). In 1974, partly in response to government pressure, Bell made Unix available to universities and released the source code, which allowed the program to be edited and expanded by budding young computer scientists (Castells, 2000). By 1985 Unix was operating on 300 000 machines and there was a considerable community writing programs for it, including for example the BBS message board software. There were also programs such as the Unix to Unix Copy protocol that allowed Unix machines to copy files stored on one computer to another computer.

However, in 1984 AT&T was looking for ways to make money. In 1985 it announced that it would begin charging a fee for Unix. This was seen as a betrayal by a computer science community accustomed to sharing new software freely and it particularly outraged a political young programmer called Richard Stallman. Stallman wrote his own operating system GNU (GNU is Not Unix) that he hoped would be a free alternative. In a game-changing moment, he released the software under a new intellectual property license he dubbed General Public License (GPL). Intellectual property licensed under GPL made its source code available, could be copied, used, edited and distributed freely, with the proviso that all derivative products would also be licensed under GPL. Although GNU itself never became popular, the GPL became hugely influential (though some felt it was still too restrictive). Stallman had effectively launched the Free and Open Source Software movement.

Similarly, the WWW was not the only system available for accessing information on remote computers. Another was Gopher, a system developed at the University of Minnesota. Also popular, it used a menu-based rather than a hypertext-based system of navigation, but in 1993 the university announced that it planned to begin charging a fee for its use. This instantly led to an unwillingness of programmers to continue developing the system (Söderberg, 2007).

Tim Berners-Lee felt that the WWW had to be free and made it freely available on his server at info.cern.ch (still available at http://info.cern.ch/hypertext/WWW/TheProject.html); he just had to get people to use it. Luckily, Berners-Lee was able to get a head start by linking the Web to existing hypertext communities. He posted information about it on the alt. hypertext newsgroup and soon interested parties began to create their own servers, listing them on info.cern.ch.

As the Web grew, Berners-Lee was concerned about the need to ensure that it remained universal. His vision demanded that it be a global information system and this required that there be recognized and standardized common protocols and especially a system of addresses like the URI, so that all computers would be able to recognize the locations of everything on the Web.

In order to steer the development of the Web, in 1992 Berners-Lee went to a meeting of the IETF, which had an open membership policy. At this meeting Berners-Lee presented the Web, attracting many interested parties and spurring the creation of a www.newsgroup to help grow the Web through grassroots engagement. Traffic on the info.cern server grew tenfold between 1991 and 1993, to 10 000 hits a day at the end of the period (Berners-Lee and Fischetti, 1999).

At this point there was still one major challenge facing the World Wide Web, which was that Berners-Lee had designed and build it for his own NeXT computer but most people were operating other systems, especially Unix. When Berners-Lee created the World Wide Web, he also created a browser, software that could be used to access the Web and that was capable of displaying images and other multimedia content, not just text. Although he had a vague intention of creating browsers for other systems, these had never materialized, so the task was left to the broader community. One of the first browsers was Viola, but the browser that perhaps truly transformed Web usage was Mosaic. Mosaic was written for Unix and created by a research team at the National Centre for Supercomputing Applications including Marc Andreessen and Eric Bina. Mosaic was a product that emphasized user friendliness through a graphical user interface. It was launched for free for Unix, and for Windows and Macintosh in 1993. Windows at that point was dominating the personal computer market and now all windows computers came packaged with software that allowed users to interface easily with the Web.

Crucially, the WWW remained free. Berners-Lee had rejected offers to turn it into a commercial program. At an IETF meeting in March 1993 Berners-Lee was asked if CERN planned to charge for the Web, a question that he had never really considered. He wanted the Web to be made available through GPL but was warned that even that could be considered too restrictive for programmers hoping to develop commercial applications for the system. What would CERN do? In April 1993 CERN approved a decision to put the Web in the public domain, making it a freely available common resource for the whole world. This was the tipping point for the Web, and by the end of 1993, one million people were using Mosaic and the number using the Internet was doubling every eighteen months. The Web and the Internet had taken off. Tim Berners-Lee left ARPA and went on to lead the World Wide Web Consortium (W3C), an organization that sets standards for Web development and works to ensure that the development of the Web stays true to Berners-Lee's vision of a free information resource open to all of humanity.

THE IMPORTANCE OF STARTING CONDITIONS AND THE STATUS OF THE MODERN INTERNET

The modern Internet remains largely free to use, openly accessible (in most countries), and easy to modify and build on to improve its functionality. It is important to understand how radically different this communication technology is from what came before. Telecommunications before the Internet were largely dominated by nationally owned companies and other large organizations. We have seen how these actors constrained the development of the Internet in the UK and France and attempted to impose their control internationally through the ISO, but they failed. That failure speaks to the power of the initial starting conditions.

ARPANET and the WWW grew up in government and university research centers, not subject to the influence of these telecommunication giants who overlooked the potential of the Internet, perhaps in part because the technology looked so different from their switchboards. Moreover, the individuals who led the development of the Internet at these centers, like Vint Cerf and Tim Berners-Lee, were influenced by the sometimes utopian philosophies of thinkers like Licklider and Vannevar Bush and worked actively to ensure the technology adhered to their vision. Today, their influence continues to be felt in the governance of the Internet through organizations like the IETF and W3C. Although the counter-factual in history is always a speculative position, nonetheless the struggles that occurred for control of the Internet strongly signal that there was nothing inevitable about its development. It is easy to imagine a world where the Internet was developed instead at the NPL, where X25 became the standard protocols, where the ISO or another traditional international standards organization oversaw new developments, and where a proprietary technology became the primary means by which to access information online.

Furthermore, we should be clear that the struggle for control of the Internet is not over. The Web is free, but as it exists in the public domain, it is also open for use by commercial interests. Today, many such companies, such as Google, Facebook and Amazon, are dominant players online and exert huge influence, alongside free and open entities like Wikipedia and Linux. Moreover, telecommunications and media companies continue to lobby Congress for greater control of the content posted online. For example, in 2012 they attempted to introduce the Stop Online Piracy Act (SOPA) and the Protect IPA Act (PIPA), generating a huge online backlash that saw many sites shut down for a day, and large public and online demonstrations that were ultimately successful in preventing the bills from passing.

An open question therefore remains. While initial starting conditions shaped the early development of the Internet, will their influence continue to be felt as strongly as it grows, or will the importance of starting conditions fade over time and give way to a new Internet, more reminiscent of the telecommunications regime of the past?

REFERENCES

Abbate, J. (1999). *Inventing the Internet*. Cambridge, MA: MIT Press.

Alvestrand, H. 2004. A mission statement for the IETF. *Internet Engineering Task Force RFC 3935*. Accessed 12 December 2016 at http://www.ietf.org/about/mission.html.

Berners-Lee, T. (1999). Answers for kids. *W3*. Accessed 11 November 2016 at https://www.w3.org/People/Berners-Lee/Kids.html.

Berners-Lee, T. and Fischetti, M. (1999). *Weaving the Web: The Original Design and Ultimate Destiny of the World Wide Web by its Creator*. New York: HarperCollins.

Bush, V. (1945). As we may think. *The Atlantic*, July. Accessed 11 November 2016 at http://www.theatlantic.com/magazine/archive/1945/07/as-we-may-think/303881/.

Castells, M. (2000). *The Rise of the Networked Society*. Chichester: Wiley.

Cerf, V. (2002). The Internet is for everyone. *Request For Comment 3271 Internet Engineering Task Force*. Accessed 1 November 2016 at https://tools.ietf.org/html/rfc3271.

Clark, D. (1992). A cloudy crystal ball – visions of the future. *Views of the Future*.

Accessed 11 November 2016 at http://groups.csail.mit.edu/ana/People/DDC/fu ture_ietf_92.pdf.

Drezner, D. (2004). The global governance of the internet: bringing the state back in. *Political Science Quarterly*, **119** (3).

Gillies, J. and Cailliau, R. (2000). *How the Web was Born, the Story of the World Wide Web.* New York: Oxford University Press.

Hoffman, P. (2012). The Tao of IETF: A novice's guide to the Internet Engineering Task Force. *IETF*, Accessed 11 November 2016 at https://www.ietf.org/tao.html.

Leiner, B.M., Cerf, V.G., Clark, D.D., Khan, R.E., Kleinrock, L., Lynch, D.C., Postel, J., Roberts, L.G. and Wolff, S. (2003). Brief history of the internet. *Internetsociety.org.* Accessed 11 November 2016 at http://www.internetsociety. org/internet/what-internet/history-internet/brief-history-internet#Origins.

Moschovitis, C., Poole, H., Schuyler, T. and Senft, T. (1999). *History of the Internet: A Chronology, 1843 to the Present.* Santa Barbara, CA: ABC-Clio.

Russell, A. (2013). OSI: The internet that wasn't. *IEEE Spectrum.* Accessed 11 November 2016 at http://spectrum.ieee.org/computing/networks/osi-the-internet-that-wasnt?

Russell, A. (2014). *Open Standards and the Digital Age.* New York: Cambridge University Press.

Söderberg, J. (2007). *Hacking Capitalism: The Free and Open Source Software Movement.* New York: Routledge.

Stewart, W. (2015). ARPANET: the first internet. *Livinginternet.* Accessed 11 November 2016 at http://www.livinginternet.com/i/ii_arpanet.htm.

8. Synthesis: self-organization, strange attractors and social innovation

Daniel McCarthy

INTRODUCTION AND CONCEPTUAL BACKGROUND

This chapter synthesizes insights from several of the case study chapters using key concepts from complexity theory to further the development of the conceptual/theoretical foundations of social innovation. Taking a broadly systemic look at three of these historic cases of social innovation or dramatic systems change, one begins to see patterns in the narratives. These patterns can be interpreted using conceptual tools, metaphors or heuristics from complexity theories so as to both help explain the phenomena and enable social innovators to recognize, and even replicate, patterns of systems behavior in the complex, evolving systems they are seeking to transform. While this chapter is not the first attempt to apply insights from complexity and chaos theories to understanding social systems, social change or innovation, it combines insights from pre-existing theories of social innovation, concepts like the "Adjacent Possible", with ideas from chaos theory and complexity theory.

Several authors have explored the concept and practice of social innovation, transformation and transition process using various forms of the Rogers (1962) diffusion of innovations theory, sigmoid curve (Geels and Schot, 2007; Geels, 2011) and Holling's adaptive cycle or panarchy cycle (Westley et al., 2006; Biggs et al., 2010). These interrelated patterns of system behavior can be usefully thought of as strange attractors – a strange attractor is a pattern of systems behavior for which the evolution through the set of possible physical states is non-periodic (chaotic), resulting in an evolution through a set of states defining a fractal set (Peitgen et al., 1992; Van Eenwyk, 1997). Strange attractors emerge out of deterministic chaos – a form of system behavior in which "patterns" or order periodically appear and disappear – as opposed to entropic chaos where a system never resolves into patterns, and simply deteriorates into total disorder. Strange attractors and deterministic chaos are useful metaphors for describing the patterns of behavior that manifest in both the human psyche and social structures, as well as the way in which social systems manifest new technologies or social innovations (Van Eenwyk, 1997).

These emergent patterns can be thought of as self-organizing, dissipative structures. Self-organization refers to a process whereby some form of order manifests from the interactions of systems components within a disordered system state. Self-organization has been explored in the disciplines of chemistry and physics, most notably by the Nobel Prize-winning Ilya Prigogine for his work on the thermodynamics of non-equilibrium systems (see, for example, Nicolis and Prigogine, 1977). Classic examples of self-organizing, dissipative structures include "Bénard Cells" and even vortices in bathtubs. Stuart Kauffman has also famously explored the concept of self-organization in several of his books, especially *Origins of Order* (1993) and *At Home in the Universe* (1995) in relation to biological evolution, and more recently in *Humanity in a Creative Universe* (2016) in relation to human creativity.

According to the second law of thermodynamics, entropy (disorder) is always increasing. Seemingly in spite of this, we see around us elegant forms of biophysical, social, economic and political order manifesting based on relatively cheap, high-quality energy (Homer-Dixon, 2007). This type of self-organization happens at the edge of chaos (Kauffman, 1995; Waltner-Toews et al., 2008) in dynamic tension between order and disorder or what Fred Spier (2011) has referred to as "goldilocks conditions". Self-organizing, emergent structures that emerge from such goldilocks conditions can often create new goldilocks conditions that allow new forms of order to emerge. In this way, self-organization can be a useful metaphor for understanding the genesis and evolution of phenomena that create the conditions for new innovations that create the conditions for further innovations.

David Bella (1994; 1997) used the concept of self-organization and a dynamic tension between order and disorder in vast, human, organizational systems such as the tobacco industry, universities and resource management to describe the behavior and evolution of organizations and institutions. Bella's work describes the behavior of large organizations or institutions as exhibiting two attractors: an ordering, amoral, rule-based, bureaucratic pattern of behavior and a disordering, critical, anti-establishment (whatever the current establishment is) pattern of behavior. As organizations or institutions evolve, rules and regulations are essential to ensure efficiency and effectiveness. However, Bella argues that the "ordering" attractor can become entrenched and self-reinforcing. If this happens the organization risks becoming ossified, overly rigid and prone to collapse. Thus, a resilient organization will allow for what Bella refers to as "credible disturbances" that question, critique and sometimes dramatically alter the existing rules of the system. At the same time Bella posits that too many credible disturbances, too much disorder, causes the system to become unstable and risks collapse or at least an inability to continue to self-organize, develop and evolve. Bella argues that this ongoing and dynamic tension between order and disorder within organizational systems is what allows them to continue to self-organize and remain resilient in the face of broader system change.

In his book *The Nature of Technology*, W. Brian Arthur describes how technology evolves in self-organizing, self-creating or "autopoietic" ways manifesting path dependencies, where the discovery of a phenomenon creates the context for new technologies to emerge, which creates new contexts for new technologies to emerge and so on. Chilean biologists Maturana and Varela (1973; 1980), in their work attempting to define the characteristics of living systems, originally defined autopoiesis as a system that is capable of self-creation, reproduction and maintenance. In one of their early works they described autopoiesis using a mechanistic metaphor:

> an autopoietic machine is a machine organized (defined as a unity) as a network of processes of production (transformation and destruction) of components which: (i) through their interactions and transformations continuously regenerate and realize the network of processes (relations) that produced them; and (ii) constitute it (the machine) as a concrete unity in space in which they (the components) exist by specifying the topological domain of its realization as such a network. (Maturana and Varela, 1980, pp. 78–9)

W. Brian Arthur described how, as a form of self-organization, autopoiesis appears to be a conceptually abstract systems property but does, in fact, tell us a lot about the nature and development of technology:

> It tells us that every novel technology is created from existing ones, and therefore that every technology stands upon a pyramid of others that made it possible in a succession that goes back to the earliest phenomena that humans captured. It tells us that all future technologies will derive from those that now exist (perhaps in no obvious way) because these are the elements that will form further elements that will eventually make these future technologies possible. (Arthur, 2009, p. 112)

These future, uncertain possible states have been referred to as "adjacent possibles" (Kauffman, 2000).

Stuart Kauffman originally defined the "adjacent possible" in the context of biochemistry by defining the current set of organic molecules, or "actual" system as "all the kinds of organic molecules on, within, or in the vicinity of the Earth, say, out to twice the radius of the moon" (2000,

p. 142). Kauffman then differentiated that "actual" set from the "adjacent possible" or "all of those molecular species that are not members of the actual, but are *one reaction step away from the actual*" (original emphasis) (2000, p. 142). Steven Johnson (2010) utilized the concept of the adjacent possible to great effect in his book on the history of innovation, *Where Good Ideas Come From*. And most recently, in his book *Humanity in a Creative Universe*, Kauffman (2016) built on his own notion of the Adjacent Possible and applied it to the evolution of human social, cultural and economic systems:

> New goods and production capacities are new Actuals that are enabling constraints that do not cause, but enable new, typically unprestatable Adjacent Possible economic opportunities into which the economy "flows," creating again new unprestatable new Actuals that enable yet new Adjacent Possibles. Economic evolution is open-ended, creative, beyond entailing law, and radically emergent. (Kauffman, 2016, p. 86)

Looking through a complexity theory lens at the development of technology and the process of social innovation tells us quite a bit about the process of innovation: that new innovations are based on existing, as well as a "pyramid" of historic, components/concepts. This implies that social innovations may exhibit both a sensitivity to initial conditions and what systems thinkers refer to as path-dependence (also explored by W. Brian Arthur in a previous work: Arthur, 1994). In this way, the notion of a system's autopoietic nature and related notions of such a system's sensitivity to initial conditions from chaos theory and the concept of path dependence, help us to understand how new ideas, behaviors and technologies were the adjacent possibles of former actual system behaviors, but also that they enable new adjacent possibles to emerge. Some of these then become new "actuals" or create the context for new forms of self-organization, self-creation or autopoiesis which can be seen as patterns of behavior or strange attractors that emerge and stabilize in the context of deterministic chaos (patterns emerging and re-emerging) extending the region of adjacent possibles along a particular system developmental pathway. It is this iterative, evolving systems dynamic of some adjacent possibles emerging as strange attractors out of deterministic chaos, becoming stabilized system actuals and creating the context for new adjacent possibles that I hope to draw out of several of the historic cases. I would assert that understanding the underlying, complex dynamics of the systems that social innovators seek to transform, using insights from complexity and chaos theories, is critical in fostering successful social innovation.

THE DUTCH EAST INDIA COMPANY AND THE JOINT STOCK COMPANY AS SOCIAL INNOVATION

As the case indicates, many scholars have highlighted the role of the Dutch and later English innovations in business and trade as laying the foundation for subsequent political, economic and social shifts, especially the emergence of individualism, the Enlightenment and the Industrial Revolution. Stuart Kauffman (2016) describes the role of the Dutch East India Company as creating the enabling conditions for the stream of adjacent possibles that we have co-created and that we are "sucked" into, including the current spreading of financial risk through the global derivatives market (see the next section). A number of key credible disturbances or disordering influences in the system at the time fed into the deterministic chaos which allowed for new strange attractors, new ordering mechanisms, to emerge, creating the enabling conditions for suites of new adjacent possibles and developing a path-dependence for subsequent innovations. The pattern of behavior or the strange attractor that was established by the joint stock company in England in the 16th century emerged or self-organized in part to dissipate a gradient of new capital that had been liberated from the deterioration of the obligation relationships of the feudal system. More specifically, joint stock companies emerged in England to dissipate the gap between the country's international ambitions and dwindling state funds. The pattern of exchange and behavior (strange attractor) that the joint stock company allowed was reinforced because of its elective affinity with the emerging social, economic and political structures in the Netherlands at the time. This disruptive strange attractor emerged out of the deterministic chaos of a shifting political economic regime described in detail in the case chapter.

At the time, Calvinism was providing a credible disturbance (disordering influence) to the existing ordering (but brittle) Catholic structures of signification through open-air sermons and even destruction of Spanish religious property. Calvinism's growth in popularity in the Netherlands co-evolved with growing political unrest with the oppressive Spanish colonial rule and burdensome taxation. Credible disturbances (disordering influences) to the Spanish structures of legitimation and domination began with Dutch military resistance in the 1570s. These credible disturbances began an era of deterministic chaos from which new ordering system behaviors, new strange attractors, would emerge in the form of the Dutch Calvinist State established by William of Orange. This new de facto Dutch state was marked by a stark shift, a new ordering influence or strange attractor, in which power and wealth had shifted from nobility and land-owning aristocracy to urban merchants. This created the enabling conditions for a suite of new adjacent possibles including the joint stock company.

Another key credible disturbance (disordering influence) that emerged at the time was the advent of *mare liberum* or open seas. As the case chapter describes, Hugo Grotius, in 1609, developed the legal case for the social phenomenon of *mare liberum*. This was in stark contrast to the existing long-established pattern of behavior or strange attractor of the joint Portuguese/Spanish claim of *mare clausum* (closed seas) that had allowed the Portuguese/Spanish to maintain a monopoly (technical, legal and spiritual) on maritime trade. Again, this legal precedent had an elective affinity with both the religious and military credible disturbances to the existing pattern of system behavior, dominated by the Spanish. *Mare liberum*, as well as human health innovations including use of lemon juice as a cure for scurvy, created the conditions for new adjacent possibles for Dutch economic expansion through extended maritime trade. While incredibly lucrative (even if three-quarters of the fleet was lost during the expedition), there was high risk associated with expensive maritime trade excursions. One adjacent possible now within reach, and a powerful new strange attractor that would become established and reinforced by social structures with strong elective affinity, was the joint stock company. The joint stock company allowed merchants to fund expensive overseas trips by pooling their capital to fund multi-ship expeditions, thereby distributing and minimizing the risk of such a large expenditure. This new social structure, pattern of behavior or strange attractor provided a new ordering influence within the system that would allow for the establishment of larger and more powerful joint stock companies such as the Dutch East India Company (VOC) as well as similar companies in France in 1604, Sweden in 1615, Denmark in 1616 and Brandenburg in 1651.

Perhaps more importantly, the joint stock company opened up the possibility, the adjacent possible, for money to play a new role in society – that money and even property (that could be purchased) could be seen as fungible and transferable. This would create a strong credible disturbance to the previous order or attractor, the land-based aristocracy associated with the feudal system. It would also create the conditions for a cascade of adjacent possibles or path-dependence that would eventually result in incredibly disembedded economic structures, including the global derivatives market.

THE GLOBAL DERIVATIVES MARKET AS A SOCIAL INNOVATION

While it may be unclear whether the emergence of the modern derivatives market can be considered a social innovation that will be deeply regretted in retrospect, it is hard to argue that options pricing and the modern derivatives market has not demonstrated impact, durability and scale – hallmarks of a social innovation. It can be argued that the modern derivatives market is but a logical extension of the systemic path created by the joint stock companies (see the previous section), that Kauffman (2016) would argue we have been "sucked" into, by the system's path-dependence, tracing its evolution back to the development of the joint stock company.

As the case chapter notes:

> In the aftermath of every major financial collapse since the early 1990s derivatives have been cited as a cause. However, the revulsion towards them has not reached a tipping point leading to stricter regulation or a withdrawal of funds from the derivative sector. Consequently, following each crash the derivatives market quickly rebounds and further expands, a trend that is currently underway following the 2008 global financial crisis.

This speaks to the resiliency of this pattern of behavior or strange attractor that emerged as a result of both the Black–Scholes options pricing model and the creation of the Chicago Board Options Exchange in 1973. For details, refer to the case chapter, but it is important to understand the development of this highly resilient strange attractor as it emerged in response to long-term tensions between centralization (ordering behavior) and decentralization (disordering behavior) of responses to addressing both financial risk and the consolidation of power in the global political-economic system. As the case notes, the modern derivatives market emerged following four different periods: the *Pax Britannica* (pre-1914); the Collapse of the Global Order (1914–29); the Rival Blocs (1930–45); and Bretton Woods (1945–71). Each of these periods marked an emergent pattern of behavior, a strange attractor that was stabilized by an elective affinity with the current political and economic pressures and trends. The Bretton Woods era was marked by an attempt to bring stability to a highly unstable post-war era and was heavily influenced by the leading thinkers of the day, in this case, John Maynard Keynes.

The Keynesian-inspired Bretton Woods attractor era was an attempt to address the economic risk around global trade and currency exchange by moving to a global standard, a gold standard with the US dollar pegged to gold and other currencies pegged to it. This pattern of political-economic behavior arose in response to wartime rival currency blocs that resulted in reduced global trade and highly imperialistic economic behavior. In contrast to both Keynes himself and the Bretton Woods system that his work inspired, a new strange attractor that emerged out of the deterministic chaos instigated by the credible disturbances marked by the Nixon shocks in the early 1970s and unpegging the US dollar from the gold standard, a deregulated, global financial market was largely inspired by the work of

Austrian economist Friedrich Hayek and the Mont Pelerin Society. As the case notes, "whereas Keynes was a scion of a weakened but still dominant British Empire, Hayek came of age in Vienna during the final years of the Austro-Hungarian Empire." Their views on what constituted "risk", the appropriate seat of power and the role of government and the market were very different.

These two perspectives, these two men and the political-economic attractors that arose out of two very different temporal periods of deterministic chaos were two different patterns of behavior that resulted from past pressures and failures within the system, the system's path-dependence, but also represented two different compromises in the dynamic tension between ordering efforts within the system (to centralize, regulate currency exchange and risk) and disordering efforts (to decentralize, deregulate). Bella (1997) might argue that these two strange attractors evolved in this dynamic tension between ordering and disordering behaviors, perhaps both to logical extremes. The Keynesian system of regulation became ossified in the face of neoliberal pressures to deregulate and so collapsed with the Nixon Shocks and loss of the gold standard. So too, the current deregulated, modern derivatives system may be verging on a similar extreme. Economic collapses in the 1990s and the 2008 economic collapse have been attributed to instabilities associated with the derivatives market. Not only does the application of these complexity-based heuristics help us to understand how innovations emerge and evolve, but they also can help us to understand how they become less resilient to change and may even collapse.

THE INTERNET AS A SOCIAL INNOVATION

The Internet as a social innovation case illustrates the utility of several of these complexity-based heuristics in understanding how innovations emerge and evolve. As identified in the case, the phenomenon that in many ways created the conditions for the phenomenal self-organizing order that has become the Internet was the concept of packet-switching. This technology, which allowed for more efficient delivery of information through a decentralized network by breaking a message down into "packets" and sending each separately to be reassembled upon arrival, had what Arthur referred to as an "elective affinity" with the emerging power of the networked computers of the day. Researchers in the well-funded think tank Advanced Research Projects Agency (ARPA) created a packet-switching network, ARPANET. ARPANET, and its founders, laid the foundations for the modern Internet and as a result, ARPANET's "initial conditions" are important in this story of innovation. ARPA was funded by the US government in an effort to keep pace with Soviet technological advances, especially Sputnik, in the late 1950s. ARPA scientists were given enormous freedom to explore projects that wouldn't necessarily result in defense applications. This could be interpreted as a context in which credible disturbances to the existing system could be explored freely. As the case notes, the ARPA scientists saw ARPANET as a research project whose intention was the sharing of information. And as Vint Cerf, one of the fathers of the Internet, wrote, "the Internet is for everyone – but it won't be if Governments restrict access to it, so we must dedicate ourselves to keeping the network unrestricted, unfettered and unregulated. We must have the freedom to speak and the freedom to hear" (Cerf, 2002).

The packet-switching phenomenon emerged and created the conditions for new emergent forms of information sharing or adjacent possibles. One of these adjacent possibles, ARPANET, ultimately grew out of the fertile conditions of a well-funded and autonomous research environment with the very clear initial conditions eloquently articulated by Vint Cerf (above). As ARPANET grew, so did several other packet-switching networks around the globe and eventually there came the need for international standards to ensure a globally connected Internet. In this competitive, and at times contentious, environment of contending approaches to standardization, a clear tension between order and disorder was evident – a tension between the need for global standardization (a form of centralization) and the need to retain a decentralized Internet for everyone. It was at this edge of deterministic chaos, this dynamic tension between order and disorder that one could see the emergence of several patterns of standardization, which could be interpreted as competing strange attractors: OSI and TCP/IP. OSI was a collaboration of major governments and large corporate entities, including IBM. While OSI was well funded, its development ultimately suffered and slowed due to the fact that its government, and especially corporate supporters, ended up embroiled in a power struggle attempting to ensure that the outcome would result in more control or competitive advantage. Bella (1997) might have interpreted OSI's development as pushing the dynamic tension between order and disorder too firmly towards an ordered, forced-control attractor and therefore inhibiting its continued self-organization or development. However, given this system's sensitivity to its initial conditions, that is, attempting to ensure an "internet for everyone", it may not be surprising that the ARPANET TCP/IP attractor was ultimately the one that became more widely adopted and subsumed the OSI system into its architecture – in the context of the dynamic tension between order (standardization and even control) and disorder (an "internet for everyone").

Ultimately, packet-switching created the conditions for the emergence of several packet-switching networks. A number of self-organizing patterns or patterns of behavior (strange attractors) emerged to take advantage of this new phenomenon. ARPANET emerged out of this period of deterministic chaos as a stable attractor that drew interest and support from around the world. This created a whole new suite of adjacent possibles, including a globally connected information network. To enable this, global standards had to be established and a new period of deterministic chaos began. In this edge of chaos state, the dynamic tension between order (standardization) and disorder (decentralization) would have to be maintained by a new pattern of behavior or attractor. And out of this period of deterministic chaos, TCP/IP emerged as the stable attractor that drew international support and reflected the system's initial conditions – erring on the side of a decentralized "internet for everyone". This stable attractor provided a new context for innovation, and a suite of new adjacent possibles emerged including email, bulletin boards, hypertext and URLs. With the advent of personal computing, no longer was it sufficient to link huge mainframe computers, thus a new period of instability, a new period of deterministic chaos arose. New patterns of organization or strange attractors developed to address the emerging need for global standards for accessing remote computers: the World Wide Web (www), Gopher and others. Ultimately, it was the free www that reflected the initial conditions of the system and became the stable attractor which has again spawned a new suite of adjacent possibles including all of the emerging uses of the Web, such as social media.

Thus, a pattern of behavior emerges, reflecting insights from complexity thinking, especially deterministic chaos and strange attractors, in which "patterns" or order periodically appear and disappear. The Internet case also highlights the importance of a system's sensitivity to initial conditions – in this case, the democratic, decentralized ethos that still undergirds the Internet today (despite many attempts to impose a centralized order).

CONCLUDING COMMENTS

This chapter attempted to integrate several heuristics from complexity and chaos theory in an effort to further buttress the conceptual/theoretical foundations of the emerging field of social innovation. Bringing together insights from self-organization theories, strange attractors, path-dependence and the dynamic tension between order and disorder within complex systems, this chapter reinterpreted some of the key events within three historic cases of social innovation: the Dutch East India Company/ Joint Stock Companies case, the global derivatives market, and the development of the Internet. In each case, credible disturbances to existing patterns of system behavior led to periods of deterministic chaos within which new patterns or strange attractors would emerge and, if there was an elective affinity within the broader system context, the attractor could become stabilized and reorder the system. In all cases, the dynamic tension between ordering and disordering behaviors within the system had an impact on the continued self-organization or evolution of the innovation. The elective affinity and path-dependence of the system, and the system's history of disturbance would at least in part dictate the selection pressure towards more ordering or disordering behaviors. However, too much "drift" towards one extreme or another might result in the ossification of the system or the deterioration of a previously stable attractor.

Scholars and practitioners of social innovation can utilize these tools or heuristics as diagnostic tools or even design tools in fostering emerging innovations. By viewing emerging social innovations as self-organizing, strange attractors that emerge out of periods of systemic instability or deterministic chaos, social innovators can see their work as managing or designing the context for self-organization rather than managing or attempting to enact a command and control strategy on their project. As such, they might view their innovation projects as fragile, emerging autopoietic (self-creating) systems that need "protected niche" spaces (Smith and Raven, 2012) within existing systems. Therefore, innovators could see the need to create credible disturbances or disordering behaviors within the existing system and at the same time ensure that their emerging innovation has some elective affinity within the system context or builds on the system's path dependence.

Within this highly dynamic innovation context, an awareness of the tension between ordering and disordering patterns of behavior is essential. While working within the system's path-dependence or ensuring that the innovation has some elective affinity, the innovator needs to ensure a healthy dynamic tension between ordering and disordering behaviors within the innovation context, avoiding the twin temptations to either control or enforce order or to allow the disordering behaviors to let the delicate, emerging attractor that is their innovation disintegrate. In this way, social innovations can usefully be viewed as self-organizing, autopoietic structures that are essentially living systems, emergent behaviors or strange attractors emerging at the edge of chaos therefore in need of constant monitoring and adaptation to an environment of deterministic chaos in which patterns can emerge and disappear. In this way, the act of social innovation is akin to the nurturing of a fragile new life form. And each time an innovation emerges and becomes stabilized, new possibilities emerge that are not necessarily prestatable: new adjacent possibles, which beget the conditions for more new adjacent possibles. And in this way, innovators create the conditions for new innovations, new life forms that can, as Kauffman (2016) indicates, "suck" us into new opportunities. These adjacent possibles can be exciting and ripe with opportunities to make the world a better place or they may be ripe with the potential to push the system to a logical extreme, as in the case of the global derivatives market. As with any innovation story, this complexity-based narrative speaks to both the hope and the potential caution imbedded in the initial conditions of any innovation. So, take hope and take heed.

REFERENCES

Arthur, W.B. (1994). *Increasing Returns and Path Dependence in the Economy*. Ann Arbor, MI: University of Michigan Press.

Arthur, W.B. (2009). *The Nature of Technology: What It Is and How It Evolves.* New York: Free Press.

Bella, D.A. (1994). Organizational systems and the burden of proof. In: D.J. Stouder, P.A. Bisson and R. Naiman (eds), *Pacific Salmon and their Ecosystems*. New York: Chapman and Hall.

Bella, D.A. (1997). Organized complexity in human affairs: the tobacco industry. *Journal of Business Ethics*, **16**(10), 977–99.

Biggs, R., Westley, F.R. and Carpenter, S.R. (2010). Navigating the back loop: fostering social innovation and transformation in ecosystem management. *Ecology and Society*, **15**(2), 9.

Cerf, V. (2002). *The Internet is for Everyone*. Memo for the Internet Society. Accessed 18 January 2017 at https://tools.ietf.org/html/rfc3271.

Geels, F.W. (2011). The multi-level perspective on sustainability transitions: responses to seven criticisms. *Environmental Innovation and Societal Transitions*, **1**(1), 24–40.

Geels, F.W. and J. Schot (2007). Typology of sociotechnical transition pathways. *Research Policy*, **36**(3), 399–41.

Homer-Dixon, T. (2007). *The Upside of Down: Catastrophe, Creativity and the Renewal of Civilization*. Toronto: Vintage Canada.

Johnson, S. (2010). *Where Good Ideas Come From: The Natural History of Innovation*. New York: Riverhead Books.

Kauffman, S.A. (1993). *Origins of Order: Self organization and Selection in Evolution*. New York: Oxford University Press.

Kauffman, S.A. (1995). *At Home in the Universe: The Search for the Laws of Self-organization and Complexity*. New York: Oxford University Press.

Kauffman, S.A. (2000). *Investigations*. New York: Oxford University Press.

Kauffman, S.A. (2016). *Humanity in a Creative Universe*. New York: Oxford University Press.

Maturana, H.R. and Varela, F.G. (1973). *De Maquinas y Seres Vivos*. Santiago: Editorial Universitaria.

Maturana, H.R. and Varela, F.G. (1980). *Autopoiesis and Cognition: The Realization of the Living*. Boston, MA: D. Reidel Publishing Company.

Nicolis, G. and Prigogine, I. (1977). *Self-organization in Non-equilibrium Systems: From Dissipative Structures to Order Through Fluctuations*. New York: Wiley.

Peitgen, H-O., Jürgens, H. and Saupe, D. (1992). *Chaos and Fractals: New Frontiers of Science*. Berlin and New York: Springer-Verlag.

Rogers, E.M. (1962). *Diffusion of Innovations*, 4th edn. New York: The Free Press.

Smith, A. and Raven, R. (2012). What is protective space? Reconsidering niches in transitions to sustainability. *Research Policy*, **41**(6), 1025–36.

Spier, F. (2011). *Big History and the Future of Humanity*. Malden, MA: Wiley-Blackwell.

Van Eenwyk, J.R. (1997). *Archetypes and Strange Attractors: The Chaotic World of Symbols*. Toronto: Inner City Books.

Waltner-Toews, D., Kay, J.J. and Lister, N.M. (2008). *The Ecosystem Approach: Complexity, Uncertainty, and Managing for Sustainability*. New York: Columbia University Press.

Westley, F.R., Zimmerman, B. and Patton, M. (2006). *Getting to Maybe: How the World is Changed*. Toronto: Random House of Canada.

9. The global derivatives market as social innovation

Sean Geobey

The way that we see risk is deeply, often unconsciously, shaped by our financial institutions. Many of these institutions and practices are quite old: saving, borrowing and lending are ancient, modern banking and insurance are almost four centuries old, and the limited liability corporation is over 150 years old. However, the defining financial instrument of the age of globalization and the neoliberal order may be the derivative contract.

These sophisticated "bets" allow the transfer of risk between people and organizations, enabling long-term investment and trade. They also allow for highly leveraged speculation, and the profitability of derivatives trading has driven the growth of highly computerized, globally integrated financial markets. Most importantly, the global derivatives market has commoditized the very concept of risk. While the ultimate social, environmental and economic impact of the dramatic growth in this market is still ambiguous, it is clear that its growth is a social innovation that has dramatically reorganized global economic and political power structures and has proved remarkably resilient despite the numerous catastrophic financial bubbles that have been blamed on it.

Though arrangements resembling derivatives have existed since ancient times, until the 1970s they were of limited use outside of the agricultural sector. Two key developments led to an explosion in their use. The first, at the institutional level, was the collapse of the Bretton Woods system of centrally managed currency exchange rates that had underpinned international trade and investment since the end of the Second World War. The instability that this change unleashed threatened to cripple the international economic order, much like the collapse that followed the toppling of the UK-dominated global economic order after the First World War.

Around the same time, the development of a new social phenomenon, the Black–Scholes–Merton options pricing model, increased the ease with which derivatives could be used to manage fluctuations in international currencies. This social phenomenon was built on developments in statistics, mathematical finance and new economic models of portfolio investments that had emerged in the mid-20th century. As Bernstein notes:

> Until the early 1970s, exchange rates were legally fixed, the price of oil varied over a narrow range, and the overall price level rose by no more than 3% or 4% a year. The abrupt appearance of new risks in areas so long considered stable triggered a search for novel and more effective tools of risk management. Derivatives are symptomatic of the state of the economy and of the financial markets, not the cause of the volatility that is the focus of so much concern. (1996, p. 305)

Derivatives appeared to be the right financial tool to manage seemingly random financial instability, and while this had always been of value in agriculture due to the unpredictable impact of weather, the new chaos emerging in the international financial system immediately expanded their application to almost all trade and investment.

The growth of the global derivatives market changed the relationship of major economic and political institutions to risk, pushing the international monetary system over a tipping point that shifted it from the Bretton Woods system of managed currencies towards the current neoliberal order. At their core, derivatives have created the impression that risk could be separated from investment, and this in turn has had three big effects on the way our economies operate. First, the derivatives market has created a highly lucrative new avenue for financial speculation, as people have stepped in to take on the risk others are trying to avoid. Second, the appearance of risk-mitigation means that investors have become more willing to take on investments that would have been considered too risky were they not able to rely on derivatives as "insurance". Third, the perception that derivatives could, for a price, eliminate risk has greatly enabled the development of a "risk society". As tools for enabling "personal responsibility", most derivatives apply to organizations rather than individuals. However, the implication that individual "bets" could be more effective than the collective risk-pooling found in more traditional insurance has certainly spread into the broader social discourse.

SHORT HISTORY OF THE EARLY 20TH-CENTURY INTERNATIONAL MONETARY SYSTEMS

International exchange rates between different currencies have always been critical to global economic integration and the systems that organize these exchange rates have largely reflected the geopolitical realities present at the time. Exchange rate stability reduces the risk of investments or trade goods being devalued and effectively incentivizes investment and trade. At the turn of the 20th century, the international system appeared quite stable and the share of global gross domestic product traded internationally reached a peak that would only be exceeded at the turn of the 21st century. However, with the start of the First World War this fragile stability shattered and started a century of international economic reorganizations that are treated here as four different periods prior to the growth of the global derivatives market: the *Pax Britannica* (pre-1914); the Collapse of the Global Order (1914–29); the Rival Blocs (1930–45); and Bretton Woods (1945–71) (see Figure 9.1).

In the pre-WW1 *Pax Britannica* period, the United Kingdom dominated international trade order, which was characterized by international monetary stability connected to a gold-backed British pound and liberal international trade policies. While this order facilitated trade, the constraints on domestic policy imposed by the gold standard tended to exaggerate boom–bust cycles, causing domestic political instability in many countries.

The First World War and the 1920s saw the *Collapse of the Global Order* as the global economic system failed to adapt to the weakening of the old European empires and the growing strength of the United States, Soviet Union, Germany and Japan. During this period the pound sterling was devalued relative to gold a number of times, and ultimately came off the gold standard in 1931, effectively eliminating the possibility of using a gold-pound as the underpinning of a new global trade system.

The economic chaos of the 1920s did not lead to international consolidation around a single global currency standard; the 1930s saw the emergence of *Rival Blocs*-led big single currencies tied to large, increasingly well-armed economic powers vying for control of scarce resources. The American dollar and the British pound were the two most important currencies, holding their respective rival trading blocs together, while the Japanese yen was rising in influence, the German Reichsmark was growing in importance as its country reindustrialized, the franc carried some weight among France's colonies, and the Soviet Union remained separate from the global economic order altogether. Trade between these single-currency blocs fell dramatically, incentivizing imperial activities that would bring the variety of resources needed to run a modern economy (such as oil, coal, iron and agricultural land) into their own economic sphere.

Following the Second World War, the victorious Allied powers, with the notable exception of the Soviet Union, sought to rebuild a global economic order that would both include the defeated powers and prevent the re-emergence of the rival trading blocs through a series of institutions known as the *Bretton Woods* system, after the location of the meetings that devised this order. Two key organizations, the International

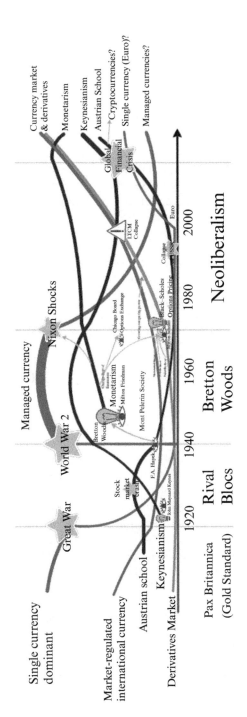

Figure 9.1   Changing international monetary systems in the 20th century

Monetary Fund (IMF) and the International Bank for Reconstruction and Development (IBRD, now World Bank), were designed to achieve exchange rate stability and facilitate international trade. The hope was that by encouraging the international flows of goods, services and investment, the Bretton Woods system could produce stronger international ties and make competitive devaluations impossible. The approach emphasized stability or even rigidity in the global economic order and was heavily influenced by John Maynard Keynes of the UK delegation and Harry Dexter White from the US Treasury Department. Pivotal to this model was the pegging of the US dollar to gold with all other major currencies' values pegged to the dollar in turn. Lawrence White notes the inherent tension arising from the multiple goals of the Bretton Woods order:

> From its inception, the Bretton Woods exchange-rate system harbored three conflicting objectives. It aimed to restore fixed exchange rates in the manner of the classical gold standard. It aimed to allow central banks more leeway to pursue independent national monetary policies. And it also aimed to restore free trade and international capital mobility. These three aims together were incompatible: only two of the three are simultaneously possible. (2012, p. 300)

CONFLICT, IDEOLOGY AND INTERNATIONAL MONETARY POLICY

The Bretton Woods system was not without its detractors and in 1971 the US dollar's pegging to gold, which had served as the cornerstone of the Bretton Woods international monetary exchange rate system, was eliminated. Quickly other global currencies followed suit and de-pegged their exchange rates from the dollar, effectively eliminating the Bretton Woods system of exchange rate pegs. Previously, the structure of international exchange rates had always been the source of ideological conflict. Former George W. Bush presidential speechwriter, David Frum, writing from a modern mainstream neoliberal perspective, argued in favor of the current post-Bretton Woods system and the trade-offs inherent in different international monetary models as follows:

> The modern currency float has its problems. There is no magical monetary cure, monetary policy is a policy area almost uniquely crowded with trade-offs and lesser evils. If you want a classical gold standard, you get chronic deflation punctuated by depressions, as the U.S. did between 1873 and 1934. If you want a regime of managed currencies tethered to gold, you get regulations and controls, as the U.S. got from 1934 through 1971. If you let the currency float, you get chronic inflation punctuated by bubbles, the American lot since 1971.

System 1 is incompatible with democracy, because voters won't accept the pain inherent in a gold standard. System 2 is incompatible with the free market economics I favor. That leaves me with System 3 as the worst option except for all the others. (2011)

This perspective marks a key difference between the Austrian and Chicago schools of economic thought. While both are strongly in favor of the free market, the Austrian School sees the gold standard or its modern alternatives, such as online crypto-currencies, as a way of restraining both government and corporate profligacy. For Austrians, the painful boom-and-bust cycles of a classical gold standard are not challenges to the system but rather desirable features that clear out unproductive economic activity. The University of Chicago Economics department contained elements of anti-Keynesian thought, beginning with Frank Knight in the 1920s; by the 1950s it had become the home of the main alternative to Keynesian macroeconomic policy, Monetarism.

Associated with Milton Friedman, Monetarism argues that monetary policy is more effective than fiscal policy in managing boom–bust cycles, directly challenging the core domestic policy implication of the Bretton Woods system of fixed exchange rates while simultaneously rejecting the Austrian approach of complete non-intervention in macroeconomic activity. During a 1999 interview, Friedman directly criticized the Austrian approach:

I think the Austrian business-cycle theory has done the world a great deal of harm. If you go back to the 1930s, which is the key point, here you had the Austrians sitting in London, Hayek and Lionel Robbins, and saying you just have to let the bottom drop out of the world. You've just got to let it cure itself. You can't do anything about it. You will only make it worse ... I think by encouraging that kind of do-nothing policy both in Britain and in the United States, they did harm. (Friedman, 1999)

The further implication of Monetarism that made it popular amongst market-oriented policy-makers is that since fiscal policy is ineffective, the macroeconomic rationale for Keynesian-style welfare state policies is weak. Thus Monetarism served as a useful macroeconomic policy framework for neoliberal policy-makers.

For advocates of Bretton Woods-style controls, the speculative costs associated with free-floating currencies have been greater than the prospective gains. The US abandoned the gold peg largely because the Vietnam War and deficit spending had made the peg untenable. While Bretton Woods imposed a series of international currency controls that made it difficult to use monetary policy to manage business cycles, it also enhanced the role of fiscal policy – taxation and public spending – in managing business cycles. Free market conservatives had long disliked this approach to macroeconomic management, though it suited the supporters of post-war welfare state policies. However, the gold peg provided a check on fiscal imprudence; running large deficits would lead to a draining of gold reserves as speculators traded in currency for gold both in anticipation of and ultimately leading to a future currency devaluation.

With free floating currencies, these checks come about through inflation, changes in interest rates and changes in exchange rates, all of which add to price instability. As Economics Nobel Laureate and post-Keynesian Paul Krugman observes:

> While a freely floating national money has advantages, however, it also has risks. For one thing, it can create uncertainties for international traders and investors. Over the past five years, the dollar has been worth as much as 120 yen and as little as 80. The costs of this volatility are hard to measure (partly because sophisticated financial markets allow businesses to hedge much of that risk), but they must be significant. Furthermore, a system that leaves monetary managers free to do good also leaves them free to be irresponsible – and, in some countries, they have been quick to take the opportunity. (1996)

As Krugman notes, sophisticated financial market tools have made it possible to manage some of these risks. The primary tools he is referring to are the derivatives that have allowed free-floating exchange rates to become the dominant global financial system rather than leading to the revival of a competing currency bloc system similar to the experience of the 1930s.

Central to this was a new social phenomenon, the development of the Black–Scholes options pricing formula. As Myron Scholes, who shared the 1997 Nobel Prize in Economics with Robert C. Merton for their development of options pricing theory, argues:

> The option-pricing technology was adopted simply because it reduced transaction costs. For without a model, traders could neither price securities with imbedded options with sufficient accuracy to compete against other traders with models, nor could they reduce the risk of their positions to employ their capital efficiently at a low enough cost to compete with other traders. Although it is hard to prove, I do think that the success of the [Chicago Board Options Exchange] and other exchanges, in part, can be attributable to option-pricing models. As traders became familiar with these models, bid–offer spreads narrowed. As traders became more familiar with risk-management techniques they could take on larger position sizes to support the market. With a deeper and more efficient market, investors began to use options to facilitate their own investment strategies. (1997, pp. 137–8)

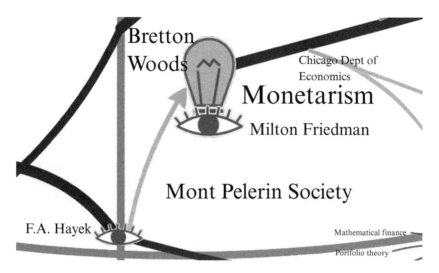

Figure 9.2   Focus on Bretton Woods

DEEP DIVE 1: BRETTON WOODS AND MONT PELERIN

The seeds of the intellectual revolution that pushed aside the Bretton Woods system were planted shortly after the Bretton Woods Conference itself at Mont Pelerin (see Figure 9.2). In 1944, the Allied powers met in Bretton Woods, New Hampshire, to design a post-war global economic order that would avoid both the rigidity of the classic gold standard and the hyper-imperialism of a rival currency bloc system. John Maynard Keynes was the most intellectually prominent participant and head of the UK delegation to the conference. Keynes first achieved prominence after publishing *The Economic Consequences of the Peace* (1919), a scathing critique of the Allies' treatment of Germany post-WWI that predicted many of the negative consequences of the Carthaginian peace imposed on the country. The 1936 publication of his *General Theory of Employment, Interest and Money* solidified Keynes as the world's most prominent economist, who stood at the center of public debates about economic policy in the UK and beyond.

Although much of the Bretton Woods framework reflected Keynes's ideas, the rising economic might of the US and their key negotiator Harry Dexter White shaped the final model in a way that was centered on the US dollar rather than Keynes's preferred model (which would have been a social phenomenon), an international currency called the Bancor as the primary currency all others would be tied to. However, the overall framework fitted with the goals of a well-regulated currency environment that combined both exchange rate stability and slow adjustments to allow those rates to shift to reflect changing economic circumstances. Shortly after the war, both White and Keynes died and were unable to defend their joint legacy personally. In 1948 White was accused of passing US government secrets to Soviet agents and died of a heart attack three days after testifying before the House Un-American Activities Committee. Keynes suffered a series of heart attacks in 1946 while negotiating an Anglo-American loan, dying that year at his home in England.

One year after Keynes's death, one of his longtime adversaries, Friedrich Hayek, organized a conference of leading pro-market intellectuals in Mont Pelerin, Switzerland. Much like Keynes, a critical phase in Hayek's development came about in the immediate aftermath of the First World War. Whereas Keynes was a scion of the weakened but still dominant British Empire, Hayek came of age in Vienna during the final years of the Austro-Hungarian Empire. Following the defeat and break-up of Austria-Hungary after the First World War, Vienna faced a massive influx of refugees from the collapsing empire, along with tightly imposed trade sanctions, and teetered on the edge of complete social and economic collapse.

Throughout the 1920s, Vienna had a radical socialist city government, and it was during this period that the prominent economist and opponent of the "Red Vienna" government, Ludwig von Mises, held a series of private market-promoting seminars that Hayek attended. Hayek later developed a theory of business cycles in *Prices and Production* (1932) that focused on malinvestment during an economic boom; his theory proposed a policy of non-intervention during an economic recession, which effectively undermined Hayek's reputation as a macroeconomic thinker during the Great Depression. However, during the 1930s, Keynes and Hayek headlined a series of debates about macroeconomic policy at Cambridge University and at the London School of Economics that established the battle lines along which Keynes's and Hayek's successors would skirmish for the next century.

While Hayek's non-interventionist prescriptions sidelined him from policy influence throughout both the Great Depression and World War II, his 1944 book *The Road to Serfdom* proved popular and in 1945 was serialized by the Reader's Digest in the United States, gaining him a large North American following. In *The Road to Serfdom,* Hayek argued that almost all policies that intervened in economic matters, including the suite of policies associated with the welfare state and Keynesianism, would put a society on a path that would ultimately lead to the extinguishing of liberty.

To combat both the spread of Marxism and Keynesianism in the postwar global order, Hayek brought together 34 attendees from Europe and

North America and three additional participants. All were pro-market philosophers and most were economists. These included Hayek's old mentor Ludwig von Mises, philosopher of the history of ideas Karl Popper, risk and uncertainty theorist Frank Knight and then neophyte economist Milton Friedman. Of the initial attendees, four would later win the Nobel Prize in Economics.

The organization they created was called the Mont Pelerin Society largely by default, as all other titles proposed were deemed either inadequate or objectionable to the participants in the initial conference; this reflected the general incoherence that resulted from various strands of pro-market thought coming together in this group. Collectively the group believed that the elite-driven non-governmentally focused strategy of the then 63-year old socialist Fabian Society had dramatically reshaped the development of economic thought and wanted to adopt similar strategies to push a market-oriented agenda. Hayek's opening address to the group reflected this ethos:

> It seems to me that effective endeavors to elaborate the general principles of a liberal order are practicable only among a group of people who are in agreement on fundamentals, and among whom certain basic conceptions are not questioned at every step. But not only is, at this time, the number of those who in any one country agree on what seems to be the basic liberal principles small, but the task is a very big one, and there is much need for drawing on as wide an experience under varying conditions as possible. (1947, quoted in White, 2012, p. 207)

Two key outcomes of the first Mont Pelerin Society conference were the organization of a series of think tanks and a renewed focus on a market-oriented research agenda.

Participant Antony Fisher in particular would go on to found a series of conservative think tanks, including the Institute of Economic Affairs in 1955, the International Institute for Economic Research in 1971 and the Atlas Economic Research Foundation in 1981, which would all help develop generations of market-oriented policy-makers. Philosophically the Mont Pelerin Society set out a research agenda comprised of the following issues, an agenda that would characterize much of the overall research agenda of the Chicago School:

1. The analysis and exploration of the nature of the present crisis so as to bring home to others its essential moral and economic origins.
2. The redefinition of the functions of the state so as to distinguish more clearly between the totalitarian and the liberal order.
3. Methods of re-establishing the rule of law and of assuring its development in such a manner that individuals and groups are not in a

position to encroach upon the freedom of others and private rights are not allowed to become a basis of predatory power.

4. The possibility of establishing minimum standards by means not inimical to initiative and functioning of the market.
5. Methods of combating the misuse of history for the furtherance of creeds hostile to liberty.
6. The problem of the creation of an international order conducive to the safeguarding of peace and liberty and permitting the establishment of harmonious international economic relations. (Mont Pelerin Society, 1947)

The agenda set by the Mont Pelerin Society would later bear fruit in the early 1970s as a strong neoliberal challenge to the set of Keynesian institutions that dominated global economics in the 1950s and 1960s.

PROCESS OF SYSTEMS CHANGE

Options contracts were not new instruments, but rather a centuries-old niche tool. Although they had always been constructed for risk management, and wars, plagues and other social-ecological uncertainty would have given them value, financial risk-mitigation tools were limited to insurance. The key social phenomenon underpinning this tool was an acknowledgement of, and effort to mitigate, risk arising from increasingly internationalized trade and currency flows.

Although it has been argued that forms of derivative contracts existed in the Code of Hammurabi, modern derivatives were first used extensively during the American Civil War for a variety of agricultural products in the North and cotton in the South (Dunbar, 2000, p. 60; Bernstein, 1996, p. 308). Prior to this, variants on agricultural options contracts were used in Holland and Japan as early as the 17th century. However, in all of these cases, options were considered shady and responsible for producing bubbles and crashes, including the Dutch tulip bubble (Capelle-Blancard, 2010, p. 9; Bernstein, 1996, p. 307). As MacKenzie and Millo argue, a concerted effort was needed to build respectability into the derivatives market:

> Economists (Baumol, Malkiel, and Quandt in the case of the Chicago Board Options Exchange; Friedman in the case of International Monetary Market) helped make the Chicago financial derivatives markets possible by providing legitimacy; Black, Scholes, and Merton provided the capstone, decisively undermining the regulatory view that derivatives were morally dubious instruments of gambling. (2003, p. 137)

The dramatic growth of the global derivatives market starting in the 1970s was central to a larger ongoing battle of ideas between Keynesian and neoliberal conceptions of the state. The Keynesian model uses regulatory, monetary, tax and public spending policies to centrally manage boom-and-bust economic cycles. The neoliberal model uses market forces and the financial instruments of savings, credit, insurance and derivatives contracts to manage the impact of economic cycles.

Embedded in both of these models are additional assumptions about how international and domestic political, economic, technological and environmental systems work. The Keynesian approach views elected governments as representative of their populations, cognizant of their incentives to coordinate, and possessing the expertise needed to manage complex economic systems. The neoliberal approach assumes that elected officials are capricious, international markets are adaptive and tend towards stability, and the expertise needed to manage complex economic systems is both decentralized and capable of coordinating itself through the price mechanism. Both approaches have shared assumptions about the unambiguously positive benefits of economic growth, limited room for environmental imagination beyond resource extraction, and tendencies towards ahistorical analyses that ignore the socio-cultural contexts their policy recommendations are often applied to. Although the neoliberal model has been on the ascent since the 1970s, the global financial crisis starting in 2008 has led to both a revival of Keynesian policies and increased room for alternatives to both models in the public consciousness.

The process of systems change in this case does not follow the process of a clear collapse at one level of a complex system and shift from one adjacent possible to another. Rather the process is driven by elective affinity between different system elements, combining at lower scales and growing to the point where they effectively displace the dominant institutions at a higher scale. Different components in the emerging derivatives market reinforced each other: first the economic and probability theory models, then computing power, market deregulation and the profitability of the Wall Street firms that used financial engineering processes. For example, increased computing power enabled new financial engineering approaches, while the profits of Wall Street's financial engineers drove private sector demand for increased computing power.

Similarly, the perceived successes of the derivative markets in managing risk increased the influence of policy-makers with a political agenda of deregulation. An elective affinity between these micro-scale developments led to the formation of an alternative system, turning the derivatives market from a function of a politically-managed international system to the driver of an international system in which political decisions are driven by market forces. While the global derivatives market has undergone a number of disruptions, including the collapse of Long-Term Capital Management (LTCM) in 1998 and the global financial crisis a decade later, so far none have been sufficiently large to disrupt the long-term growth of the derivatives market or the neoliberal economic model of which it is a part. However, the state-managed Keynesian model appeared to have hit its limits immediately prior to the 1971 Nixon Shocks.

OPTIONS CONTRACTS

Prior to the advent of the modern derivatives market, options and other derivative financial tools were rarely used niche products. Demand for risk-mitigation options contracts was low in the context of the post-war Bretton Woods economic system due to the international regime of fixed exchange rates and the macroeconomic policies countries followed in order to maintain them. However, on the eve of the development of the Black–Scholes formula, three major changes at the macro scale opened a window of opportunity. First, the 1971 "Nixon Shock", in which the US moved off the gold standard, effectively ushered in the age of deregulation, the weakening of the Bretton Woods system and exchange rate volatility, generated demand for risk-managing financial instruments like derivatives (Bernstein, 1996, p. 305). Second, the Chicago Board Options Exchange began listing stock and commodities options in 1973, and Chicago's International Monetary Market began trading currency futures in 1972, providing markets that allowed derivative exchanges. Finally, the ongoing development of computing power meant the technological capacity existed to undertake the complicated calculations needed to make the Black–Scholes–Merton model work (Lowenstein, 2000, p. 30). All three combined to open a window of opportunity for pushing the system over a tipping point.

As a starting point, it is useful to clarify what an options contract is and how they are used. An options contract is a tradable security that provides its holder with the right to buy (call) or sell (put) a fixed number, usually 100 units, of some security by a given time. For example, a call option on Microsoft shares at $100 on 11 December 2012 would give its holder the right to buy 100 shares of Microsoft at $100 per share, on 11 December 2012. The contract itself is just the right to a future exchange rather than an actual exchange, making the value of the contract dependent on the price of the underlying security. Because of this, options are a type of *derivative*, meaning that their value is derived from the value of some other item. What is really being turned into a tradable commodity here is risk, which the derivative is attempting to separate from the underlying item.

To further the example, if on 11 December 2012 Microsoft shares are valued at $120, then fulfilling the contract ("exercising" the option) would enable the holder of the option to purchase 100 shares at $100 each and instantly sell those same shares on the market for $120 each for a profit of $2000, or $20 per share. However, if shares of Microsoft are trading at $90 per share on 11 December 2012, then exercising the option would be at a loss, so the holder would just let the option expire. Allowing the option holder to either exercise the contract or let it expire is what makes the contract optional, hence the name "option". Note that the value of the trade the contract enables can vary greatly. Here, if the contract was purchased for $1000 and Microsoft went up to $120 per share, then the purchaser's investment would double, while if the price went down to $90, the investment would disappear. As a contrast, the same $1000 could buy 10 shares at $100 per share and if the shares went up to $120 each the total investment would only go up by $200 (20 percent), while if the shares went down to $90 each the investment would go down by $100 (−10 percent). For the same dollar amount, the potential gains and losses are far greater when using an option contract compared to investing in the underlying security, making the investment a highly leveraged one.

In effect an option allows investors to trade risk on a future outcome. Originally, in the mid-19th century, options contracts were primarily applied to commodities, especially agricultural commodities, allowing farmers to moderate the impact of unpredictable weather. Basically the option-issuer placed a bet by writing the option. For a farmer, this reduced the amount the farmer could make if wheat prices went up, while increasing the amount he could make if wheat prices went down. Ultimately the contract is a zero-sum wager, because the option-holder makes money off the contract whenever the farmer loses and vice versa. The bet works because the farmer and the option-holder are likely to have different views on the future price of wheat. As importantly, the contract allows the farmer to transfer some of his risk onto the option-holder, making it easier for him to plan investments for the farm. While agricultural options and other commodities had been the primary use for options contracts since their invention, the Black–Scholes–Merton options pricing model allowed for a wider variety of risks to be priced and the application of derivatives to markets where they had never been used before.

GLOBAL DERIVATIVES MARKET

The global derivatives market has emerged in the past 40 years to become a central pillar of the world economic order. A direct line can be drawn between the collapse of the Bretton Woods system and the rise of derivative contracts. As of June 2012, the notional value of outstanding over-the-counter derivatives contracts in the world stood at $639 trillion dollars, of which $565 trillion were either interest rate or foreign exchange contracts, the two types of derivative contract most directly tied to the volatility of national currencies. For comparison, in 2012 the World Domestic Product, that is the Gross Domestic Product of all countries in the world combined, stood at just under $72 trillion.

An idea that played a key role in transforming the global financial market into one that heavily uses derivatives was the Black–Scholes options pricing model. Prior to its creation, there was not a single method for pricing options. Options are the simplest type of financial derivatives and the Black–Scholes model's adoption led to the growth of the derivatives as a financial tool around the world. This model, and those derived from it, enabled the widespread use of financial derivatives by allowing traders to easily estimate their prices. This change also started a shift in the perception of risk in the financial sector and in society at large, leading to a change in how risk is now managed. Beck puts the shift in perspective:

> The Bretton Woods institutions established following World War II were conceived as global political answers to global economic risks, and the fact that they functioned was a key factor in the emergence of the European welfare state. Since the 1970s, however, those institutions have been largely dismantled and replaced by a succession of ad hoc solutions. Thus we face the paradoxical situation that, whereas markets have never been more liberal and more global, the powers of the global institutions that monitor their effects have been drastically curtailed. Under these conditions, we cannot rule out the possibility of a worldwide financial disaster on the scale of 1929. (2009, p. 201)

The Black–Scholes formula was built using early- and mid-20th century ideas, disseminated through global financial markets. It has dramatically changed the institutions of risk and finance. The formula itself is built using naturalistic phenomena identified and developed in the early and mid-20th century, in particular the statistical concept of the random walk, the application of mathematical modeling to financial problems (Samuelson, 1970) and the development of modern portfolio theory (Markowitz, 1952).

Since its creation, the dissemination of the Black–Scholes model has come about through market competition, academic dissemination channels and finance programs. Additionally, the model and the derivatives market demonstrated an elective affinity with changing regulatory environments and advancements in computing. The spread of options pricing, and the broader shift towards the use of derivatives in the financial markets, has had a number of broad social impacts including the rise of quantitative analysis in financial companies, commodification of risk, and the rise of systemic risk. It has also contributed to the ideological shift towards neoliberal regulatory practices. MacKenzie and Millo argue that it is difficult to underestimate the importance of the Black–Scholes model, as the theory itself changed the way markets functioned:

> Black, Scholes, and Merton's model did not describe an already existing world: when first formulated, its assumptions were quite unrealistic, and empirical prices differed systematically from the model. Gradually, though, the financial markets changed in a way that fitted the model. In part, this was the result of technological improvements to price dissemination and transaction processing. In part, it was the general liberalizing effect of free market economics. In part, however, it was the effect of option pricing theory itself. Pricing models came to shape the very way participants thought and talked about options. (2003, p. 137)

What is the Black–Scholes Equation?

The Black–Scholes equation is a somewhat intimidating formula that does not need to be known in detail to understand this case. However, this particular formulation of it is taken from Bodie et al. (2008, pp. 670–71), and reads as follows:

$$C_0 = S_0 N(d_1) - Xe^{-rT} N(d_2)$$

where

$$d_1 = \frac{\ln\left(\dfrac{S_0}{X}\right) + \left(\dfrac{r\sigma^2}{2}\right)T}{\sigma\sqrt{T}}$$

$$d_2 = d_1 - \sigma\sqrt{T}$$

and where
 C_0 = current call option value
 S_0 = current stock price
 $N(d)$ = the probability that a random draw from a normal distribution will be less than d
 X = exercise price
 e = the base of the natural log function
 r = risk-free interest rate (the annualized continuously compounded rate on a safe asset with the same maturity as the expiration date of the option)
 T = time to expiration of the option, in years

In = natural logarithm function

σ = standard deviation of the annualized continuously compounded rate of return of the stock.

The calculation of the current option value using the Black–Scholes equation directly would be a computationally difficult task and the contribution from Merton was to couple this equation with an estimation technique that makes the calculation of the option value less burdensome. It was this contribution that led to the 1997 Nobel Prize in Economics being awarded to both Robert C. Merton and Myron Scholes; Fischer Black was not included because he passed away in 1995. In much of the literature, the model is referred to as the Black–Scholes–Merton model.

As important for this case is the set of assumptions that are used in the Black–Scholes model, most of which are innocuous most of the time. First, the model is for pricing European options, which means that the options can only be exercised on their due date, whereas American options can be exercised at any time on or before their due date. Second, the market does not present any arbitrage opportunities, as arbitrage is assumed to "enforce" the options pricing (Dunbar, 2000, p. 37). Third, it is possible to borrow or lend cash at a constant risk-free interest rate. Fourth, any amount of the underlying security can be bought or sold, including fractional shares. Fifth, there are no fees applied to any transactions. This assumption, although it does little to impact prices for trading purposes, is worth noting as the existence of many high-paid derivatives traders and quantitative analysts could not be supported without these fees. Finally, and most importantly, the price of the underlying security is assumed to follow a geometric Brownian motion model with constant drift, volatility and a normal distribution of random effects. This is important because if the actual movement in the price of underlying securities does not follow a normal distribution, derivatives markets may be mispricing risk.

In particular, Taleb argues that actual movements tend to follow a power law distribution, with one consequence being that large movements are far more likely in practice than a normal distribution would assume (2007, p. 29). Capelle-Blancard argues that although Black–Scholes has seeded a great deal of academic study, its breadth has been limited:

Since the decisive articles of Black and Scholes (1973) and Merton (1973), a whole theory has been built and it is not exaggerated to say that academic research has significantly contributed to the growth of derivatives markets. However, the overwhelming majority of research is devoted to asset pricing, while very few papers deal with the destabilizing impact of derivatives. Yet, the exceptional growth of the market alone justifies some concerns, not to mention the opacity of [over-the-counter] markets. (2010, p. 13)

BLACK–SCHOLES DEVELOPMENT

Shifting the financial system through the growth in the derivatives market involved the development of the Black–Scholes options pricing model through a combination of existing naturalistic and social phenomena. First, naturalistic early 20th-century developments in probability theory, particularly Brownian motion, were needed for the assumptions of randomness used by the model. Second, the social phenomenon of Samuelson's models for the valuation of financial investments made the idea of a pricing model tractable by applying a set of assumptions to the behavior of financial products, including Gaussian distributions and Brownian motion. Finally, the construction of modern portfolio theory by Markowitz opened up the possibility of managing risk by holding on to multiple investments simultaneously, a key insight used in constructing the Black–Scholes model (Dunbar, 2000, p. 18). Black and Scholes would use these concepts as a bricolage to pull together their options pricing model (see Figure 9.3).

Samuelson's application of mathematics to economic theory included the formal modeling of financial phenomena. Up until that time, finance was primarily the domain of practitioners, and theoretical advancements in the field were rare. However, with the development of financial modeling, the pricing of stocks, bonds, loans and other financial instruments fell into the domain of financial economics. While these models are often of little value for short-term predictions, they are often useful in longer-term financial planning (Dunbar, 2000, p. 18). These models, and the assumptions

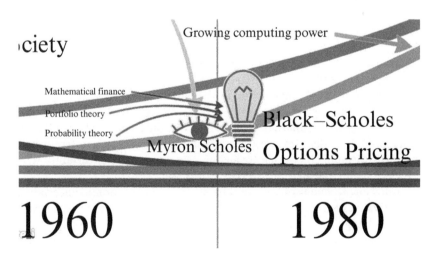

Figure 9.3   Focus on Black–Scholes options pricing

(phenomena) that underlie them, were important in establishing that a pricing mechanism could be extracted from and used in financial data.

Although Samuelson's theories were important for individual investments, it was Markowitz's idea of mitigating risk through multiple investments in a portfolio that was of particular importance for the development of the Black–Scholes model (Bernstein, 1996, p. 6). Modern portfolio theory, the idea that multiple uncorrelated investments held simultaneously can mitigate the risk of being over-dependent on returns from a single investment, underpins most financial risk mitigation strategies. It suggests that risk itself can be quantified and managed (Markowitz, 1952) – an incredibly powerful social phenomenon, as risk shifts from an external force (an act of God) uniquely to a question of probabilities, with great utility. Options and other derivative instruments take the idea of managing risk to an extreme by isolating risk and turning it into an instrument itself.

These changes have been profound, setting in place many of the central tools underpinning the post-Bretton Woods, post-Keynesian neoliberal regime of the late 20th and early 21st century. At the beginning of the 1970s the post-war consensus was under serious threat. Politically, the Vietnam War undermined the belief that the political leadership in the West was capable of maintaining international peace and stability. Economically, the stagflation arising from wartime deficit spending, oil crises and creaking welfare state programs was combining with domestic civil rights and anti-war movements to undermine the credibility of the establishment in domestic politics.

Hence, the status quo became untenable and this led directly to the 1971 Nixon Shocks in which the United States sought to respond to its domestic and international economic challenges by unpegging the dollar from gold and, since most major world currencies were pegged to the dollar, undermined the set of fixed exchange rates that were at the center of the Bretton Woods international economic order. The shift to a world of floating exchange rates greatly increased uncertainty in international trade patterns and from that grew fears about the stability of the international political order. Trade uncertainty in the 1930s and the international political–economic blocs that formed in response to that uncertainty were seen as a major cause of the Second World War.

In this environment of tremendous international economic uncertainty the derivatives market would rise to fill a key role in managing risk arising from exchange rate uncertainty. Indeed, even today the majority of the global derivatives market is comprised of exchange-rate management tools. By providing the key tool for managing uncertainty without coordinated government regulation, the derivatives market responded to one of the key concerns arising from a shift to a post-regulatory, neoliberal world economic order. Ferraro, Pfeffer and Sutton claim that the assumptions and models built into Black–Scholes did more than predict, they constructed the market's behavior:

> The same year the CBOE opened, Black and Scholes (1973) and Merton (1973) published what were to become the most influential treatments of option pricing theory, for which the authors were to win the Nobel Prize in Economics. The formula developed in this work expressed the price of an option as a function of observable parameters and of the unobservable volatility of the price of the underlying asset. It is important to note that this formula originally did not accurately predict option prices in the CBOE, with deviations of 30 to 40 percent common in the first months of option trading. Yet, as time passed, deviations from the model diminished substantially so that, for the period August 1976 to August 1978, deviations from the Black–Scholes price were only around 2 percent (Rubinstein, 1985). (2005, p. 13)

In effect, the mathematical modeling provided prophetic starting conditions for how the market would then develop.

DEEP DIVE 2: 1973 CHICAGO

By 1973 the seeds planted at the first Mont Pelerin Society meeting in 1947 were flowering. In the US, the University of Chicago had become the focal point for market-oriented economic thinking, particularly in the economics and law departments. While not all members of the Chicago School of thought were at the University of Chicago and not all University of Chicago economics and legal faculty were members of this school, the university had become an intellectual hotbed of pro-market thought and counted the movement's most prominent spokesman, Milton Friedman, among its faculty.

Friedman founded the Monetarist school of macroeconomic policy-making, which argued that central bank management of the money supply is more effective at managing growth and inflation than the use of fiscal policy, effectively allowing macroeconomic management while simultaneously avoiding large welfare-state expenditures. This approach was appealing to members of the Nixon administration, as were Friedman's calls to remove the US dollar from the Bretton Woods system of exchange rate controls. The 1971 Nixon Shocks effectively ended the Bretton Woods exchange rate regime and key Chicago economists, including Friedman, helped establish the International Monetary Market in 1972 as a spin-off of the Chicago Mercantile Exchange and as a response to the currency fluctuations brought about by the collapse of Bretton Woods (see

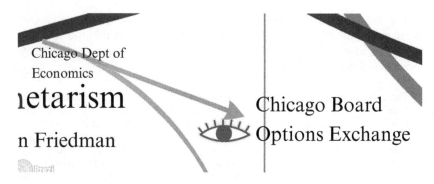

Figure 9.4   Focus on the Chicago Board Options Exchange

Figure 9.4). While these victories for the Chicago School in 1971 and 1972 were important, 1973 marked a major turning point for the spread of Chicago School-designed institutions and policies.

1973 saw three major developments that advanced the Chicago School agenda: the installation of the Pinochet Regime in Chile, the establishment of the Chicago Board Options Exchange and the publication of the Black–Scholes options pricing formula. On 11 September 1973, the democratically elected socialist government of Salvador Allende in Chile was overthrown by General Augusto Pinochet, who then served as President of Chile until the restoration of elections in 1990. Pinochet appointed many young economists who trained under Friedman in Chicago, or who studied at the Chicago-affiliated economics department at the Catholic University of Chile, to positions of political authority. From here this group, dubbed the Chicago Boys, initiated a radical deregulatory agenda that would serve as a model later picked up by both Ronald Reagan in the US and Margaret Thatcher in the UK.

Earlier that year on 26 April the Chicago Board Options Exchange (CBOE) launched its first day of trading. Prominent Chicago School economists, including William Baumol, helped establish the exchange as an offshoot of the Chicago Board of Trade. Trade on the CBOE grew quickly in response to the economic fluctuations largely triggered by the collapse of Bretton Woods. As previously noted, the development of the Black–Scholes model was critical to the adoption of options and served as intellectual cornerstone for the growth of the entire derivatives market. Fischer Black and Myron Scholes originally devised the options pricing model in 1970 but the article they submitted to the *Journal of Political Economy*, based at the University of Chicago, was rejected without being reviewed. Two of Scholes's PhD advisors, Chicago School economists and future Nobel laureates Merton Miller and Eugene Fama, persuaded the editors of the journal to reconsider the paper and it was ultimately published in 1973. Mathematical economist Robert C. Merton published modifications to the original Black–Scholes model later the same year and would share the 1997 Nobel Prize in Economics with Scholes for the development of this theory, with Black being honored at the ceremony but ineligible to receive the prize due to his death two years earlier. In his Nobel lecture, Scholes argued for this model as being critical to the success of the CBOE:

> The option-pricing technology was adopted simply because it reduced trans-action costs. For without a model, traders could neither price securities with imbedded options with sufficient accuracy to compete against other traders with models, nor could they reduce the risk of their positions to employ their capital efficiently at a low enough cost to compete with other traders. Although it is hard to prove, I do think that the success of the [Chicago Board Options Exchange] and other exchanges, in part, can be attributable to option-pricing models. As traders became familiar with these models, bid-offer spreads narrowed. As traders became more familiar with risk-management techniques they could take on larger position sizes to support the market. With a deeper and more efficient market, investors began to use options to facilitate their own investment strategies. (1997, pp. 137–8)

CO-EVOLUTIONARY AND SELECTIVE PRESSURES

The Black–Scholes equation's development in 1973 unleashed an explosion in the use of options and other derivatives. Alongside, and independent of, the publication of this model, the Chicago Options Exchange allowed over-the-counter trading of options and other derivatives, a change that spread to financial exchanges around the world by the end of the 1990s (Dunbar, 2000, p. 60). Prior to this change, options trading mostly involved unique non-standard contracts, making trading difficult even if there had been pricing models available. However, this combination of a regulatory change and the introduction of a pricing system any trader could use started the ascent of derivatives to their central place in the global financial markets. As of June 2011 the total amount of outstanding over-the-counter derivatives exceeded $700 trillion globally, up from under $1 trillion in the early 1980s and following an annual average increase of 30 percent (Bank for International Settlements, 2013; Capelle-Blancard, 2010, p. 10), making the total value of the assets tied to derivatives worth more than ten times the global domestic product.

Technological change further contributed to the dissemination of the Black–Scholes model. Rapid advances in computing technology allowed for the quick calculation of derivative prices in a way that had never been possible previously, and these complicated models helped drive the demand for calculating power among Wall Street traders. Indeed, in one particular instance the first widely available handheld calculator that Texas Instruments produced for market traders in the mid-1970s included the Black–Scholes equation as a built-in function (Lowenstein, 2000, p. 30).

Furthermore, the Black–Scholes model was a combination of ideas that enabled the development of more complicated pricing models for a wider variety of financial instruments (Dunbar, 2000), providing a strong example of Arthur's (2009) model of technological evolution in which a new innovation creates an adjacent possible for the development of further innovations. These intellectual developments were cited by Scholes in his Nobel lecture explaining the adoption of derivatives by global financial markets thus, "To date, the major growth in the use of derivatives has been fueled by trends toward securitization and the increased understanding of the role that derivatives can play in the unbundling, packaging, and transferring of risks" (1997, p. 141).

In addition to the elective affinity demonstrated here, the options pricing model was directly disseminated through market competition, as financial companies mimicked the successes of competitors who put the Black–Scholes model to use. Most notable among these firms was Long-Term Capital Management (LTCM), a hedge fund whose principals included Myron Scholes and Robert Merton and whose spectacular collapse in 1998 led to two of the books providing the source material for this case study, Dunbar's *Inventing Money: The Story of Long-Term Capital Management and the Legends Behind it* (2000) and Lowenstein's *When Genius Failed: The Rise and Fall of Long-Term Capital Management* (2000).

LTCM was a key vehicle for spreading derivatives pricing models and its spectacular 1998 loss of $4.6 billion in four months triggered a global financial crisis that revealed the dangers in using these models inappropriately. Founded in 1994, LTCM quickly built a reputation for its solid year after year performance and for hiring the best and brightest in Wall Street from a variety of mathematical disciplines in academia. While other Wall Street firms had used highly technical people in their operations, they were usually relegated to support roles. In LTCM these mathematical analysts, colloquially called *quants*, were put in charge. Their central position was based on their relatively rare technical expertise, which made these usually young technicians particularly valuable (Dunbar, 2000, p. 16).

One of the consequences of the assumption of a normal distribution in the prices of underlying assets is that although derivatives are designed to minimize exposure to financial risk, a misperception of randomness can magnify risk. According to Taleb, built into the options pricing model is an assumption of normal distribution of random events rather than the power law distribution which is more common in complex adaptive systems like the financial markets. He argues that the ease of use and simplicity of the Gaussian distribution – plus the institutional power bestowed by Nobel Prize wins for Markowitz, Samuelson and Black–Scholes – spread its adoption, rather than the validity of the modeling (2007, p. 277).

The specific roles of Black, Scholes and Merton in developing the options pricing model and its importance in the development of the derivatives market is clear, whereas the importance of LTCM in its development is more ambiguous. Even before the founding of LTCM, the financial industry had adopted both the Black–Scholes model and the broad range of derivative financial instruments it enabled, making it unlikely that the company was necessary for the growth of the derivatives market and financial engineering. Despite LTCM's reputation as the hotbed of financial engineering on Wall Street, the influence of the quants had been steadily growing in most financial companies during the 1980s and 1990s (see Figure 9.5).

While LTCM may have been the first and largest provider of financial engineering services, it was not the only financial firm to do so. Moreover, given the hyper-competitive culture of Wall Street, its strong selective pressures and the elective affinity between these developments, LTCM's innovations probably would have been developed without LTCM. It is likely that the focus of LTCM and the clout of its founders sped up the adoption of financial derivatives and financial engineering mostly by example. It is

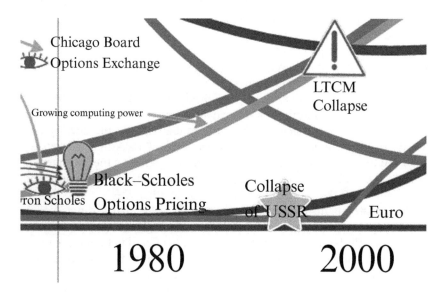

Figure 9.5   Focus on the long-term capital management collapse

also certainly possible that the broad adoption of derivatives could have been slowed following LTCM's fall. However, the American political apparatus maintained its deregulatory instincts and ultimately encouraged the growth of this market.

EFFECTS OF OPTIONS PRICING AND THE GLOBAL DERIVATIVES MARKET

Although it would be difficult to pin down an exact date, by the end of the 20th century the neoliberal model had overtaken the Keynesian model as the dominant financial system in the world economic order. Prior to the growth of the global derivatives market and the related policy and technological systems that support it, financial markets operated as separate niches within a state-managed international economic regime. However, at some point there was a shift and states now compete with each other as individual niches within a market-based international economic order. Consequently, the impact of options pricing and the derivative markets it enabled extend far beyond the financial markets. Because financial markets conduct long-term economic planning in the private sector and determine the cost of capital for government borrowing, changes in financial markets ripple outwards. Here we focus on just four effects: the rise of the quants; commodification of risk; increase in systemic risk; and the neoliberal shift from public long-term economic planning towards market-based economic planning.

With the development of the options pricing model and the concurrent growth in computing power, the importance of sophisticated mathematical techniques in the financial markets and the number of people trained in them increased dramatically. This produced a number of additional impacts. First, the addition of that capacity has changed markets by enabling the addition of new trading techniques. Second, the development of these new techniques has changed the type of risks that markets are exposed to. For example, high-frequency trading relies on the placement of automated trades, with the consequence that crashes and spikes in prices occur far faster than would have been possible otherwise.

Third, the quants are usually drawn from fields that are not directly financial–economic, such as mathematics, engineering and physics. Consequently, because of the outsized rewards offered in finance, many of the best and brightest technical people are building trading models instead of designing the cars, consumer technologies and alternative energy systems of the future. The reasons for this shift are not only the financial rewards. For example, Fischer Black left academia in 1984, almost a decade before Scholes and Merton had left to join LTCM, in part because of the pace of academia, noting that unlike the real-time experiments in finance, "the option problem in my last paper took three weeks to solve, but two years to get into print" (quoted in Dunbar, 2000, p. 87).

The second effect, commodification of risk, has transformed unpredictability into a financial instrument. Well before the pricing of options was a possibility, options still involved the transfer of risk from the risk intolerant to the risk tolerant for a price. However, before the Black–Scholes model was widely adopted, it was difficult for the producers and purchasers of options to come to agreements that both sides found workable. This meant that options themselves were rare, making the market for options illiquid. As a consequence, it was often difficult to find options appropriate for a variety of investment strategies and to appropriately price that risk transfer.

With a more accurate price revelation mechanism, the size of the options market increased quickly and enabled the development of more complex financial derivatives, increasing the variety of trades exponentially. These newly engineered financial tools include instruments made by combining multiple options to create new derivative financial instruments to cover possible outcomes that were not available for sale (Dunbar, 2000, p. 78). As a consequence, the range of instruments that investors have available to them has expanded dramatically, allowing trading in assets such as commodities that might not otherwise be available, and on balance this appears to have made the market for those assets more liquid (Capelle-Blancard, 2010, p.15). However, baked into these models are assumptions about probability that underestimate the fragility of and inherent risk in the financial system (Taleb, 2007) and lead to an overconfidence in the assumptions of mathematical models that cannot possibly capture the true underlying complexity at play (Bernstein, 1996, p. 219).

The expansion of the derivatives market has also increased systemic risk. This third consequence means that the global financial market is now exposed to types of risk that did not previously exist. Generally, the consensus of current research is that derivative instruments used by non-financial companies increase real value by mitigating general risk (Capelle-Blancard, 2010, p. 18). However, they do not address systemic risk. Counterparty risk, often most worrisome for financial regulators, is the risk that arises when one of the parties tied to a derivatives contract is unable to fulfill its side of the contract. Because of the scale of the global derivatives market and the number of times many contracts are traded, determining the counterparty is not always straightforward.

Furthermore, the failure of one options contract reduces the assets of the company holding the contract, which may weaken its capacity to honor its part of a separate contract, possibly by pushing the company into insolvency, further spreading contagion. Former US Federal Reserve Chairman Alan Greenspan worried that the withdrawal of traders in response to market contagion could cause "a seizing up of the markets" (quoted in Lowenstein, 2000, p. 195). This counterparty systemic risk is further compounded by the probability assumptions inherent in the Black–Scholes formula. Knowable risks and uncertainty within markets are confused, as measures of volatility only include the first, rather than the uncertainty arising from systemic change. However, confusing the two leads some traders to underestimate the true uncertainty and take larger risks than they otherwise would (Bernstein, 1996, p. 335). As Beck argues:

> there are the global economic risks, the imponderabilities of globalized currency and financial markets which have commanded increasing public attention in recent times. This global market risk is also a new form of "organized irresponsibility." Facilitated by the information revolution, the financial flows determine the winners and the losers. Because of the structural dominance of competition in this sector, no player is sufficiently powerful to change the direction of the flows. Nobody controls the global market risks. Because there is no world government, the market risk cannot be curbed on national markets. On the other side, no national market can seal itself off completely from the globalized markets. (2009, p. 13)

Finally, the commodification of risk and rise of systemic risk changed the way the financial markets are regulated. In particular, the possibility of trading risk coupled with the efficient markets hypothesis has led many regulators to believe that the financial markets are able to self-regulate without substantial government regulation. This contributes to the neoliberal assumption that financial markets are better at long-term planning than governments, further entrenching the primacy of the market over public policy decision.

Alan Greenspan cited the growth of the derivatives market and its capacity to manage financial risk as a reason to avoid tightly regulating them, stating that "I see no reason to question the underlying stability of the over-the-counter markets, or the overall effectiveness of private market discipline" while in the midst of the LTCM meltdown (1998). While there is strong evidence that derivatives themselves do not contribute to the volatility of markets, they do create incentives for other actors in the system to take greater risks. Importantly, the remuneration schemes for traders encourage excessive risk-taking (Taleb, 2007, p. 19) which, when coupled with weaknesses in models and the taking of second-order risks because derivatives were assumed to lessen first-order risks, may concentrate risk and uncertainty in the financial system far more acutely than prior to the

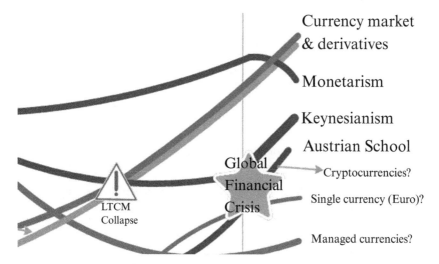

Figure 9.6   Focus on the 2008 global financial crisis

expansion of derivatives markets, though evidence of whether the costs outweigh the benefits is murky (Capelle-Blancard, 2010, p. 23).

However, the belief in their efficacy is broad enough that derivative and derivative-like instruments are proposed for a broad number of macroeconomic indicators like employment and GDP (Shiller, 2004; 2008; Gürkaynak and Wolfers, 2006) and even social or environmental indicators (Horesh, 2000) rather than just financial assets. It is unclear if the emergence and expansion of the modern derivatives market can be considered a social innovation to be reviled in retrospect; whether it is or not depends primarily on the perspective of the observer. In the aftermath of every major financial collapse since the early 1990s, derivatives have been cited as a cause. However, the revulsion towards them has not reached a tipping point leading to stricter regulation or a withdrawal of funds from the derivative sector. Consequently, following each crash the derivatives market quickly rebounds and further expands, a trend that is currently underway following the 2008 global financial crisis (see Figure 9.6).

REFERENCES

Arthur, W.B. (2009). *The Nature of Technology: What It Is and How It Evolves.* New York: Free Press.
Bank for International Settlements (2013). *BIS Quarterly Review.* March.

Beck, U. (2009). Critical theory of world risk society: a cosmopolitan vision. *Constellations*, **16**(1), 3–22.

Bernstein, P. (1996). *Against the Gods: The Remarkable Story of Risk*. New York: John Wiley.

Bodie, Z., Kane, A., Marcus, A., Perrakis, S. and Ryan, P. (2008). *Investments*, 6th Canadian edn. Toronto: McGraw-Hill Ryerson.

Capelle-Blancard, G. (2010). Are derivatives dangerous? A literature survey. *Centre D'Etudes Prospectives et D'Information Internationales*, No. 2010-24.

Dunbar, N. (2000). *Inventing Money: The Story of Long-term Capital Management and the Legends Behind it*. Chichester: John Wiley.

Ferraro, F., Pfeffer, J. and Sutton, R. (2005). Economics language and assumptions: how theories can become self-fulfilling. *Academy of Management Review*, **30**(1), 8–24.

Friedman, M. (1999). Mr. Market. Accessed 20 December 2016 at http://www.hoover.org/research/mr-market.

Frum, D. (2011). What really went wrong with the Nixon Shock? (Updated). Accessed 30 July 2014 at http://www.frumforum.com/what-really-went-wrong-with-the-nixon-shock.

Greenspan, A. (1998). The regulation of OTC derivatives. Testimony before the Committee on Banking and Financial Services, U.S. House of Representatives, 24 July.

Gürkaynak, R. and Wolfers, J. (2006). Macroeconomic derivatives: an initial analysis of market-based macro forecasts, uncertainty, and risk. *NBER Working Paper*, No. 11929.

Hayek, F.A. (1932). *Prices and Production*. London: Routledge.

Hayek, F.A. (1944). *The Road to Serfdom*. Chicago, IL: University of Chicago Press.

Horesh, R. (2000). Injecting incentives into the solution of social problems: social policy bonds. *Economic Affairs*, **20**(3), 39–42.

Keynes, J.M. (1919). *The Economic Consequences of the Peace*. New York: Harcourt, Brace and Howe.

Keynes, J. M. (1936). *The General Theory of Employment, Interest and Money*. London: Macmillan and Co.

Krugman, P. (1996). The gold bug variation: the gold standard – and the men who love it. Accessed 30 July 2014 at http://web.mit.edu/krugman/www/goldbug.html.

Lowenstein, R. (2000). *When Genius Failed: The Rise and Fall of Long-term Capital Management*. New York: Random House.

MacKenzie, D. and Millo, Y. (2003). Constructing a market, performing theory: the historical sociology of a financial derivatives exchange. *American Journal of Sociology*, **109**(1), 107–45.

Markowitz, H. (1952). Portfolio selection, *The Journal of Finance*, **7**(1), 77–91.

Mont Pelerin Society (1947). Statement of Aims. Accessed 13 December 2016 at https://www.montpelerin.org/statement-of-aims/.

Samuelson, P.A. (1970). The fundamental approximation theorem of portfolio analysis in terms of means, variances and higher moments. *The Review of Economic Studies*, **37**(4), 537–42.

Scholes, M. (1997). *Derivatives in a Dynamic Environment*. Nobel Lecture, 9 December, pp. 137–8.

Shiller, R. (2004). *The New Financial Order: Risk in the 21st Century*. Princeton, NJ: Princeton University Press.

Shiller, R. (2008). Derivatives markets for home prices. *NBER Working Paper No. 13962*.

Taleb, N. (2007). *The Black Swan: The Impact of the Highly Improbable*. New York: Random House.

White, L.H. (2012). *The Clash of Economic Ideas: The Great Policy Debates and Experiments of the Last Hundred Years*. New York: Cambridge University Press.

10. Indian residential schools

Katharine McGowan

> After a while along came a young boy rolling a horse clippers into the room and that horse clippers bounced over my head and gave me a bald head. After he got through, he said, "Now you are no longer an Indian," and he gave me a slap on the head. I don't know how to explain it but it really hurt my feelings.
>
> (Charlie Bigknife, 7 December 2001, as quoted in Callahan, 2002)[1]

INTRODUCTION

From the mid-19th century until the late 20th (specifically 1998), the Canadian federal government and many Canadian religious institutions ran schools to Christianize and Canadianize Indigenous children; from 1880 onwards, this effort took the official, standardized form of the Indian Residential Schools.[2] Residential Schools sit significantly closer to social engineering than social innovation on a spectrum of agent-driven social change. Yet, if we understand social innovations as including efforts to target isolated or disadvantaged populations, to improve their standard of living and shift them towards greater inclusion and ultimately resilience, then Residential Schools certainly warrant consideration, even if the process of examination is fundamentally unsettling. Consider this study a cautionary tale of how attempts at social change can be fatally flawed and eventually fall out of favor when new ideas (social phenomena) emerge and unseat our current assumptions and beliefs.

This story is especially important to emergent or active social entrepreneurs and their allies – those interested in social innovation work. To replace assumptions with knowledge, to learn from the system as we engage it, is important; it is also useful to remember that when attempting to shift the system, we must not replicate or reinforce power imbalances. Residential Schools were an obvious failure, in every respect: the schools did not for the most part provide a useful education, they did not assimilate Indigenous children into Canadian society, and they were sites of horrific – and tacitly state-sponsored – physical, emotional and sexual abuse. It should serve as a constant reminder, especially for those in public policy and social innovation, of the great risks associated with making decisions *for* an entire marginalized population rather than with them. The case fully supports John Milloy's (1999) claim that Residential Schools represent "a national crime", one committed in the name of inclusion with the intention of improving the lives of a minority population, so we in social innovation must grapple with its story.

The recently completed Truth and Reconciliation should be required reading for anyone seeking to build innovative policy for complex social problems. The view from Ottawa (or Washington or London or Brussels) is not always the best lens, and over time the commitment to a policy must be based on evidence of empowerment and impact, and on community feedback, rather than on ideology or faith in one's convictions as a change agent. It is also best when policy is community-driven. This is a difficult message for those excited by the prospects of triggering change and who feel empowered by social innovation language; that is exactly why it is important.

BACKGROUND: WHY RESIDENTIAL SCHOOLS? A LANDSCAPE DIAGNOSIS

By the third quarter of the 19th century, North America had largely completed a major landscape-level shift (see Figure 10.1) that fundamentally changed resource and authority flows across the continent. It had, in the course of four hundred years or so, gone from a continent populated by many Indigenous nations, to one of Indigenous–European competition and cooperation (alternating and often in flux), to the institutional

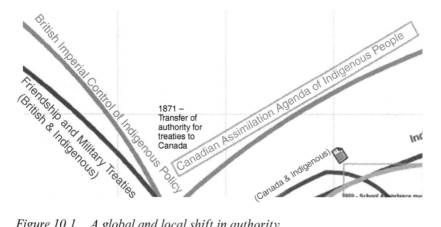

Figure 10.1   A global and local shift in authority

structure in place today, dominated by European-inspired states. Since at least the Pequot War of 1636–37 (but in some ways since the first Spanish arrivals), North America was caught between multiple competing European and Indigenous powers – through various wars and treaties, shifting alliances and disputed sovereignties.

After the American Revolution and the War of 1812, however, there emerged an increasingly dominant American and British institutional norm across the northern portion of the continent. These nations could claim de facto monopolistic control over their territories, regardless of the continued Indigenous presence. During the 19th century, America and Canada expanded and settled westward from the Ohio Valley into more and more Indigenous nations' territory (Mortin, 1958; Berger, 2013). This expansion was often violently contested, but there was significantly less ambiguity in the power relationships between these Western Indigenous nations and the expansionist states than there had been in previous centuries in the east.

Many American and Canadian observers perceived Indigenous nations as impediments to economic prosperity. Living on lands that could be farmed or that were needed to build railroads, they were not legitimate owners and occupiers of that land (Daschyk, 2013; Carter, 1990). Although it took different forms, generally speaking there was a common, centuries-old belief that European societies (including their religions, political practices, social expectations, etc.) were inherently better than Indigenous ones.

Many consequently believed that it was incumbent on white (European) settlers/evangelicals to "correct" or "civilize" the behavior of the peoples they encountered. This goal was partially motivated by the proselytization of most Christian churches. Throughout the 19th century, North

---

BOX 10.1 A NOTE ON TREATIES

The history of treaties is still evolving in Canada; new treaties are still being negotiated and old ones re-examined by the courts. Part of this current flux can be attributed to a shift in how the Supreme Court has interpreted treaties. In 1886, through *St Catherine's Milling and Lumber Co.* vs. *R*, the Judicial Committee of the Privy Council (then Canada's last level of appeal) decided First Nations only had usufructuary rights to their land prior to signing treaties. This significantly limited First Nations' capacity to argue land claims – and in 1927 it became illegal to use band funds to file land claims in court at all. This was reversed in 1951, and the landmark Calder case of 1973 opened the possibility of Aboriginal title, thereby fundamentally changing the legal interpretation of treaties.

American society was being reshaped by a trifecta of mutually reinforcing forces: missionaries, the expansion of white-dominated democracies, and economic-infrastructure shifts (railroads). The modern North American landscape was, for all intents and purposes, fully born. How would it grow?

In the United States, the movement westward was facilitated through armed conflict (Brown, 2007). British (and later Canadian) authorities in Canada did not (and could not) mount a similar violent campaign of expulsion/settlement. They chose to continue their established pattern of signing treaties with individual Indigenous nations to determine the terms and character of the latter's acquiescence to the former's extended authority. Even the nature of treaty signing – a legal obligation the British Crown guaranteed in the Royal Proclamation of 1762 – became largely a pretext for settlement.

The North American landscape shifted enough that Indigenous peoples were outnumbered on their land. Emerging and established institutions were undermining or outright threatening Indigenous ways of being and livelihoods. And the two states, Canada and America, showed little interest in respecting different sovereignties in the lands they claimed.

BRIEF DIVE: THE EDUCATIONAL REGIME IS CAPTURED BY THE STATE, WITH SIGNIFICANT IMPLICATIONS

The history of education is one characterized by competing social phenomena and bricolage; religion, technology, political and social trends and gender expectations are all important to understanding the pathways that education and especially public education took. Even something like literacy is the product of a confluence of events, trends and contexts: "Far from being an isolated phenomenon, it was the resultant of many forces, most of which – political, religious, economic, technological – seem on first glance to have little bearing on the growth of the reading habit" (Altick, 1957, p. 3).

In the case of the English reading public, even something as seemingly foreign as the French Revolution stoked the elite's fears and impeded the development of public education (Altick, 1957). For these decision-makers, French philosopher Helvétius's declaration *"l'education peut tout"* (education is capable of anything) (Heater, 2004, p. 39) had proven true, not in terms of social progress, but in terms of furthering a frightening journey into chaos.

Education had long been seen as training for elites (especially clergy). Many of the French philosophers advocating for education still saw it as primarily an elite pursuit, even as they linked schooling with citizenship (Heater, 2004, p. 39). In early European America, heavily informed by radical Reformational sects, there were a surprising number of community schools; education was perceived as a means of saving the souls of children, and later of transforming colonists into citizens (Heater, 2004, pp. 46–7; McClellan, 1999; Cremin, 1970). By contrast, the eventual shift to universal education in England was impressive, given the powerful belief, held by many as late as the 19th century (and certainly in the 18th), that the poor were born into the condition God intended for them and were therefore either unable or unworthy of educational opportunities (Stuart, 2013, pp. 1–3). In England, the Reformation-inspired belief that literacy was essential to ensure people could read the Bible, which was so important in America, seems to have resonated less with key decision-makers. Social prejudice, not just cross-cultural prejudice (as we will discuss below), permeated the development of education.

Social concerns were not, however, insurmountable obstacles. Throughout the 19th century, schools (especially public ones) were increasingly seen as a means to end poverty through vocational training, build national wealth by creating a more effective workforce, and, for Canada and the United States, integrate immigrants into the emergent national plurality (Cremin, 1961, p. 106; Spring, 2008, pp. 5–7). The demand for and perceived benefits of education were not limited to the working classes by any means. This was a time of a burgeoning middle class, which demanded and iteratively fostered a commensurate boom in professional education, especially professionally focused universities (Bledstein, 1976).

Therefore, public schools emerged as one of the key institutions in the modern era, national systems devoted to training children to become "citizens for an industrial economy" (Jarman, 1951; Barrow, 2011, p. 105; Vinovskis, 1985, pp. 10–11; Spring, 2008; Heater, 2004, p. 45). Whether the pupils were young Englishmen to be sent to fight for Empire or young Indigenous children whom their teachers hoped to convert to Christianity (Haig-Brown, 1988, p. 31) schooling was (and is) the popularly-agreed upon pathway from (relative) tabula rasa to desired outcome.

Education as a tool for assimilation was actually a Tudor idea; English history and institutions heavily informed Canada's. In the 16th century, English authorities recognized they could not conquer the Irish people uniquely through force, and they certainly could not eliminate Irish culture and language through war. The colonial imperative demanded an educational approach: "they [the Irish] must be instructed to be the king's true subjects, obedient to his laws, forsaking their Irish laws, habits and customs, and setting their children to learn English" (as quoted in Stuart, 2013, p. 64). England spent tens of thousands of pounds annually on Irish education long before they looked to educate their own population (Stuart, 2013). Educational *economic and nationalistic* capacity actually lags in practice behind its *cultural* force, at least as concerns one of England's oldest colonies.

ADJACENT POSSIBLE? SHIFTING WORLDS REQUIRE NEW INSTITUTIONS

Contrary to the historical path residential schools eventually took, and the evidence experience in Ireland might suggest, the window of opportunity that allowed their creation was triggered by Indigenous leaders. The new social phenomenon at the core of residential schools was a realization that the Indigenous peoples were living in a world dominated by Anglo-European dynamics, and that the landscape had been disrupted as Canada became a legal, economic and practical reality for many First Nations. The Garden River Ojibwa (Anishnaabe) chief Augustine Shingwauk explained his rationale to the Anglican authorities in Toronto in 1871:

> I hoped that before I died I should see a big teaching wigwam built at Garden River, where children from the Great Chippeway Lake would be received and clothed, and fed, and taught how to read and how to write; and also how to farm and build houses, and make clothing; so that by and bye they might go back and teach their own people. (Miller, 1996, pp. 5–6)

Shingwauk's father, also called Shingwauk or Shingwaukonse, had worked with the Anglicans to create a day school for about twenty pupils in 1830 (Hele, 1996, p. 157), so this declaration was likely the result of decades of observation and analysis. Based on this understanding of a new reality, Chief Shingwauk's teaching wigwams were to be a bridge between his people and a survivable future. Shingwauk and his brother Bukhwujjenene worked with the missionary Edward Francis Wilson throughout England to raise money for a school for Native children in 1872; on 22 September 1873, they opened the Shingwauk Industrial Home at Garden River (Nock, 1998).

Whether Shingwauk was a social entrepreneur or institutional entrepreneur is up for debate. He did not invent a new organizational form, and although he clearly articulated an understanding of the shifting Indigenous/non-Indigenous landscape and its implications, and therefore has loomed large in histories of the schools, the idea did not necessarily originate with him. In many ways Shingwauk was a representative of many different Indigenous political leaders, rather than a discrete actor with a unique perspective. Hence, Shingwauk's realization – and similar ones – came at different times to Indigenous nations across the continent, as Euro-Canadian settlers grew in number and the federal government sought to enforce its authority across the lands it claimed; it required adaptation and innovation to survive (Miller, 1996, pp. 76–7).

Importantly, from an Indigenous perspective, the teaching wigwam was not a pathway away from traditional life and identity, but an effort to maintain their culture in the new context. It was therefore an attempt at bricolage – to combine two cultures or perspectives in a proactive and positive way. Advocating for this pathway required a basic shift in perspective that placed Indigenous peoples in a Canadian, rather than Indigenous, context.

PHENOMENA: THE INDIVIDUAL, THE STATE AND HUMANITY

Chief Shingwauk imagined an adjacent possible wherein the children of his community could be wholly themselves as Anishnaabe peoples, while succeeding in the new Euro-Canadian reality. He sought to create a path to that adjacent possible with his teaching wigwams. However, in his words and his work negotiating a treaty with the federal government, Shingwauk inadvertently created the space for a very different adjacent possible (see Figure 10.2), based on oppositional and contradictory

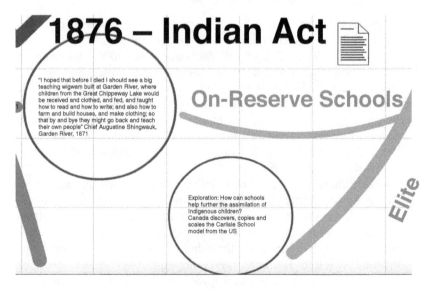

Figure 10.2   Teaching wigwams vs. the Indian Act

founding phenomena. This space contained assimilation policies directed at Indigenous youth, specifically via residential schools. The power imbalance between Indigenous nations and the Canadian state after the signing of treaties allowed for the latter to impose their interpretation of the adjacent possible on the former.

The British disregard or outright hostility for other cultures, especially non-European ones, was long-standing. It was a basic assumption in the settlement of North America that excused treaty-breaking and promoted missionaries' work to "civilize" the populations of North America (Dickason, 2009). Their work included individual schools as early as the 17th century, although not as a continuous or cohesive organization (Miller, 1996, p. 39). The schools and eventually the policies of Canada and the United States were informed by the social phenomena that human societies are hierarchically organized, from the most civilized to the most savage, and the belief that Christianity was a moral truth (the one true faith) that must be disseminated and must dominate (Castellano et al., 2008: pp. 53–4).

Confederation distanced Indigenous communities from their British allies. The new Canadian government took over Indian administration, signaling a shift in focus from the "civilization" of Indigenous peoples to the "assimilation" of them (Milloy, 2008; Castellano et al., 2008, p. 50). Canada's first Prime Minister, John A. Macdonald, is often lamented today for his openly hostile statements about First Nations and Metis people. Although he was not without contemporary critics, his sentiments reflected the views of many at the time. Consider the following, offered in the House of Commons:

> When the school is on the reserve the child lives with its parents, who are savages; he is surrounded by savages, and though he may learn to read and write, his habits and training and mode of thought are Indian. He is simply a savage who can read and write. It has been strongly pressed on myself, as the head of the Department [it not being separate from the Prime Minister's responsibilities], that Indian children should be withdrawn as much as possible from the parental influence, and the only way to do that would be to put them in central training industrial schools where they will acquire the habits and modes of thought of white men. (Macdonald, as quoted in Canada, *Debates*, 9 May 1883, pp. 1106–107)

Macdonald was Prime Minister of Canada from 1867 to 1874 and then again from 1878 to 1891, times of significant treaty-signing. Although it is inappropriate to suggest the head of the government's sentiments automatically translated into policy, Macdonald's government (and subsequent ones) frequently adopted policies closely aligned with his views on Indigenous peoples.

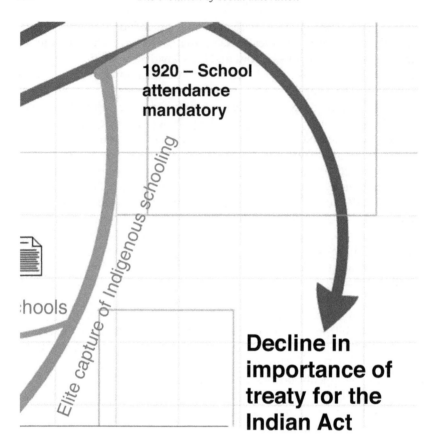

Figure 10.3   The Indian Act basin

Macdonald does not meet the standard of a social entrepreneur, and probably not an institutional entrepreneur in this case, although he certainly took on that role with other early Canadian legislative items (including the creation of Canada as a Dominion in 1867). However, he was one of many legislators and bureaucrats who thoroughly supported and believed in the social phenomena that supported Residential Schools. These actors, enthusiastic observers at the very least, played a crucial role in the schools' development and survival over time, disregarding contrary evidence in favor of an unwavering commitment to assimilation. These cheerleaders played a key role in maintaining one set of relationships, social phenomena or basin of attraction over time, contributing to an emergent window of opportunity for change. The voting and buying public, key decision-makers and social standard-bearers were frequently targeted by entrepreneurs – and for a century they were firmly pro-Residential Schools.

Residential Schools were a paradox. If we remember Chief Shingwauk's aspirations, Residential Schools were "from the Native perspective, a chance to acquire the practical skills needed to compete in a white-dominated society while retaining economic and cultural hegemony", while missionaries and bureaucrats alike believed the schools were assimilationist tools (Wall, 2003, p. 10). As a program, however, Residential Schools were a bricolage of ideas about children and humanity, and organizational forms open to the nation-state and participant churches. Residential schools represented the culmination of the state's belief that it could shape its subjects through schooling, and that Indigenous society and people needed to be changed. J.R. Miller argued that these schools "typified the totalitarian and assimilative spirit of Canada's Indian policy" at the time, with a simply stated (but not easily achieved) goal to: "educate and colonize a people against their will" (1990, p. 396).

AN EVOLVING INDIAN POLICY REGIME

How can a basin of attraction be created that is so deep and sticky that a century of abuse and failure is almost insufficient to dislodge it (see Figure 10.3)? The social phenomena that contributed to the creation of an Indian Policy Regime in Canada held that regime in place with a surprising resilience to landscape shifts and potentially disruptive evidence, experiences and voices. Importantly, this basin was iteratively reinforced by the fact that as a matter of policy, Canadian legislators disempowered Indigenous peoples from being participants in or critics of their own conditions.

As the federal treaty-makers made their way across the Prairies in the 1870s, each treaty negotiation could be considered a niche that contributed to building a broader national Indian Policy Regime. This regime was crystalized in the 1876 *Indian Act* that Canadianized and standardized the relationship between Indigenous peoples and the Canadian government, regardless of treaties (Leslie, 2002; Milloy, 2008; Coates, 2008; Miller, 1990; Adams, 1995; Robertson and Quinney, 1985). Once a treaty was signed, the Indigenous treaty signatories entered the Indian Act regime, becoming status Indians (still a legal identity today), under an Indian Agent who ultimately controlled access to supplies, aid, movement and power in council. This regime was still in the process of crystalizing when the first teaching wigwams appeared.

Many historians have debated the degree of freedom Indigenous negotiators enjoyed in their dealings with their federal counterparts, but the results

---

BOX 10.2   SELECTIONS FROM TREATY 1

Whereas all the Indians inhabiting the said country have . . . been convened at a
meeting at the Stone Fort, otherwise called Lower Fort Garry, to deliberate upon
certain matters of interest to Her Most Gracious Majesty, of the one part, and to
the said Indians of the other, and whereas the said Indians have been notified and
informed . . . that it is the desire of Her Majesty to open up to settlement and immigration a tract of country bounded and described as hereinafter mentioned, and to
obtain the consent thereto of her Indian subjects inhabiting the said tract, and to
make a treaty and arrangements with them so that there may be peace and good
will between them and Her Majesty, and that they may know and be assured of
what allowance they are to count upon and receive year by year from Her Majesty's
bounty and benevolence . . . And further, Her Majesty agrees to maintain a school
on each reserve hereby made whenever the Indians of the reserve should desire
it . . .

Source: Courtesy of http://www.aadnc-aandc.gc.ca/eng/1100100028664/1100100028665,
Aboriginal Affairs and Northern Development Canada.

(the numbered treaties) suggest that both sides acknowledged they had
learned from previous treaties, and to some extent, both sides contributed
to the treaties' content (Carter, 1990, pp. 118–27). Support for schooling
of some sort was a common element of the treaty promises: for instance,
Treaty 1 eventually promised to maintain a school, whereas Treaty 4 promised to pay for teachers (Miller, 1996). As in Chief Shingwauk's case, these
promises largely seem to have emerged from the Indigenous (rather than
Canadian) negotiators (Miller, 1996).

Although some point to the Carlisle School in Pennsylvania as the
prototype and precursor for all North American Indian schools, the
similarity between schools may simply have been the result of a shared
intellectual tradition (MacDonald and Hudson, 2012, p. 431). In the first
years after the numbered treaties, on-reserve schools often closely paral-
leled Shingwauk's "teaching wigwams" (MacDonald and Hudson, 2012,
p. 431). This concerned some observers in Ottawa, who felt "the influence
of the wigwam was stronger than the influence in the school" (Castellano
et al., 2008, p. 52).

Prime Minister MacDonald's government commissioned a report on the
industrial board schools (such as Carlisle) being established in the United
States (Castellano et al., 2008, p. 52; Haig-Brown, 1988, p. 26). The report's
author, Nicholas Flood Davin, believed that the long-term removal of
children (as in the American example) would facilitate assimilation. He
negotiated with religious representatives to form church–state partnerships to run the new Canadian schools (Castellano et al., 2008, p. 52). The

shift to off-reserve residential schools reflected the government's belief that on-reserve schools were not assimilating children, that to transform Indigenous children into Canadian workers they needed to be separated from their parents, their communities and therefore their way of life (Miller, 1996, p. 103: MacDonald and Hudson, 2012, p. 432).

This was more than a semantic difference; the focus shifted from "lifting up" a whole community to actually changing individual Indigenous people through pathways such as enfranchisement, private land ownership and off-reserve schooling. The partnerships with various religious denominations to run the schools reflected a broad joint commitment to assimilation, as well as an attempt to save money on the part of Indian Affairs. It was also characteristic of the generally anaemic (or, more generously, nascent) state of Canadian social policy in the 19th century (professionalism in the delivery of services became the norm in the post-Second World War period, especially for Indigenous people) (MacDonald and Hudson, 2012, p. 431; Millon, 2000, p. 92; Leslie, 2002, pp. 24–6).

An important advocate and champion of the residential school, with the power and position to ensure this model was universally adopted, was Indian Affairs' head bureaucrat, Deputy Superintendent General Duncan Campbell Scott (D.C. Scott). Scott was a career bureaucrat who rose through the ranks of Indian Affairs (Titley, 1986, pp. 17–25; Dominion of Canada, 1909, p. 601). A prolific poet, prone to romanticizing Indigenous people, as a bureaucrat "Scott concerned himself with improving the existing policy in order to render it more effective in achieving the assimilation of Native peoples into the general population" (Salem-Wiseman, 1996, p. 124). Indeed, to Scott, assimilation was inevitable (Monture, 2002, p. 125).

Scott is perhaps the best example of an institutional entrepreneur in the Residential Schools' creation. He and his department, over which he had significant control, advocated for assimilation policies and against other forms of schooling, including day schools, which many Indigenous parents preferred. Departmental employees often blamed parents for disobedient children; so deep was the prejudice against Indigenous peoples' self-determination that resistance to and criticism of the schools were interpreted as unacceptable and even conspiratorial (TRC, 2015a, pp. 113–15). This attitude was made even more pernicious as status Indians (the parents) were legal wards of the state, unable to vote and with severely limited rights in the courts, which blunted avenues for resistance. Hence the deep basin of attraction: those most affected by the schools' problems were unable to undermine their conditions or seek adjacent possibles.

Contemporaneously, evidence was pointing at least one Departmental employee away from the schools. Dr Peter Bryce, the Department's chief medical officer, observed a shocking disparity between Indigenous and non-Indigenous Canadians: the former were dying at twice the rate of the latter, and the Residential Schools were key breeding grounds for deadly diseases like tuberculosis (TRC, 2015a, pp. 95–6; Titley, 1986, pp. 56, 83). Scott and his department, from Ottawa down to the officers at the schools, blatantly ignored Bryce's warnings (TRC, 2015a, p. 96). Bryce's report was suppressed until 1922, when Bryce published his findings. Despite constant efforts, Bryce was unable to destabilize the Residential Schools, which resided in a deep basin of attraction created by the social phenomena associated with assimilation.

THRESHOLDS AND FAILURE: "A LOST CHILDHOOD"[3]

Unlike the United States' Indian Wars, Canada's assimilation plan was bureaucratic, guided by a basket of legislation (Dyck, 1997, p. 333). Residential schools were no exception, and unlike the on-reserve schools that arose from treaties, the 80-odd (at any given time) off-reserve schools were imposed by Ottawa (Miller, 1990, p. 396; MacDonald and Hudson, 2012, p. 431). These quickly scaled out from an experiment to the norm when attendance was made mandatory in 1894–95; in the 1920 revision to the Indian Act, children between 7 and 15 could be forcibly removed from their parents to attend school (Miller, 1990, p. 389; Castellano et al., 2008, p. 23; Haig-Brown, 1988, p. 27). During the schools' more than a century of existence, 150 000 Indigenous children passed through their gates, more often by force than by choice, and increasingly without their parents' consent (MacDonald and Hudson, 2012; Miller, 1990, pp. 396–7). This coercion highlights a simple fact: rather than bringing Indigenous communities more into the Canadian fold, Indian residential schools did much harm and little good for their targeted population.

Residential Schools failed by nearly every metric. Beyond obviously failing Chief Shingwauk and other Indigenous leaders' expectations as a pathway for young Indigenous peoples to navigate the white man's world while fundamentally maintaining their identities, culture and communities, the schools failed to either assimilate or educate their pupils. These failures are partly attributable to the pedagogical and physical structure of the schools themselves. The various Christian denominations ran the majority of schools, and therefore teachers were members of these orders; their enthusiasm for their faith and mission were more important qualifications than classroom experience (MacDonald and Hudson, 2012; Millon, 2000). Consider the pedagogical approach that survivor Margaret Paulette recalled:

The nuns put a piece, a wedge about this big in his mouth and he hadn't eaten all day and he was drooling and all that and then later on in the day they took it out and told him to read, "Now you can open your mouth. You'll be able to read." Poor guy wasn't able to read. And today that guy still stutters. (As quoted in TRC, 2015b, pp. 122–3)

Even for the most passionate, most skilled teacher, the ability to teach was limited; each instruction day was divided in half, between instruction (of which religious education formed an important part) and "training", which usually translated into domestic work for girls and farm labor for boys (MacDonald and Hudson, 2012; Millon, 2000; Haig-Brown, 1988, pp. 57, 64).

Refusal to allow your children to go was punishable by incarceration, which created a terrible choice: lose your children to school or have them lose you to jail and they will probably still have to go to school. Consider the words of survivor Donna Antoine: "We were sort of caught in, in wanting to stay home, and seeing our parents go to jail, and we thought, we must have thought, who's gonna look after us if our parents go to jail?" (As quoted in TRC, 2015b, p. 13). The schools were frequently located at a significant distance from the children's families, but also from society generally, and this isolation, combined with lenient attitudes, allowed sexual predators in the system to procure young victims (Haig-Brown, 1988; Miller, 1996).

One of the profound common memories amongst survivors is the loneliness of separation from family, especially as young, vulnerable children. Large dormitories proved to be isolating and despair-ridden places, especially at night, as survivor Betsy Annahatak recalled:

I remember the, the time the first few nights we were in the residential school, when one person would start crying, all the, all the little girls would start crying; all of us. We were different ages. And we would cry like little puppies or dogs, right into the night, until we go to sleep; longing for our families. That's the memory I have. (As quoted in TRC, 2015b, p. 111)

Students frequently experienced physical, sexual and emotional abuse (Cairns, 2003; Carter, 1990). The buildings and living conditions themselves were unsanitary, and at least 3000 children died on school premises, largely from tuberculosis (Cairns, 2003).

Yet these problems did not destroy the residential schools. Instead, intellectual and practical considerations and a new worldview (partially) repudiated the old one. After World War II, Canadians aware of their country's policies became increasingly uncomfortable with the coercive cultural genocide. Some historians have attributed this discomfort to the unsettling

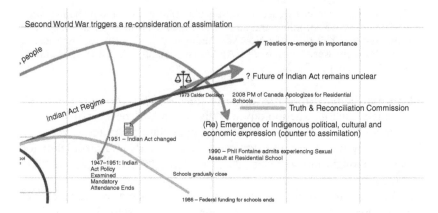

Figure 10.4   A change in regimes, landscape

similarities between the Nazis' policies and those of the Canadian government. Residential school alumni, now community leaders, joined in the criticism and expanded upon it (Millon, 2000; Leslie, 2002; Plant, 2009). At the same time, Indian Affairs officials realized that the Indigenous population under their jurisdiction was growing, not shrinking (they were not disappearing through assimilation) (Plant, 2009).

Between 1946 and 1971 the federal government explored multiple options for changing its Indian policy, with many false starts and underutilized reports (see Figure 10.4). After a pronounced Indigenous backlash against a plan to end treaties and assimilate status Indians completely, and after a significant set of court victories in the 1970s established the treaties' enduring legal status, assimilation ceased to be an acceptable policy goal (Leslie, 2002; Coates, 2008; Haig-Brown, 1988). Closing the schools was a gradual process: some were transferred to Indigenous control beginning in the 1970s, new federal funding ended in 1986, and the last school officially closed in 1998 (Miller, 1996; Castellano et al., 2008).

In 1990, then leader of the Association of Manitoba Chiefs, Phil Fontaine, disrupted an unofficial silence on Residential Schools when he began openly discussing the sexual abuse he'd experienced while at school (CBC, 2008). In the quarter century since, a once deafening silence has begun to give way to a national awakening – albeit through fits and starts and not yet universally. In the same year that the last school closed, the Aboriginal Healing Foundation received $350 million for residential-school related projects, the first of many such funds, projects and initiatives meant to resolve the problems created by this failed innovation. In

2002, Ann Callahan declared that the "gripping accounts of the punitive measurements used by staff of these schools are numerous, too numerous to infer that abuse was conjured up by those who have come forward" (Callahan, 2002, p. 16).

Survivors drove their stories out of the shadows and into the nation's political (if not always popular) consciousness when they negotiated the Indian Residential Schools Settlement Agreement with the Canadian federal government, which included financial settlements for many survivors (although not all, as an ongoing lawsuit indicates) and mandated the creation of a Truth and Reconciliation Commission (TRC) starting in 2007 (TRC, 2015a, p. 6). The TRC held hearings, as well as national and storytelling events across the country from 2010 to 2014; in all, 238 days of local hearings were held in 77 communities across Canada, where over 9000 survivors registered to speak, and many more spoke without registering (TRC, 2015a, p. 25). Many of the survivors' reflections included in this narrative come from the TRC testimonies. The TRC produced 94 recommendations, which have inspired many universities across Canada to explore Indigenizing their curriculum, and many other initiatives (MacDonald, 2016). Hopefully we are in a new window of opportunity, one characterized by reconciliation rather than assimilation.

CONCLUSION

In 2008, then Prime Minister of Canada Stephen Harper rose in the House of Commons to publicly apologize to Residential School survivors and their families on behalf of the Canadian government. The entirety of the apology can be found on the TRC's website, but one point bears repetition in reference to social innovation: "The government now recognizes that the consequences of the Indian Residential Schools policy were profoundly negative and that this policy has had a lasting and damaging impact on Aboriginal culture, heritage and language" (TRC, 2015a, p. 370). This declaration highlights the terrible paradox of the Residential Schools: they were meant to be transformative, but instead of building resilience, the schools tested and damaged the resilience of most of their students. They brought disempowerment rather than inclusion and undermined Indigenous peoples' values and capacity.

The Indian Residential Schools failed to equip their pupils with the tools to join Canadian society. Attendance did significant damage to the traditional practices and languages that the schools sought to eradicate, but the schools did not assimilate "Indianness" out of existence. On the individual level, the schools could be vile, damaging and destructive places. They also operated under a belief in Indigenous peoples' inherent inferiority, a belief that has since been replaced (or is being replaced) by a vision of a multicultural, multi-perspective Canada.

This shift has created the space for an emergent social phenomenon in Canada, one that is not yet universal but has transformative potential. This social phenomenon is the belief that as Canadians "we are all treaty people" (TRC, 2015a, p. 8). Implicit in this social phenomenon is the idea that all Canadians benefited (and continue to benefit) from the treaties, not just some Indigenous peoples (as is occasionally the belief). Additionally, this social phenomenon demands that reconciliation be a universal responsibility, much of which hinges on the legacy and evolving meaning(s) of the Residential Schools. The phenomenon then was born in part out of a reflection on the schools, and may inspire new innovations that create connections between Indigenous peoples and non-Indigenous Canadians and build Indigenous peoples' resilience.

Not all Residential School survivors fully rejected education. Many did – and this absence of education, both physical and cultural, has been a major contributing factor to the frequently deplorable conditions many Indigenous peoples continue to endure in an otherwise wealthy Canada. However, this rejection was not universal. Roy Bear Chief, a survivor and significant contributor to this narrative (through extensive conversations with the author) has repeatedly lamented that learning would have inspired him, if only he could have gone home at night. Thankfully for everyone who has had the privilege to know him in recent years, Roy eventually broke through the ceiling of lowered expectations (what he calls the mentality baseline) and now has a Master's degree in social work and frequently lectures in university classrooms. It is this author's sincere wish he will eventually become Dr Bear Chief.

NOTES

1. Throughout this case, Residential School survivors have been quoted; this is a paltry attempt to give the reader an understanding of the human toll of these institutions and to celebrate voices that were silent too long. However, it is important to note that these are only small excerpts from much wider personal reflections, and it is possible that some will be offended and see the selected quotations as an example of appropriation. This is not the intention and access to full narratives is included in the works cited.
2. Throughout this case, "Indian" is only used in reference to policy (Indian Residential Schools, Indian Affairs, the Indian Act and the Indian Policy Regime); elsewhere this chapter refers to Indigenous peoples.
3. Callaghan (2002, p. 3).

REFERENCES

Adams, H. (1995). *A Tortured People: The Politics of Colonization*. Penticton, BC: Theytus Books.

Altick, R. (1957). *The English Common Reader: A Social History of the Mass Reading Public, 1800–1900*, 2nd edn. Columbus, OH: Ohio State University Press.

Barrow, T. (2011). Undesirable citizens: education, care and control of the "feeble-minded" in the Swedish Prince of Malmöhus, 1900–1950. *European Journal of Disability Research*, **5**, 104–15.

Berger, C. (2013). *The Sense of Power: Studies in the Ideas of Canadian Imperialism, 1867–1914*, 2nd edn. Toronto, ON: University of Toronto Press.

Bledstein, B. (1976). *The Culture of Professionalism: The Middle Class and the Development of Higher Education in America.* New York: W.W. Morton.

Brown, A.D. (2007). *Bury my Heart at Wounded Knee: An Indian History of the American West.* New York: Henry Holt.

Cairns, A. (2003). Coming to terms with the past. In J. Torpey (ed.), *Politics and the Past: On Repairing Historical Injustices.* Lanham, MD: Rowman & Littlefield, pp. 63–90.

Callahan, A.B. (2002). On our way to healing: stories from the oldest living generation of the File Hills Indian Residential School (Masters dissertation). Winnipeg, MB: University of Manitoba.

Canada, House of Commons (1883). *Debates*, 46 Vict. (9 May 1883) 14, pp. 1107–108.

Canadian Broadcasting Company (CBC) (2008). A history of residential schools in Canada, 16 May. Accessed 16 September 2016 at http://www.cbc.ca/news/canada/a-history-of-residential-schools-in-canada-1.702280.

Carter, S. (1990). *Aboriginal People and Colonizers of Western Canada to 1900.* Toronto, ON: University of Toronto Press.

Castellano, M.B., Archibald, L. and DeGagné, M. (2008). *From Truth to Reconciliation: Transforming the Legacy of Residential Schools.* Ottawa, ON: Aboriginal Healing Foundation.

Coates, K. (2008). *The Indian Act and the Future of Aboriginal Governance in Canada.* West Vancouver, BC: National Centre for First Nations Governance.

Cremin, L.A. (1961). *The Transformation of the School: Progressivism in American Education 1876–1957.* New York: Knopf.

Cremin, L.A. (1970). *American Education: The Colonial Experience, 1607–1783* (Vol. 2). New York: Harper & Row.

Daschyk, J. (2013). *Clearing the Plains: Disease, Politics of Starvation and the Loss of Aboriginal Life.* Regina, SK: University of Regina.

Dickason, O. (2009). *Canada's First Nations: A History of Founding Peoples from Earliest Times*, 4th edn. Don Mills, ON: Oxford University Press.

Dominion of Canada (1909). *Annual Report of the Department of Indian Affairs for the Year Ended March 1909.* Ottawa, ON: King's Printer.

Dyck, N. (1997). Tutelage, resistance and co-optation in Canadian Indian administration. *The Canadian Review of Sociology and Anthropology*, **34**(3), 333–48.

Haig-Brown, C. (1988). *Resistance and Renewal: Surviving the Indian Residential School.* Vancouver, BC: Tillacum Library.

Heater, D. (2004). *Citizenship: The Civic Ideal in World History, Politics and Education*, 3rd edn. Manchester: University of Manchester Press.

Hele, K. (1996). "How to win friends and influence people": Missions to Bawating, 1830–1840. In B.L. Guenther (ed.), *Historical Papers 1996: Canadian Society of Church History*, pp. 155–76.

Jarman, T.L. (1951). *Landmarks in the History of Education: English Education as Part of the European Tradition*. London: John Murray.

Leslie, J.F. (2002). Indian Act: an historical perspective. *Canadian Parliamentary Review*, **25**(2), 23–7.

MacDonald, D. and Hudson, G. (2012). The genocide question and Indian residential schools in Canada. *Canadian Journal of Political Science*, **45**(2), 427–49.

MacDonald, M. (2016). Indigenizing the academy. *University Affairs*. Accessed 6 April 2016 at www.universityaffairs.ca.

McClellan, E. (1999). *Moral Education in America: Schools and the Shaping of Character From Colonial Times to the Present*. Williston, VT: Teachers College Press.

Miller, J.R. (1990). Owen Glendower, Hotspur, and Canadian Indian Policy. *Ethnohistory*, **37**(4), 386–415.

Miller, J.R. (1996). *Shingwauk's Vision: A History of Native Residential Schools*. Toronto, ON: University of Toronto Press.

Millon, D. (2000). Telling secrets: sex, power and narratives in Indian residential school histories. *Canadian Woman Studies*, **20**(2), 92–104.

Milloy, J.S. (1999). *A National Crime: The Canadian Government and the Residential School System, 1879 to 1986*. Winnipeg, MB: University of Manitoba Press.

Milloy, J. (2008). *Indian Act Colonialism: A Century of Dishonour, 1869–1969*. West Vancouver, BC: National Centre for First Nations Governance.

Monture, R. (2002). Beneath the British flag: Iroquois and Canadian nationalism in the work of Pauline Johnson and Duncan Campbell Scott. *Essays on Canadian Writing*, 75, January, 118–41.

Mortin, W.L. (1958). *The West and Confederation, 1857–1871*. Toronto, ON: Canadian Historical Association.

Nock, D.A. (1998). Wilson, Edward Francis. *Dictionary of Canadian Biography* (vol. 14). Toronto/Montreal: University of Toronto/Université Laval.

Plant, B.K. (2009). A relationship and interchange of experience: H.B. Hawthorn, Indian affairs and the 1955 BC Indian research project. *BC Studies*, **163**, Autumn, 5–31.

Robertson, E. and Quinney, H.B. (1985). *The Infested Blanket: Canada's Constitution – Genocide of Indian Nations*. Winnipeg, MB: Queenston House.

Salem-Wiseman, L. (1996). Verily, the white man's ways were the best: Duncan Campbell Scott, native culture and assimilation. *Studies in Canadian Literature*, **21**(2), 120–42.

Spring, J. (2008). *The American School: From the Puritans to no Child Left Behind*, 7th edn. Boston, MA: McGraw-Hill.

Stuart, M. (2013). *The Education of the People: A History of Primary Education in England and Wales*. London: Routledge.

Titley, E.B. (1986). *A Narrow Vision: Duncan Campbell Scott and the Administration of Indian Affairs*. Vancouver, BC: University of British Columbia Press.

Truth and Reconciliation Commission of Canada (TRC) (2015a). *Final Report of the Truth and Reconciliation Commission of Canada. Volume One: Summary. Honouring the Truth, Reconciling for the Future*. Winnipeg, MB: Truth and Reconciliation Commission of Canada.

Truth and Reconciliation Commission of Canada (TRC) (2015b). *The Survivors*

Speak: A Report of the Truth and Reconciliation Commission of Canada. Available at www.trc.ca.

Vinovskis, M.A. (1985). *The Origins of Public High Schools: A Reexamination of the Beverly High School Controversy*. Madison, WI: University of Wisconsin Press.

Wall, S. (2003). "To train a wild bird": E.F. Wilson, hegemony, and native industrial education at the Shingwauk and Wawanosh residential schools, 1873–1893. *Left History*, **9**(1), 7–42.

11. "A fever for business": Dutch joint stock companies

Katharine McGowan

INTRODUCTION

Seventeenth-century Amsterdam was known internationally for its *handelaars* – those engaged in commerce; they were largely responsible for transforming a small, medieval port town into a center for international trade. Commerce was such a feature of the town that one foreign transplant (the mathematician Descartes) reflected, "there is no one in this city, except me, who is not engaged in trade; everybody is so concerned with his profits, that I could stay here all my life, without seeing anyone" (Descartes, as quoted in Regin, 1976, p. 92). The Italianate Stock Exchange or *Beurs* building saw nearly daily trade in spices, wines, jewelry, pottery, hardware, wool, fish, gunpowder, flint, picks, swords, helmets, and harnesses – and no doubt this is an incomplete list (Descartes, as quoted in Regin, 1976, p. 92). There was an unknown quantity of coin stashed (and much speculated about) in a vault under the town hall. Amsterdam was popular for foreign exchange (thanks to a limited tax on the export of silver), and the *Bank van Leening* lent money to private companies at 5–6.25 percent (Descartes, as quoted in Regin, 1976, p. 92). These factors were the pillars of the Dutch Golden Age, and they emerged from a niche that provided circumstances for meaningful bricolage and scaling.

New and emergent social phenomena can be powerful forces, creating the intellectual impetus to glimpse and eventually move into the adjacent possible. Yet not all contexts are equally ripe to receive and capitalize on an emergent social phenomenon. New scientific discoveries and social facts are more likely to emerge in some areas than others. They are similarly likely to grow in the most fertile soil, which may or may not exist in their place of origin. Social phenomena can occasionally float on the intellectual breeze until they find receptive conditions and less opaque opportunities contexts. Understanding this movement of ideas can help us grasp why innovations emerge in one place and not another (or sometimes in multiple, seemingly independent circumstances), and at certain times. In this case, long-, medium- and short-term socio-economic, political, and even ecological and geographical circumstances created a receptive niche for an emergent social phenomenon to become a disruptive social innovation.

THE NORTHERN NETHERLANDS AS FERTILE SOIL FOR INNOVATION

Europeans' perception of and engagement with the globe, which had been cracking for more than a century, opened up in the 1590s. The Dutch were best positioned of all the European nations to sail into the newly available space. This was much less a question of global geography than of political, economic and technological possibilities: new phenomena, new adjacent possibilities and ultimately systems-shifting innovations. Importantly, the economic, political and cultural conditions of the northern Netherlands, in comparison to those in countries like France or England, contributed to a significantly riper, hazier opportunity context in the former than in the latter two states.

A moment of systems insight sparked significant historical disruption. A reflective sailor observed that the Portuguese spice trade network was not an impermeable monopoly but that the seas were open to anyone who could navigate them. This realization raised an important question: how? Ships and sailors are expensive, and highly risky – the entire plot of the contemporaneous play *The Merchant of Venice* focuses on the financial (and personal) risks associated with sea-going trade missions. One solution to this problem, the joint stock company, had a transformative effect in the Netherlands, triggering clusters of innovations around financial tools and ship building that strengthened the emerging Dutch Independent state.

In England, the joint stock company model was an adaptation, reinforcing the linked merchant (guild-based) and Crown relationship. The situation in the Netherlands was different. Dutch merchants, especially in Amsterdam, had excess resources (freed from Spanish taxes) and a new, relatively weak government system. In this society in the process of release and reorganization, the confluence of new religious expectations and technological knowledge allowed joint stock companies to become truly transformative, freeing capital from land and labor and transitioning a society away from medieval feudalism towards modern capitalism and representative (rather than monarchical) government.

This case focuses on the macro- and meso-level conditions that can contribute to the creation of a niche for transformative innovation. These are not *prescriptive* but *descriptive* conditions, that can contribute to understanding why the joint stock company emerged in England and appealed to the merchants in the Netherlands. The goal is to explain how external and internal shocks can destabilize a stable configuration and tip a system into a new space, allowing the exploration of an adjacent possible.

Scale is important to this story: at the continent-wide scale, the landscape in the late 16th century can explain elements of the joint stock company story, but not the whole story. Instead, one must understand how local and regional conditions contributed to different outcomes. The journey across the medieval and early modern landscape of Europe is varied, even bumpy, and marked with occasional pockets of potential for transformation.

A SYSTEM AND A NICHE: FEUDAL ATTRACTORS AND OVERLAPPING STRUCTURES OF LEGITIMATION AND DOMINATION

For the most part, Europe in the medieval period was caught in a surprisingly resilient system, the feudal system. A good portion of this resiliency can be attributed to a strong, nearly perfect overlap of the structures of legitimation and domination and the dense network of economic, social, political and spiritual institutions and practices. The primary form of economic relationship and social structure in this system, the manor house, was also its primary political and military unit – a powerful set of structures of domination. A lord or religious institution (monastery, bishopric) possessed a portion of land, which was farmed in smaller lots by individuals (serfs and freemen) who paid the lord in kind and in labor for their protection, in rent, and for the use of such labor-saving and wealth-generating infrastructure as roads (built by peasants for the lord) and mills (Hunt, 1990, pp. 4–5). Although towns and hamlets produced artisanal goods, this was primarily an agrarian economy: ergo, wealth was largely trapped in non-fungible land rather than in cash.

The lord was responsible to the next level up in the socio-political hierarchy in the case of military necessity. So in theory, justice and protection flowed downward (so it was not in the peasants' immediate interest to challenge the system, lest they find themselves on the brunt end of a military and justice-dispensing class' displeasure), and resources flowed upwards, to support the military classes in their effort to maintain order. Some elements of this collective, hierarchical, reciprocal flow existed in most towns, where guilds dominated the processes of training and the career paths of members, including living arrangements and family structures; to sell or buy services and products, one needed to go through a guild (Hunt, 1990; Roper, 1989).

Unsurprisingly, this was a conservative culture, with several reinforcing social phenomena. One of the most foundational was, as discussed above, the reciprocal obligation between the landed elite and their peasant worker base; the privileged had to use their wealth to protect and nurture those beneath them, and serve those above them. Accumulated wealth outside of this system was perceived as bad for the social order, and therefore sellers should only charge a "just price", which included the cost of production and just enough profit to support their families in the social position they occupied. Wealth was not necessarily wrong, but earned wealth, especially beyond the expectations of one's position, was deeply suspect.

Lastly, to ensure no one was ever without support, it was expected (albeit this would be difficult to enforce) that a worker's tools should not be accepted as payment for a debt because that would deprive the worker of his livelihood (Hunt, 1990, pp. 8–10; Beaud, 1983; Howell, 2010, p. 11). Underlying many of these expectations was the authority of the Catholic Church, which provided powerful structures of legitimation in the feudal system and its many interactive parts (see Figure 11.1). What could be more effective than the carrot of eternal salvation and the stick of eternal damnation?

These social values were deeply held by many. One observer in 1480 declared that the wide base of rural peasants and urban artisans worked "to pourveye for the clerkes and knyghtes suche thinges as were needful for them to lyve by" (William Caxton, as quoted in Rowlands, 2001, p. 31). While relatively neat and tidy, and certainly understood at the time as

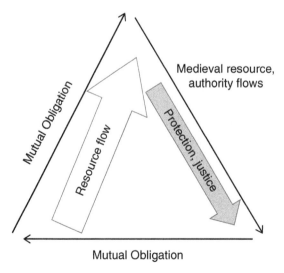

Figure 11.1   Medieval Europe's mutual obligations and resource flows

broadly representative, this model is an oversimplification of European society (see Figure 11.1).

If the above describes Europe, especially Western Europe, in general terms, the structures of legitimation and domination did not reach everywhere equally, due to local conditions. It is actually examples of cracks or disparities in the social phenomena across Europe that advance this narrative. The internal variability had a direct impact on the sites ripe for experimentation and innovation. Consider the following deep dive into the economic complexities of late medieval Europe.

DEEP DIVE: WEAK ATTRACTORS? PRECONDITIONS FOR A SYSTEMS SHIFT

Many historians have correctly challenged the colloquial understanding of feudalism as a deep, dark, impenetrable system, but the feudal system seemed resilient enough that a shock as significant as the Black Death in the 1340s and 1350s and the estimated one million deaths could not fully destabilize the continental socio-economic and political systems (Hatcher, 2008; Peschke, 2007). Peasant revolts could not effectively undermine monarchies' monopolies on the use of force, or the centrality of land-based labor as the primary source of wealth, although they did lead to some long-term improvements in the quality of life (Hatcher, 2008, pp. 285–7; Jones, 2010).

Instead these revolts more often produced terrible and numerous deaths (of both rich and poor, but more often poor) and temporary disruptions in intra-continental trade (Cohn, 2007). As Samuel Cohn points out, monarchies and governments passed wage and price controls to essentially lock in pre-Plague economic relations, laws that "defy any obvious patterns of economic or political rationality" but benefited the socio-political states of their authors, and played especially on their fears of the lower classes (2007, p. 457).

If we move away from a continent-wide perspective to look at different regions of Europe, we can see how in some areas local conditions reduced the power of legitimation and domination structures, and the attractors that reinforced the feudal system. This variance can be connected with the early emergence of new institutions in those areas. In the Netherlands, especially the northern portions of the area, the strength of relationships between lords and peasant farmers/serfs and the concentration of wealth and resources in the medieval political hierarchy weakened much earlier than in other parts of Europe.

While the late 16th and early 17th centuries are this case's primary focus, some of the important pre-conditions to the Dutch joint stock companies' emergence existed in previous centuries. Over time, economic and technological innovations built on each other towards a crucial tipping point, and differences in geography and ecology funneled human activity and ingenuity down certain channels and away from other possible outcomes. For instance, real wages dropped significantly across the continent beginning in 1500, but in England, the Netherlands and (modern) Belgium, they either rose or only slightly declined (Allen, 1998). This is a signifier of other, deeper systems conditions.

The Netherlands

In the 16th century, 85–90 percent of Europe's population farmed the land (Rowlands, 2001, p. 32). Belgium was the most urbanized part of Europe in the late Middle Ages, but by 1500 the Netherlands was virtually identical to Belgium, and about 45 percent of the population of the northern Netherlands lived in cities. Urban population growth overtook rural in 1580 (Allen, 1998; De Vries and Van der Woude, 1997, p. 63). The Netherlands was a comparatively urban, densely populated area, where the little land available for farming had relatively high per acre yields because of advanced technology. Much of this was the result of necessity; the northern Netherlands flooded and required significant technological intervention (and therefore investment) to farm effectively. Even Amsterdam, the city that would emerge as so crucial to the Dutch Golden Age, somewhat inelegantly "rose from a swamp" (Regin, 1976, p. 1).

Unlike the manor house economic model, at the beginning of the 16th century the Netherlands bore little relationship to a cohesive state; it was more a loose connection of town economies oriented towards the river systems by which they engaged in trade with the wider economic world (De Vries and Van der Woude, 1997, p. 10). Even before intense urbanization, the settlement patterns in the northern Friesian lands (land that required frequent drainage) undermined feudal institutions and relationships, where peasants were offered land and freedom in one. Instead, free peasants organized into *buurschappen*, which managed local affairs under the respective and often distant authority of the closest representative of royal rule (De Vries and Van der Woude, 1997, p. 10).

The little Ice Age of the mid-16th century, with its cold winters and uncertain flooding, favored the more diversified economy of the northern Netherlands over the more agrarian economies to its west and south-west (De Vries and Van der Woude, 1997, pp. 19–22). It also encouraged that diversification trend with new opportunities. Changing water temperatures drew more Dutch to the northern fisheries. Fewer people farmed, and more lived in cities located largely on the coast or on major rivers.

Even Amsterdam, the smaller cousin of the then-more-significant Antwerp, was already bringing thousands of visitors from across Europe, both sailors and merchants, to its ports (which brought in herring and wheat from the Baltic). Pilgrims also flocked to the "miracle of Amsterdam", a host (communion wafer) from a mass in 1345 that could not be destroyed by fire (or apparently eating) along the city's Heiligeweg (Holy Way), today's Overtoom Street (Shorto, 2013, pp. 30–31, 37). These foreign sailors, traders and pilgrims "presaged what Amsterdam would become: a place of mixed languages and backgrounds" (Shorto, 2013, p. 37).

From the early 15th century, merchants in Amsterdam had essentially exited the feudal system with the approval of local governments, who allowed preferential trade practices for local merchants, relatively free of export controls, coupled with high import duties for foreign merchants (Shorto, 2013, p. 62). But it would take several important shocks for Amsterdam to emerge as a dominant force in the European economy, as will be discussed below.

Italy

Certain key trade-related innovations made later explorations possible. Many Italian city-states were free from feudal domination, so capital was liberated from the mutual obligation networks, and could be put into trade (Bryer, 2000, p. 331). Geography was also important in Italy, specifically the position of several city-states on the Mediterranean. The proximity to the Levant (Red Sea-based) trade route facilitated international trade for Italian merchants, making some city-states the first points of contact between Europe and the world. These Italian businessmen adopted some foreign tools that helped them develop trade. For example, using Arabic rather than Roman numerals allowed for the innovation of double-entry bookkeeping (simultaneous calculations of assets and liabilities) (Benjamin, 2009, p. 66).

Innovations and improvements – new forms of business partnerships that mixed different types of trade, marine insurance, more robust commercial and contract law and deposit banks – emerged in these city-states, as mechanisms to further new business ventures (Benjamin, 2009, p. 66). English merchants may even have learned about transferable shares from Italian investment pools (Gevurtz, 2011).

England

The strength of the attractors – the reciprocal obligations – of the feudal system started to erode across England in the 15th century. Across the island state, churches and boroughs could be granted royal charters, which allowed them to opt out of feudal obligations to a lord, and granted them the freedom to own property and practice limited forms of self-government *in addition to* the Crown authority (Dullard and Hawtrey, 2009, p. 19). These arrangements are often perceived in retrospect as examples of proto-corporations.

To manage and foster foreign trade, the Crown offered an exclusive franchise to merchant collectives. "Foreign" denoted European, meaning that these collectives undertook generally short journeys that did not require large investments to exchange and sell goods. These were precursors to joint stock companies, where merchants shared access to that exclusive franchise as members of a "regulated company" (Gevurtz, 2011, pp. 475–521). Regulated companies' only collective or cooperative quality was membership; partners did not share work or goals. They were something between guilds (limited access to markets) and companies (collective action) but shy of a modern joint stock company.

The Netherlands, certain Italian city-states, and south-eastern England were less distinctly feudal than other parts of Europe. In some ways, this could be seen as a great disadvantage; those areas in Europe that lent themselves more naturally to an agrarian economy could thrive (relatively speaking, especially for the aristocratic classes) in the feudal system. Exploring new ways of doing business, new forms of wealth creation, and new political arrangements is not necessarily in the interests of those who benefit from the current circumstances. These areas where the relationships between the structures of legitimation and domination were weaker either shed the feudal system earlier than others, or were more prepared to take advantage of shocks as opportunities.

SHOCKS

The feudal system's variance in the strength, resilience and universality of the structures of legitimation and domination was historically insufficient to explain why joint stock companies emerged and why they flourished in the Netherlands. Several key disruptions or shocks to the European system helped further the creation of key niches for the innovation.

A MAJOR SHOCK IN THE CHANGE OF FAITH

The Reformation represents one of the key shocks to the bonds of mutual obligation that made the feudal system so resilient. It also significantly undermined the structures of legitimation across the continent. Disruption rarely comes as spectacularly as in the Reformation. As Euan Cameron so succinctly put it, "In 1500 the people of Western Europe belonged to an international Church theoretically serving them all ... In complete contrast to this near-uniformity, by 1600 many, perhaps most of Europe's people were acutely conscious of being Roman Catholics, Lutherans, or reformed" (2006, p. 145).

Importantly, this was not just a question of labels or categories. In a time of low literacy, the number of people who self-identified with a fractional religious identity speaks to the Reformation's penetration and importance to many Europeans. Regardless of their spiritual sophistication, the Reformation-inspired peasant revolts beginning in 1525 indicate the importance of new religious avenues for many within Europe (Cameron, 2006, p. 145). Religion mattered, and differences in religion divided the continent's populace.

Not only did the Reformation effectively shift the Catholic Church from a covering or common institution to one competing with rival religious institutions, but several new social phenomena emerged in the growing cacophony of religious theology that allowed for significant exploration of the adjacent possible. The Reformation did not affect all parts of Europe equally, especially over time; many areas remained Catholic. However, that does not mitigate the fact that the Reformation affected those areas – and its differing impact contributes to the regional variability identified above.

Perhaps most important to this discussion, Calvinism presented several social phenomena that fundamentally undermined the strong attractors of the feudal system and its structures of legitimation and domination. John Calvin (the originator of Calvinism) believed money could be used to glorify God and distinguish between the elect (those going to heaven) and the reprobate (the damned). This was a new, disruptive constructed phenomenon (Hugill, 1993, p. 21; Beaud, 1983, p. 18).

In the northern Netherlands, where Calvinism became very popular, the adoption of the new religion and its associated values by the Duke of Orange, many of Amsterdam's inhabitants and eventually its government, further reduced the barriers to leaving the feudal system, weakening the Catholic Church's capacity to act as a set of structures of domination.

Calvinism linked lenders and borrowers in the northern Netherlands, as both groups were among the early adopters of the new religion. The business between the co-religious in a competitive environment drove down the cost of borrowing and made the process more reliable. Medieval lenders were primarily Jews, and their Christian clients could claim usury when it was time to repay the loan, whereas Calvinist borrowers had no such recourse against Calvinist lenders (Hugill, 1993, p. 21). The Calvinists of

Amsterdam also took a very liberal approach to other religions, not insisting on the conversion of immigrants and refugees, although religion was still an important element of trade networks and communities.

England also became a centre of new religion. The Church of England was less theologically distinct (or fixed) than Calvinism, but it still affected the connection between England and the rest of Europe. The Church of England encouraged a sovereign outlook in the Crown and the merchant class, which influenced trade and maritime activity (Vlami, 2010, p. 68). National interests overlapped with religious–cultural values. If a Dutch or English merchant or collective of merchants were Calvinists or Anglican, what did it matter to them that they violated papal bulls that divided the world outside Europe between the Spanish and Portuguese? (Erlichman, 2010, p. 418; Boxer, 1965, p. 2).

A POLITICAL SHOCK WITH SURPRISING RESULTS

We need a compelling explanation for the variations across the secondary seafaring nations – particularly England and the Netherlands – on the transformative effects of an innovation and the ability to explore adjacent possibles made evident through new social phenomena. An important shock to the political structures of the northern Netherlands, an alchemical mix of religion, urban geography and demographics, among other factors, helped reveal an important adjacent possible for Dutch merchants that was not apparent or available to English merchants at the same time.

In the middle of the 16th century, Dutch merchants lived and worked under Spanish rule and its international trade regime (which had subsumed the Portuguese trade empire). The Dutch population, and especially its minimal political establishment, was constrained within the rigid bounds of the Spanish Empire, limited in its ability to raise new capital, to explore new political/power arrangements, or even to benefit fully from the wealth they created, thanks to high imperial taxes. The Dutch ports subsidized the Spanish empire. Provincial delegates from the northern towns and communities could, in theory, only meet in The Hague at the request of the Spanish Governor General of the colony (Hart, 2014, pp. 12–15).

The northern Dutch territories disrupted their political and economic institutions/systems when they effectively rebelled, which opened up opportunities in the social, political, economic and even spiritual sphere. Economic controls and taxes were loosened, undermined or completely removed by the Dutch when they rejected their colonial masters. As the society began to reorganize, innovations like the joint stock company, developed in England to compensate for the gap between the country's (both the Crown's and merchants') international ambitions and anemic state funds, was adopted, with transformative effects on Dutch society. This organizational form scaled to the northern Netherlands and grew in a supportive context.

NEW IDEAS AND NEW INSTITUTIONS AND REORGANIZATION

Over the course of the 16th century, the political structure of the Habsburg Empire reached a zenith, and yet its rigidity suggested a possible fragility. The Habsburg Charles' inheritance folded Netherlands into Spanish Crown possession in 1516, and royal revenues from the Dutch provinces increased fivefold in half a century, while the prices Dutch merchants could command for their goods increased only twofold (Benjamin, 2009, p. 229). The Spanish Crown took money from the Netherlands at a rate much higher than that at which their businesses and revenue grew. Spanish tax collectors took advantage of the Netherlands' sophisticated and diverse economy. Agricultural practices in the Netherlands were significantly more productive and efficient than in many other parts of Europe, and Antwerp had become the major hub for bringing Asian spices from Portuguese traders to European markets (Smith, 1991, pp. 98–101; Benjamin, 2009, p. 229).

Meanwhile, Charles was a largely absentee ruler, appointing friends to important government positions in the Dutch counties (Ames, 2008, p. 98). The Habsburgs took advantage of the Netherlands' prosperity and near complete lack of political autonomy. Charles "could raise taxes [in the Netherlands] in an almost arbitrary fashion", so that Dutch profits paid for Spanish largesse (Smith, 1991, pp. 102–103). The perceived burdens of Spanish rule on the Dutch decreased the Habsburgs' legitimacy in the Netherlands. Whatever relationships reinforced the Spanish hold on the Netherlands became increasingly brittle.

Religion was the spark that lit a federal flame: although the Netherlands were still technically Catholic (as a Spanish possession), Calvinism became increasingly popular in the northern Netherlands. During the 1560s, large open-air Calvinist sermons and (possibly related) furies of iconoclastic religious property destruction seemed to demand a response from the Spanish Crown (Benjamin, 2009, p. 230; Hart, 2014, p. 13; Gunn, 2001, 129). In 1567, the King appointed the Duke of Alva as the Netherlands' new governor general; Alva took a very particular stance in his new position, and his "Council of Blood" executed thousands of rivals and rebels (Hart, 2014, pp. 13–14).

The first Dutch military challenges to Spanish authority occurred in Holland and Zeeland provinces, where radical rebels, "the Sea Beggars", seized several towns in the 1570s (Davies, 1961, p. 24). In 1572, the rebels formalized their rejection of Spanish authority in the small, old town of Dordrecht, where representatives of the States of the Province of Holland gathered to declare their sovereign control over their territory and to proclaim William of Orange as their new *stadholder* (royal representative), thus rejecting Alva's choice of Count Bossu (Hart, 2014, p. 15).

From the Dutch perspective, the rigid structures and relationships that characterized Spanish authority in the Netherlands began to collapse in key structures of domination (and wealth, freed from the heavy Spanish tax burden). When the Sea Beggars took Amsterdam in 1578, they declared the city officially Calvinist (Shorto, 2013, p. 83), replacing one set of structures of legitimation and domination (albeit weak ones) with a new set, a federal Dutch Calvinist state. Two years later, William of Orange actually re-enacted a medieval ceremony by entering Amsterdam via the water, "standing on the foredeck of a galley draped with his noble colors", specifically orange, "at the head of a flotilla that entered the harbor and sailed majestically into the city centre" (Shorto, 2013, p. 83). The colorful ceremony marked this systems shift with seeming prescience: it was known as the Alteration.

As the legitimacy of Spain receded, the northern Dutch counties perceived the possibility of a Dutch state outside Spanish control and Crown-based, strictly inherited authority. This idea crystalized in 1581, when the new federal council at The Hague, the States-General, affirmed the emergent Dutch state's existence:

> We have unanimously and deliberately declared, and do by these presents declare that the King of Spain has forfeited, ipso jure, all hereditary rights to the sovereignty to these countries, and are determined henceforth not to acknowledge his sovereignty or jurisdiction, nor any act of his relating to the domains of the Low Countries [the Netherlands]. (Benjamin, 2009, p. 230)

Economic historians Jan de Vries and Ad van der Woude caution against the perception that the Dutch economy was a traditional nation-state structure; the state was not, strictly speaking, the unifier in the Dutch economy (1997, p. 10). Indeed the state apparatus seemed to emerge, at least in part, to accommodate the confluence of economic, spiritual and political needs of the northern Netherlands.

After the Duke's Army of Flanders sacked Antwerp, 60 000 to 100 000 Protestant refugees fled for the safety of the north, which was partially protected from the Army of Flanders by the Rhine, Waal and Meuse Rivers (Davies, 1961, p. 29; Erlichman, 2010, p. 405; Furber, 1975, p. 189).

This mass migration further divided the Netherlands along sectarian lines, with an independent Protestant, merchant capitalist United Provinces in the north and the largely Catholic south under heavy and taxing Spanish control (Smith, 1991, p.103). It also meant a concentration of merchant money and connections in Amsterdam, an important trend for the United Provinces' shipping economy. At the same time, ships from the northern Netherlands were barred from ports in Seville and Lisbon, undercutting one trade route and inadvertently incentivizing the search for another (Prakas, 2014, p.9).

As the United Provinces pulled away from the Spanish throne and medieval political relationships, another world was figuratively opening. In 1598 the Habsburg Crown (controlling both Spain and Portugal) placed an embargo against Portuguese trade with the United Provinces (Erlichman, 2010, pp.403–405). This gave new impetus to the Dutch rebellion against the Habsburgs and made a compelling case for Dutch merchants to bypass their Iberian middlemen and trade directly with Asian markets.

Although the war with Spain extended well into the 17th century, the Dutch United Provinces operated as a de facto independent state from this point forward (Ames, 2008, p.98). The new Dutch federal republic reflected a feature of Dutch society: the nobility and land-owning aristocracy lacked significant power in comparison with urban merchants. As the traditional source of authority – inheritance – lost its exclusive dominance and absolute power in the northern Netherlands, the Dutch reorganized government authority brought together the different estates of society.

A NEW PHENOMENON CREATES A LINK TO THE ADJACENT POSSIBLE

Mare Liberum

In the 1590s, Dutch sailor Jan Huyghen van Linschoten published a widely popular account of his nine years in the Portuguese trade, wherein he detailed the strengths and, more importantly, the weaknesses of Portuguese operations: they were significantly overextended and being crushed by the costs of maintaining military installations across the globe (Ames, 2008, p.97; Erlichman, 2010, p.417). Linschoten's conclusion shook the entire European economy and political system, a landscape-level disruption. It became common knowledge that the Portuguese empire was deeply vulnerable, but who would best take advantage of this new opportunity? What adjacent possibles were made visible in this collapse?

It became well known in interested circles around Europe that the Portuguese overseas Empire was vulnerable to competition. In 1609, Hugo Grotius outlined the legal case for the constructed phenomenon/social fact of *mare liberum* (open seas). This was in contrast to the joint Portuguese/ Spanish claim of *mare clausum* (closed seas), that they had a monopoly (technical, legal and spiritual) on maritime trade (Benjamin, 2009, p. 214; Ames, 2008, p. 97).

Mare liberum did not open the way for Dutch ships, for they were already actively navigating the oceans. However, Grotius crystallized an emergent constructed phenomenon, in response to the combination of Calvinism (breaking Catholic control) and challenges to Spanish (and Portuguese) political and economic hegemony, that ability, not papal dispensation or monarchical authority, determined endeavor, facilitated by the technological capabilities that permitted long-distance sea voyages.

INNOVATION

The reality of *mare liberum* was an exploration frenzy among a class of individuals who had previously been unable to undertake such risky endeavors. New knowledge was a pull, but merchants outside of Spain and Portugal required a new approach to exploration and shipping beyond Europe, outside of the power and resources of a Crown. The solution to this problem was the joint stock company, which allowed merchants to fund otherwise prohibitively expensive overseas trips. Investors pooled their capital to fund multi-ship expeditions, and by extension they distributed and minimized the risk of such large expenditures.

One such company founded to explore the East was formed in London in 1591. Although this mission was largely unsuccessful, its sailors discovered that lemon juice cured scurvy, an important discovery that facilitated more overseas trade (Erlichman, 2010, p. 422). This new naturalistic phenomenon/scientific fact opened up the possibility for longer, less interrupted sea voyages.

Elizabethan mariners did not seek to change the flow of resources internationally at a systems level; they were privateers/pirates, who, with the Crown's blessing, sought to redirect the flow of individual ships away from Spanish and Portuguese ports and into English ports and English pockets (Barbour, 2008, p. 258). This was a foreign policy of peskiness, but any policy that extended overseas was expensive, and the English Crown's resources were considerably smaller than those of their Spanish rivals, so they offered licenses and charters to private individuals and groups willing to take the financial risk (Vlami, 2010,

p. 68). Hence, the development of the joint stock company in the mid 16th century.

England's joint stock companies represented an adaptation for the resilient merchant guild, rather than any tipping point towards capitalism. For instance, the Chancellor–Willoughby voyage had 200 subscribers in 1551, but the 1553 royal charter, which eventually empowered the resultant Muscovy Company, reduced investor membership to 12 (Bryer, 2000, p. 332). A north-west passage explicitly sought to *avoid* existing routes dominated by the Portuguese.

The joint stock model was brought in line with the extant Merchant Adventurers Guild model, where the Crown offered monopolies to regulated companies that reinforced the guild quality of membership in the merchant class (Bryer, 2000, pp. 331–2; Dullard and Hawtrey, 2009; Vlami, 2010, pp. 67–8). This was not a significant challenge to resource flows, but merchants seeking to "economize on the high level of recurrent transactions" in international trade (Carlos and Nicholas, 1988, p. 399). In the English context therefore, the early joint stock company model was an adaptation meant to build the resilience of the English Merchant regime.

FROM ADAPTATION TO TRANSFORMATION

Although the English minimized risk for any one merchant, joint stock companies in that market drew from traditional sources of wealth, and repaid them. The joint stock company had yet to become "the type of institutional innovation that transformed the European economy and gave it an advantage over the rest of the world" (Harris, 2005). Potential hyperbole aside, the innovation needed to seek out a more supportive and fertile niche.

For the joint stock model to be transformative, it had to shift the resource flows. Dutch and English merchants traded commodities, ideas (including theology), and the concept of joint stock companies. With tens of thousands of Protestant merchant refugees flooding north to escape the Duke of Parma, Amsterdam became increasingly awash with merchants who lacked businesses but had connections (Smith, 1991, p. 103; Davies, 1961, p. 29; Erlichman, 2010, p. 405; Furber, 1975, p. 189). The Calvinist merchants' interest in growing capital, as good for business and good for their souls, the articulation of *mare liberum* and the newly independent United Provinces meant that Amsterdam and the surrounding area was in a particularly good position to capitalize on the English invention of joint stock companies (see Figure 11.2).

A good investor should do due diligence; this truism certainly applied to

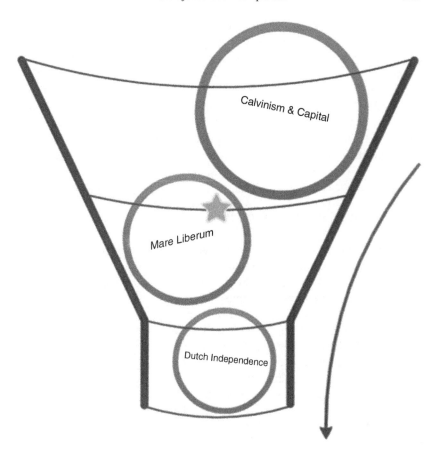

Figure 11.2   Combination of phenomena, events that led to a Dutch transformation

a Dutch investor in the 1590s. Take Cornelius de Houtman as an example: laden with merchandise as a cover, he was sent to Lisbon (where Dutch ships were no longer permitted) to collect information on the state of the Portuguese trade system and the possibilities for Dutch merchants (Shorto, 2013, p. 95). Under this guise he collected information for two years; he identified specific targets across the globe where the Portuguese were vulnerable to Dutch merchants undercutting their connections with local sources.

How could De Houtman and his employers exploit their new knowledge? Learning from the English experiment encouraged a similar niche of Dutch investors to form a joint stock company. The Compagnie van Verre funded a 4-ship fleet in 1595 under De Houtman (who was not a professional sailor or commander, which may be relevant to the trip's ultimate outcome). This was both a great failure and a success. Although only one of the four ships and 89 of the 249 crew survived, reduced to near skeletons and hating their commanders, including De Houtman (one ship was burnt in a mutiny), the cargo that ship brought back to the United Provinces was sufficient to make the voyage profitable, albeit only modestly (Erlichman, 2010, p. 423; Furber, 1975, p. 31). If a fleet could lose three-quarters of its ships and still turn a profit, imagine what a more successful voyage could achieve.

CLUSTERS OF INNOVATIONS

Throughout much of the period described above, the northern Netherlands was actively at war, a fact that contemporary observers and historians alike have found remarkable given the area's amazing productivity. Consider 17th century Amsterdam burgomaster Pieter Corneliszoon Hooft's view: "Whereas it generally is the nature of war to ruin land and people, these countries have been noticeably improved thereby" (as quoted in Hart, 2014, p. 1). Indeed, the improvement Hooft observed is powerfully captured in the city's physical and wealth expansion, and the cluster of innovations the frenzy for trade required and inspired.

As niches of merchants explored potential avenues to make money, within the related area of shipbuilding, technological innovations furthered Dutch exploration. Dutch shipyards had mastered the building (partially mechanized, using wind-powered sawmills and cranes) of high-quality, low-cost ships, built on the *fluyt* or *fluitship*, a common design that was light but able to carry heavy cargo (100–900 tons), as well as hiring foreign workers and paying them less than their Dutch-born counterparts (Benjamin, 2009, p. 229; Hugill, 1993, p. 21; Beaud, 1983, p. 26). The *fluyt* could be built at essentially half the cost of its nearest rival ship, significantly benefiting Dutch merchants. Wages higher than in most of the rest of Europe drew many of the best skilled and unskilled workmen to satiate the hunger for ships (although then, as now, the cost of living in Amsterdam significantly undermined workers' salaries) (Israel, 1998, p. 351).

The extent of shipbuilding in Amsterdam was significant enough that travelers in the early 17th century remarked on the ever-present smell of pitch in the city – tar used to cover newly-built or repaired ship hulls (Shorto, 2013, p. 100). By the 1610s, Amsterdam was a boomtown, as English Ambassador Dudley Carleton described:

I saw the whole town and observed this difference from Antwerp [the former trade center] that there was a town without people and here a people as it were without a town. Such are the number of all nations, of all professions and all religions there assembled, but for one business only, of merchandise. Their [refugees, immigrants and merchants] new town goeth up apace. (As quoted in Goldgar, 2008, p. 10)

The city was bursting in all possible ways. The tightly packed medieval townhouses could not accommodate the flood of entrepreneurial refugees and immigrants; the population grew from less than 42000 in 1585 to 106500 in 1620, and 200000 in the 1660s.

This growth was so acute that in the 1610s city officials began an organized expansion beyond the medieval walls and canal. The original settlement became the tiny core of a modern, sprawling, planned city, with large, well appointed gardens; the fashion of the time for exotic flowers was fueled and supported by a public ordinance that insisted a portion of all new lots must be reserved for gardens (Goldgar, 2008, pp. 44–6). It was a city of increasingly abundant luxury – with tastes facilitated through burgeoning international trade.

Many individuals looked to make money through the growing spice trade; the influxes of cash and people required key institutional developments to facilitate effective, efficient exchange. The government, no longer based on the will of God or the Church, had to deliver effective services to its taxpayers in order to be considered legitimate. These services included the expansion of Amsterdam, physical protection for traders and reliable financial services for businesspeople (Hart, 2014, p. 6; Goldgar, 2008, pp. 44–6). Similarly, financial organizations emerged to provide regularity and reliability in the potential chaos of international trade: a chamber of assurance was founded in 1598, followed by a public exchange bank and a lending bank within the next twenty years, including the *Bank van Leening* (Goldgar, 2008, p. 9).

Traders needed accurate information and reasonable predictions about new and existing trading companies, their expeditions and their prospects. As a new system of information developed, including journals that published reliable stock prices as early as 1606 and a formal stock exchange in 1611, niche experimentation scaled up (Smith, 1991, p. 104; Kyriazis and Metaxas, 2011). While many deals were done in pubs or in the open-air square, these organizations regularized, ordered and legitimized exchange. Thus they essentially undermined the old community-based ethos and promoted individualism and abundance (Goldgar, 2008, pp. 12–15).

As the United Provinces' population was largely urbanized and land was limited, many Dutch invested in the stock market, rather than property, as a way to store and grow their wealth (Hammal, 2008, pp. 20–21).

Speculation emerged as a behavioral pattern quick on the heels of the markets' creation, as demonstrated by the Great Tulip Mania of 1636–37 (Hammal, 2008, p. 21). It seems that within one generation, the new economic institutions had already been captured by *windhandel* – a business deal of empty wind (Goldgar, 2008, p. 2).

EXPANDING THE NICHE

Ownership in some of these corporations was so dispersed that few would lose their shirts if one ship or many in a fleet never returned to Amsterdam (Hugill, 1993, p. 21; Hammal, 2008, p. 19). The sheer number of corporations (often one-offs) and fleets led to excessive and deleterious (for the Dutch) price competition among traders (as spices became more plentiful in Europe and European traders competing for monopolistic trade relationships became more plentiful in Asia) (Erlichman, 2010, p. 424).

A business arrangement that made sense in the niche of early traders was proving deeply problematic as a basic arrangement for the shipping economy. In an effort to prevent Dutch merchants undercutting each other (and highlighting the state-based approach to foreign trade), the United Provinces created the Dutch East India Company (VOC) in 1601, essentially homogenizing and nationalizing the spice trade into one corporation (Erlichman, 2010, pp. 424–5). This is, in a way, the end of the exploration of and experimentation with organizational form, although it was not the end of wealth generation.

The early enthusiasm about the VOC project was such that initial subscribers came from a wide range of Dutch society (from the very wealthy and influential businessmen to their domestic help), although large, more affluent interests quickly bought out smallholders (Boxer, 1965, p. 4). At first this may seem like an alternative path to a national trading company like the Portuguese system. However, the character of the VOC reflected the elements of the Dutch federation that broke with traditional European feudal structures. In particular, merchant capitalism and the oligarchy of burgers (Ames, 2008, pp. 102–103; Hammal, 2008, p. 19; Furber, 1975, pp. 186–7) were at the VOC's core, both of which reflected a shift away from the linked land, privilege and obligation of the feudal economy. In a public–private partnership seeking to both undercut the Spanish and enrich the Dutch United Provinces, the VOC harmonized local and national interests, business and political goals (Boxer, 1965, p. 2).

Many countries followed England and the Netherlands' example. East India companies were founded in France in 1604, Sweden in 1615, Denmark in 1616 and Brandenburg in 1651 (Gevurtz, 2011, pp. 475–521). The ubiquity of the stock market itself as one of modernity's primary sources of wealth speaks to the transformative power of the Dutch innovation.

CONCLUSION

Multiple authors have pointed to the Dutch and later English experimentation in business and trade as laying the foundation for changes in the associated realms of politics, economics and social relations, including the emergence of individualism, the Enlightenment and the Industrial Revolution (Smith, 1991, p. 6; Wallerstein, 1974, p. 67; Hart, 2014, pp. 1–6; Goldgar, 2008, pp. 12–13). Martha Howell (2010) offered perhaps the most direct discussion of what might be considered the emergence of a new social phenomenon (our term, not hers), as merchants matched and soon radically eclipsed the wealth of landowners. Howell argues that the ascendancy of trade (a multifaceted trend) meant that money and property began to be seen as fungible capital (a new phenomenon), having value in the abstract, which disrupted basic assumptions and arrangements in medieval Europe.

The potential profits of a successful overseas trading venture (or even an unsuccessful one such as the Compagnie van Verre) dwarfed the annual rents even the greatest estates could claim. This challenged the dominance of land as the primary source of wealth. As trade expanded in scope it lost its personal quality (credit could no longer be based on the honor of the creditor in international trade). As land shifted from immovable to movable property (with the associated innovations in marriage and inheritance law), it lost its hold on the social order as the bastion of authority and stability (Howell, 2010, pp. 29–45).

An important constructed phenomenon/social fact in the shift from medieval to market economies was therefore the idea that property was capital and therefore was as movable as any other. Not only did the joint stock company model open up the potential for exploration and trade on a level and to an extent that individual and family-based trade networks could never support, but it also established a different role for money. These were partnerships of money, and membership was transferable (Braudel, 1979, p. 439). This new concept of exchange was derived from the obvious contradictions between the emerging market economies and the socio-economic and political system of manorial land tenure. In its definition, this new social phenomenon, like those before it, created the need and opportunity for new innovations in economic exchange, political power and social arrangement. And so, as new truths emerge, society changes.

In 1776, nearly two centuries after the seas opened up, Adam Smith, in *The Wealth of Nations*, declared the Dutch Republic (as it was then) was "a country that had acquired that full complement of riches which the nature of its soils and climate and its situation with respect to other countries allowed it to acquire" (as quoted in De Vries and Van der Woude, 1997, p. 1).

REFERENCES

Allen, R.C. (1998). The great divergence: wages and prices in Europe from the Middle Ages to the First World War. University of British Columbia Department of Economics Discussion Paper, 98-12.

Ames, G. (2008). *The Globe Encompassed: The Age of European Discovery, 1500–1700*. Upper Saddle River, NJ: Pearson.

Barbour, R. (2008). The East India Company journal of Anthony Marlow, 1607–1608. *Huntington Library Quarterly*, **71**(2), 255–301.

Beaud, M. (1983). *A History of Capitalism 1500–1980*, trans. T. Dickman and A. Lefebvre. New York: Monthly Review Press.

Benjamin, T. (2009). *The Atlantic World: Europeans, Africans, Indians and their Shared History*. Cambridge: Cambridge University Press.

Boxer, C.H. (1965). *The Dutch Seaborne Empire: 1600–1800*. London and New York: Penguin.

Braudel, F. (1979). *Civilization and Capitalism, 15th –18th Century: The Wheels of Commerce*, Vol. II, trans. S. Reynold. Cambridge: Harper & Row.

Bryer, R.A. (2000). The history of accounting and the transition to capitalism in England. Part two: Evidence. *Accounting, Organizations & Society*, **25**, 327–81.

Cameron, E. (2006). The turmoil of faith. In E. Cameron (ed.), *The Sixteenth Century – Short Oxford History of Europe*. Oxford: Oxford University Press, pp. 145–73.

Carlos, A. and Nicholas, S. (1988). Giants of earlier capitalism: the charter trading companies as modern multinationals. *The Business History Review*, **62**(3), 398–419.

Cohn, S. (2007). After the Black Death: labour legislation and attitudes towards labour in late-medieval western Europe. *Economic History Review*, **60**(3), 457–85.

Davies, D.W. (1961). *A Primer of Dutch 17th Century Overseas Trade*. The Hague: Martinus Nijhoff.

De Vries, J. and Van der Woude, A. (1997). *The First Modern Economy: Success, Failure and Perseverance of the Dutch Economy, 1500–1800*. Cambridge: Cambridge University Press.

Dullard, S. and Hawtrey, K. (2009). Corporate virtue and the joint-stock company. *Journal of Market and Morality*, **12**(1), 19.

Erlichman, H. (2010). *Conquest, tribute & trade: the quest for precious metals & the birth of globalization*. Amherst, NY: Prometheus.

Furber, H. (1975). *Rival Empires of Trade in the Orient, 1600–1800*. Minneapolis, MN: University of Minneapolis Press.

Gevurtz, F. (2011). The globalization of corporate law: the end of history or a never-ending story? *Washington Law Review*, **86**(3), 475–521.

Goldgar, A. (2008). *Tulipmania: Money, Honour and Knowledge in the Dutch Golden Age*. Chicago, IL: University of Chicago Press.

Gunn, S. (2001). War, religion and the state. In E. Cameron (ed.), *Early Modern Europe: An Oxford History*. Oxford: Oxford University Press, pp. 102–34.

Hammal, R. (2008). Dutch Tiger: the booming economy of the Dutch Republic, 1579–1650. *History Review*, **62**.

Harris, R. (2005). The formation of the East India Company as a cooperation-enhancing institution. Working Paper, December. Accessed 5 September 2016 at http://ssrn.com/abstract5874406 or http://dx.doi.org/10.2139/ssrn.874406, 2.

Hart, M. (2014). *The Dutch Wars of Independence: Warfare and Commerce in the Netherlands, 1570–1680*. London and New York: Routledge.

Hatcher, J. (2008). *The Black Death: A Personal History*. Philadelphia, PA: Da Capo Press.

Howell, M.C. (2010). *Commerce Before Capitalism in Europe, 1300–1600*. Cambridge: Cambridge University Press.

Hugill, P.J. (1993). *World Trade Since 1431: Geography, Technology and Capitalism*. Baltimore, MD: Johns Hopkins University Press.

Hunt, E.K. (1990). *Property and Prophets: The Evolution of Economic Institutions and Ideologies*, 6th edn. New York: Harper & Row.

Israel, J. (1998). *The Dutch Republic: Its Rise, Greatness, and Fall, 1477–1806*. Oxford: Oxford University Press.

Jones, D. (2010). *Summer of Blood: The Peasant Revolt of 1381*. London: Harper Press.

Kyriazis, N. and Metaxas, T. (2011). Path dependence, change and the emergence of the first joint-stock companies. *Business History*, **53**(3), 363–74.

Peschke, Z. (2007). The impact of the Black Death. *ESSAI* 5: Article 32.

Prakas, O. (2014). *The Dutch East India Company and the Economy of Bengal, 1630–1720*. Princeton, NJ: Princeton University Press.

Regin, D. (1976). *Traders, Artists and Burghers: A Cultural History of Amsterdam in the 17th Century*. Amsterdam: Van Gorcum.

Roper, L. (1989). *The Holy Household: Women and Morals in Reformation Augsburg*. Oxford: Clarendon Press.

Rowlands, A. (2001). The conditions of life for the masses. In E. Cameron (ed.), *Early Modern Europe: An Oxford History*. Oxford: Oxford University Press, pp. 31–62.

Shorto, R. (2013). *Amsterdam: A History of the World's Most Liberal City*. New York: Doubleday.

Smith, A. (1991). *Creating a World Economy: Merchant Capital, Colonialism, and World Trade, 1400–1825*. Boulder, CO: Westview Press.

Vlami, D. (2010). Corporate identity and entrepreneurial initiative: the Levant company in the 18th and 19th Century. *The Journal of European Economic History*, **39**(1), 67–99.

Wallerstein, I. (1974). *The Modern World-System I: Capitalist Agriculture and the Origins of the European World-Economy in the Sixteenth Century*. New York: Academic Press.

12. Synthesis: tracking transformative impacts and cross-scale dynamics

Michele-Lee Moore

INTRODUCTION

A significant focus in the field of social innovation is on the notion of needing to scale an innovation – meaning to make change across multiple scales. The notion that a social innovation process will involve more than one scale makes intuitive sense, since interdependencies and interconnectedness amongst people, places, economies, goods, services and ecosystems are omnipresent (Challies et al., 2014; Berkes, 2002). So why is it even worthwhile to discuss cross-scale dynamics? What does the topic reveal about the history or unfolding of different social innovations over time, other than the obvious: that everything is connected to something or someone else?

As central as cross-scale dynamics are to the complex systems perspective on social innovation (see Chapter 1), the actual definition and nature of those dynamics have been difficult to "pin down" analytically (see Vervoort et al., 2012 for a detailed discussion). In this chapter, I posit that by examining cross-scale dynamics in detail, we can better understand why certain social innovations take root and may be more transformative than others.

Different disciplinary traditions use different terms and methods to describe and study scales and the interactions across those scales. The ecologist Levin (1992) identified scale as a methodological issue suggesting that ecologists are interested in patterns in ecosystems and those patterns will depend on the scale of observation used. It is understood that large-scale patterns have consequences for fine-scale phenomena, such as climate change affecting the hydrological patterns of a single creek. Thus, having research that crosses scales – particularly the large and the fine scales – is essential. In the scholarship of sociology, previous research focused on either the macro scale, which includes structures, institutions, stratification and social order, or the micro scale, which includes individual interactions, morality and emotions. Many scholars now argue that the micro–macro link is essential – that micro phenomena can help explain the macro and vice versa (e.g. Giddens, 1984; Collins, 1988). In geography, although scale is often focused on quantifiable spatial units, ongoing discussions have also focused on the notion that scale is socially produced (Delaney and Leitner, 1997). Scholars have built evidence to demonstrate how discourse, actions, authority and structured power relations are leveraged by actors to deliberately establish and periodically transform scales – such as the boundaries by which local or global, rural or urban, or developed and developing nations are defined – to serve their own interests (Swyngedouw, 1997; Smith, 1998).

Moreover, previous scholars have also attempted to describe connections across scales and the changing nature of those connections – referred to here as cross-scale dynamics – in rather "neat" terms. Linkages are frequently described as vertical in reference to connections across levels of organization, or horizontal, meaning similar units that are connected across space (see, for example, Berkes, 2002; Adger et al., 2005). However, the cases of social innovations discussed here reveal cross-scale dynamics as a complex web of layered and nested connections that cross the typical space, time and sector boundaries highlighted in previous discussions of scale (e.g. Cash et al., 2006; Cumming et al., 2006; Wyborn and Bixler, 2013), and that cross scales bounded by knowledge, moral and philosophical principles, identities, resource types, and of course, the constructed boundaries of ideas. Such dynamic webs of interaction do not demonstrate chaos; in fact, the layers and strands of cross-scale connectivity often emerge due to strategic intent by individuals exerting agency (see Olsson, Chapter 4). But deliberate intent and strategic agency do not necessarily equate to linear, tidy connections that can be categorized as simply vertical or horizontal.

In order to capture this complex and dynamic web, and recognizing that the chapters in this book combine numerous disciplinary perspectives, analytical methods and discourses, and deal with cases from across different temporal and spatial scales, this book combines frameworks to achieve a different approach to describing cross-scale dynamics. In Chapter 1, McGowan et al. describe the use of the multi-level perspective (MLP) framework involving the niche, regime and landscape scales (see also Geels, 2002). Although the MLP framework has typically been dedicated to social-technological transition studies, the tool is applied here beyond the technological, and considers the niche as a micro scale of individual interactions in social innovation processes. The niche is generally understood to be a "safe" space for experimentation and a scale in which grassroots innovations are likely to emerge, while the regime involves legal and policy institutions and how we organize ourselves as humans – in communities, in organizations, and in governance processes (Hegger et al.,

2007; Geels, 2002; Frenken et al., 1999). I use the landscape as the macro scale, which involves broad social, cultural, economic and political beliefs, values, norms, ways of knowing and being. The MLP framework is then layered further to include Giddens's theory of structuration (1984), so that each niche, regime and landscape is understood to involve their own structures of domination, legitimation and signification, which themselves form boundaries of scale. The combination does not create perfectly neat boundaries, and yet, the analytical usefulness is apparent in the insights which this layered cross-scale framework provides.

Specifically, the analysis stemming from the combined frameworks includes an examination of the type of cross-scale dynamics that characterize the social innovations explored in this book. I use those dynamics to assert that although innovation is often thought to emerge in a niche that is associated with small scales or local scales, in fact, the size of a niche is not a fixed variable, and expands and contracts over time. Moreover, patterns across the cases demonstrate a certain amount of inter-temporal agency at a niche scale: actors combining and building on others' ideas even though they may never meet or live in the same time period. Having described the niche patterns across cases, I examine the niche-regime dynamic and contend that in order to achieve durability and transformative change across scales, those working within a niche will draw on specific landscape structures of legitimation and signification – and are most successful when they eventually begin to operate alongside the dominant regime, as a type of proto-regime. The paths and processes for doing this differ across cases, but simply trying to convert, take down, or disrupt the existing regime without first establishing a proto-regime that fits with meaningful, broader structures of legitimation and signification results in a struggle to have the social innovation recognized; it is often opposed or rejected. Lastly, I argue that when social innovations are "niche-less" and introduced or developed by a regime, it is rare that they actually radically alter the regime or have a transformative effect. Rather, social innovations that are created and implemented by the regime are undoubtedly *for* the regime and thus tend to strengthen the regime's structures of domination, legitimation and signification, reducing the innovative or transformative quality of what could be introduced.

CHARACTERIZING THE NICHE AND ITS ROLE IN CROSS-SCALE DYNAMICS

As there is still limited theorization of cross-scale dynamics in complex systems and in social innovation processes, the need exists for a more substantive description of the nature or type of interactions involved. Together, these case studies demonstrate that such interactions are not just about one scale interfering with another, such as a national government using a top-down approach, or about a lower level resisting something "above" in a vertical hierarchy of power. Likewise, social innovations do not arise simply because one scale provides resources and support to another scale, and "scaling" a social innovation for impact is not just about expanding the number of people adopting a particular innovation.

If these statements describe what cross-scale dynamics are not, with respect to social innovation in complex systems, we still need to understand what exactly they are and how they matter. Therefore, I use the niche as a starting point to discuss the nature of cross-scale dynamics and outline four new insights generated by the findings of these cases.

Previous scholars in socio-technological transitions studies have discussed the importance of creating innovative niches, which are understood as safe spaces within an organization, protected from the everyday operational concerns, where innovations can be created, tested and refined (Kemp et al., 1998; Verbong et al., 2010). The rationale is that innovations may not yet: (1) have a proven track record of success; (2) be feasible; and (3) be either profitable or clearly meet the mandate of an organization. Therefore, a niche or safe space ensures that these concerns do not limit the efforts to generate innovations (see, for example, Van der Laak et al., 2007; Schot and Geels, 2008; Smith and Raven, 2012).

In general, socio-technical transitions scholars treat the niche as an entity within an existing organization, but niches could also serve as the roots of an eventual organization. For instance, some grassroots non-profits and start-up tech firms were not recognized as formal organizations when their innovations were being generated. The story of Steve Jobs and Stephen Wozniak developing key products and ideas that would later form the building blocks for Apple, while working in a garage and without much recognition, is a familiar example. The concept of novel, groundbreaking innovations emerging in poorly resourced but creatively safe spaces has arguably become somewhat romanticized (Audia and Rider, 2005), but the practice of deliberately dedicating a small group of staff and space to innovation is now well-established, particularly in technology firms.

The case studies in this volume highlight four main characteristics for social innovation niches that depart from existing scholarly viewpoints.

First, the cases make it clear that the niche scale is not necessarily bound within a single organization, and the forms and sizes of niches vary across cases. For instance, in the creation of the first national park, the acceptance of the idea and the management and institutionalization of protected areas involved a geographically large space, and the idea was embedded in national government, policy and law early on (that is, not just as a pilot project that operated "under the radar"). But this differs significantly from the size or magnitude of the niches involved in the establishment of the Dutch East India Company and financial derivatives, or the number of niches critical to the birth control case study. Thus, the notion that niches are always small groups of people working on the fringe of an organization or dominant regime, without notice or reliance upon large numbers of people at the beginning of an initiative, does not always hold true.

Beyond the notion of the niche as a space for the creation of an innovation, previous social innovation research has begun to differentiate between the notion of effect and scale with regard to the adoption and implementation of an established innovation. That is, having a transformative effect is not singularly about getting many people to adopt a particular innovation across different geographies or different niches (see Ross, 2014; Bradach and Grindle, 2014; Moore et al., 2015). Although key agents and system entrepreneurs are associated with each case study niche, the number of people who would actually be involved in the emergence of the niche, the maintaining and sustaining of that niche, and the possible links that some niches made across scales in order to ensure an innovation became established at the regime level, is far beyond the number typically associated with a small, hardworking set of social or tech entrepreneurs. Moreover, when larger numbers of people are involved, they are not just passive consumers or recipients of a social innovation "impact", adopting an innovation that has been put before them in a final, polished state. Rather, large numbers may be involved in the niche during the innovation generation phase.

Secondly, the fragility of the niche and its own contraction and expansion dynamic are central to understanding the niche throughout history. For instance, when examining the formation of the Duty to Consult principle regarding settler–Indigenous relations in Canada, the historical perspective portrays that some attempts were made to create "safe spaces" over time to examine, question and challenge the dominant settler regime. Prime Minister Laurier is claimed to have made one such attempt when he proposed examining the question of Aboriginal title in the province of British Columbia, despite the protests by the provincial Premier at the time. A short time later, when the federal election resulted in a new Prime Minister, the opportunity to work within that niche, with support from the federal government, closed.

Similarly, the case goes on to highlight the role of Prime Minister Pierre Elliott Trudeau's White Paper. A White Paper itself could potentially represent a "safe space" for governments to test ideas, discourse and policy approaches with the public and to launch debate and dialogue. Yet, as the results demonstrate, this discourse was not considered "safe" or appropriate by Indigenous peoples because the White Paper proposed abolishing the colonial *Indian Act* and the recognized status of Indigenous peoples within Canada. In doing so, the proposal failed to honor the special rights of Indigenous peoples (now contained in Section 35 of the Constitution) and did not recognize the history of conflict over Aboriginal rights and title to land. As McGowan describes, key alliances emerged to resist the government's proposal and were successful, but the proposal did temporarily create a contraction in the niche where such ideas could be discussed. While the White Paper may have been an attempt to heed key signals from within the system that the current status quo was failing Indigenous peoples, it did not propose an acceptable alternative. The debate over dismantling the federal legislation continues today, now often initiated by Indigenous leaders, but the justification is based upon, *inter alia*, the premise of strengthening the self-determination of Indigenous nations, not the elimination of their status.

This latter example raises a third characteristic of niches and cross-scale dynamics in the history of social innovation: the inter-temporal "bricolage" that occurs in some cases. While bricolage is discussed in more detail in previous chapters, the concept relates to cross-scale dynamics in so far as it showcases a pattern in which people who may never have met, who may never have existed in the same space or time, all contributed to preparing the system for the transformative effects of the social innovation by sustaining, protecting and expanding the niche when possible by interacting through ideas, discourse and efforts to shape the innovation.

In the case of national parks, Antadze (Chapter 2) traces the dynamic variables that led to the establishment of Yosemite Park, which can be considered a niche, given that it initially operated without a formal parks management regime, was not part of a broader national strategy, and was an experiment in only one region of the country where the idea of a protected area was tested. The variables that Antadze highlights include the role of Romanticism, through the artists and poets who captured the beauty of a range of ecosystems from across the US, and in particular the role of Catlin, who was one of the first to propose the idea of national parks in the United States. Environmental philosophers, naturalists and conservationists also played key roles in shaping ideas and debates about human connection to nature, wildness and naturalness, and conservation or preservation, ranging from Aldo Leopold's Deep Ecology and Thoreau and Emerson's beliefs in transcendentalism, to the more recent ideas of the self-described "half-hearted fanatic" Edward Abbey. But John Muir's efforts to establish Yosemite as a state park took place in between these writings and efforts. Furthermore, Olmstead's work on landscape architecture and parks design at municipal, state and national levels took the niche created by the establishment of Yosemite and began to support the emergence of a regime, or proto-regime. Despite these individual efforts, history does not show a collaborative effort by this group of actors and in many cases they would never have crossed paths, given the differences in age, location and vocations.

However, variation exists, as in the case of financial derivatives where the cross-scale dynamic involved deliberate and direct interactions amongst people. The meeting of actors through the Mont Pelerin Society, the Chicago School and, eventually, among academic economists and political administrations was instrumental in the diffusion of ideas related to the market-based approach to pricing risk. But ultimately, both of these cases illustrate that the notion of a niche as the domain of a close-knit group of actors operating in a small, safe space for a short period of time to generate an innovative intervention is challenged by the findings of history. Instead, it appears that social innovations rely on cross-scale interactions that involve inter-temporal agency in creating a niche and possibly shaping a regime, and this dynamic may occur over a century, with actors who may, in some instances, only be indirectly linked.

Fourth and finally, the role of, and even the need for, crisis or some type of major disturbance in creating an opportunity for transformative change is often raised in relation to social change (Crossley, 2002; Olsson et al., 2004; Biggs et al., 2009; Gelcich et al., 2010). The importance of crisis is associated with the often repeated Winston Churchill quote "never let a good crisis go to waste". However, the social innovation history cases demonstrate that niche-level efforts do not necessarily benefit directly from a crisis, nor do innovations only cross scales to effect regime change when there is a crisis. Although protracted crises were present in many of the cases – the health of women seeking illegal abortions and of both men and women having unprotected sexual intercourse in the birth control case, the environmental degradation caused by human developments that national parks would eventually protect against in small pockets of the world, and the economic quagmire that engulfed the world's dominant economies as the Bretton Woods institutions collapsed – these were not the type of sudden shocks or extreme events that shake up world orders, decimate communities in natural disasters, or completely change human belief systems in short time periods. Although history can point to pivotal moments, the slow variables in system dynamics may explain as much about how social innovation unfolds within niches, and then across regimes or landscape levels, as the fast or punctuated moments associated with crises.

EMERGING FROM DIFFERENT SCALES: FROM NICHE TO PROTO-REGIME

If the success of a social innovation is defined by whether it transforms resource and authority flows, practices, and norms, values and beliefs in ways that have durability across different scales (Westley and Antadze, 2010; Westley et al., 2006), then those cases that seem to have achieved that have done so in ways that, *prima facie*, may seem counterintuitive. Often, discussions about social innovation begin by justifying the need for change in society, and point to lamentable, complex problems that humans have created as the motivation for such innovation, including climate change and rising inequality (Mulgan et al., 2007; Murray et al., 2010). Social innovations are then proposed as a means to solve such enduring problems, by halting the way we currently operate in society, giving voice to those not currently heard, and beginning to do things differently. Niches provide the place to experiment with doing things differently, and if activities within the niche are undertaken with effective learning, networking and visioning processes, scholars have proposed that the innovation will be more likely and more "ready" to diffuse across scales (Schot and Geels, 2007; Hegger et al., 2007) and become the mainstream way of operating.

However, cases such as the national parks, derivatives, the Dutch East India company, and the Internet show a different pattern in relation to the role of the niche and the nature of the cross-scale dynamics. In all of these cases, actors do not seem fixated on attempting to solve a problem, nor are they resisting the authority of a powerful actor perceived as responsible for how the problem endures in the existing system. Instead, the activity within the niches tended to contribute to the construction of entirely new knowledge and this led to new actors acquiring a level of authority. For example, in both the derivatives and Internet cases, those with the technical knowledge – the *quants* and various engineers and physicists, and those who originally developed packet switching, TCP/IP and hypertext – competed and negotiated with each other to be the first to develop the formulas and codes that would make everything, from the implementation of the Black–Scholes model and automated trades to the World Wide Web and free, open software, possible.

During the development of the various technologies that contributed to the creation of the Internet and World Wide Web, these technical experts were simultaneously the underdogs and the technical elites. The anti-authoritarian sub-culture and deep philosophical commitment to open access within the community shaped what was possible, but what was also socially acceptable to develop. As Tjörnbo describes, this led to a rejection of those systems that came to include fees, such as the University of Minnesota's attempt to price Gopher and the attempt by AT&T to charge for Unix. By the point in time when AT&T made such an attempt, the innovation associated with Unix was into the adoption phase with approximately 300 000 users. Therefore, a rejection of fees was likely pragmatic. Why tolerate paying when you were used to getting access for free? But given that only about 300 000 users existed, and millions more would come to adopt the technology, one can imagine that new members at least could pay the fee, with existing users falling under a grandfather clause. The intolerance towards the monetization of access possibly also stemmed from early and ongoing commitments to ensure that everyone had access, with a belief that this in itself would help the innovative technology be further developed and refined, and would also ensure that it could not be controlled by governments and royalty. Likewise, decision-makers in companies such as AT&T were probably fully aware that these technical experts could simply create their own alternative system should they choose to do so. Thus, it could be surmised that typical power-holders within the telecommunications regime recognized that technical knowledge equated to a certain amount of new power.

For all the power that the construction of new knowledge may have bestowed and the eventual proto-regime that emerged, the establishment of the knowledge and proto-regime did not require a dismantling of pre-existing structures of domination, legitimation and signification at the regime level. There was no other form of the internet, and thus, its creation did not diminish the authority or power of an existing regime, because there was no internet regime. Instead, it could operate alongside of and with regime-level actors, including the US Department of Defense, academia, and telecommunications giants.

As another example, the creation of Yosemite as a park, and later the creation of an entire national parks system as a proto-regime, created tensions at the existing regime level, with ministries related to resource development for instance, but there was no pre-existing protected areas regime. Other ministries, and the authority of government to make decisions about land use, had to be altered but not completely dismantled as a result of the new knowledge generated by combining concepts from landscape design and environmental philosophy with tourism development. This was markedly different from the initial struggles undertaken in the launch of birth control, given that reproductive rights and related medical processes were the very domain of regime-level actors in religious and medical professions.

The most successful social innovations were developed by actors within niches that used the construction of new knowledge as a form of authority in establishing a proto-regime, and operated alongside of the existing regime, challenging that regime but also being strengthened by interactions

with it, and never directly aiming to supplant it. Conversely, the least successful, and most negative in terms of social, cultural and ecological consequences were not led by a niche group of actors and activities, but were
introduced by the regime itself, as is evident in the cases of the intelligence
tests, the residential schools and the duty to consult.

EMERGING FROM DIFFERENT SCALES: REGIME-LED SOCIAL INNOVATIONS

Although links are drawn by McGowan (Chapter 10) between Chief
Augustine Shingwauk's teaching wigwams at Garden River and the roots
of the residential schools, it is challenging to characterize this as much of
a niche. Olsson (Chapter 4) highlights the potential role that co-optation
may have played in the development of residential schools, but a cross-
scalar lens may also reveal that the residential schools case is arguably one
that is niche-less. The teaching wigwams were not sufficiently developed at
the niche level, and were not protected in a "safe space" in which experimentation occurred over time and space, with refinement and further
testing of the school's governance, teaching pedagogy, or for any goal
related to improving Indigenous–settler relationships. Certainly, the teaching wigwams never came to be established as a proto-regime. Instead, the
Anglican Church of Canada and the Government of Canada drew upon
ideas and ways of thinking about assimilation that existed long before the
teaching wigwams and directly tied them to the dominant education and
religious regimes to create the residential schools. The regime level appears
to have generated, adopted, scaled out and institutionalized the residential
school as an innovation.

Furthermore, closer scrutiny indicates that residential schools did
not shift authority, norms, beliefs or values within any niche, regime or
landscape level, and did not fundamentally alter financial resource flows;
religious institutions were already powerful financial actors. Instead, the
concept of residential schools relied on existing regime-level structures of
domination, signification and legitimation for a new purpose: to achieve
assimilation. Despite the attempts within the regime level's discourse to
frame assimilation as something positive, the process for accomplish-
ing assimilation was tantamount to attempting to dismantle Indigenous
structures of authority, legitimation and signification at the family and
nation level. Numerous, clear signals were present throughout the lifespan
of the residential schools that positive social benefits of assimilation were
not accruing, and in fact, individuals and families have demonstrated that
the opposite was true (Truth and Reconciliation Commission of Canada,

2015). Nonetheless, dominant and powerful actors within the regime level ensured the "innovation" remained institutionalized. Instead of altering the social structures of the regime, the regime appears to have been committed to exerting the full strength of its existing social structures and processes of domination, legitimation and signification in the hopes of making colonial ways of knowing and being ever more dominant.

Today, the legal duty to consult may be characterized in a slightly more positive light by McGowan, but arguably would not be deemed a successful innovation by numerous Indigenous (and non-Indigenous) communities (Lawrence and Macklem, 2000; Natcher, 2001; Sossin, 2010; Promislow, 2013). Again, the duty to consult is linked by McGowan to numerous efforts by Indigenous peoples to forge a different kind of relationship with the Crown, including the delegation of chiefs visiting London in the early 1900s, and later in the combined effects of the *Calder, Sparrow, Van der Peet, Delgamuuw, Haida, Taku* and *Mikisew Cree* decisions that unfolded in the courts over more than three decades. However, the emergence of the duty to consult was in many respects a niche-less social innovation – one created by the existing colonial legal regime and some of the most powerful actors within it (judges in the Supreme Court). In this instance, the regime level created the legal principle without testing it within a protected niche, and the precedent-setting nature of case law meant that it immediately *was* the new regime for governments across Canada, at local, provincial and national levels, for all to implement.

Although the principle was created in direct response to a legal challenge brought forward by Indigenous peoples and thus shaped by Indigenous peoples, in fact, Indigenous peoples have long articulated a need for the colonial regime actors to recognize their rights, their self-determination, and their title/ownership of territories that were not ceded (Callison and Hermida, 2015; Corntassel and Holder, 2008). The duty to consult, as created through the courts, requires that the "Crown" (federal and provincial governments) consult and accommodate concerns of Indigenous peoples for activities and developments on lands which affect Indigenous peoples, but does little to recognize or reaffirm the self-determination and authority of Indigenous people, nor that the land may in fact not be owned by the Crown but be unceded and owned territories of Indigenous peoples.

If ongoing legal cases today are to be characterized as experiments in applying this principle, attention thus far has mostly focused upon determining what activities "count" as consultation and accommodation. For instance, settler governments have struggled to understand what the duty entails and what level of engagement or effort is sufficient to prove in court that they have attempted to meet their duty to consult (e.g. Ritchie, 2013). These "experiments" or legal battles are hardly creating opportunities for niche-level actors to refine and further develop social innovations, construct new knowledge, and eventually establish a new proto-regime. Nor has the principle opened up a vast adjacent possible. Instead, consultation processes have come to be yet another bureaucratic process controlled by the existing regime level, which continue to frustrate actors on all sides (Promislow, 2013; Moore et al., 2016).

Similarly, although the intelligence test has the roots of a niche in that it was created within a lab by two academics, the manner in which it was quickly adopted without evidence or testing amongst the existing medical and education regimes in the US makes this case more similar to the residential schools than to the creation of the Internet in terms of the cross-scale dynamics.

Ultimately, it can be hypothesized from these cases that when innovations are primarily generated by the regime level, and then adopted and institutionalized within the regime, the social innovation is unlikely to truly alter the structures of domination, legitimation and signification at the niche, regime or landscape levels. Previous scholarship has argued that governments – which arguably are a dominant actor within regimes – have an essential role to play in both enabling and generating social innovations (e.g. Moore et al., 2012; Foxon and Pearson, 2008). But the cases of residential schools, intelligence tests and the duty to consult add a more nuanced perspective on their role. If a government is going to generate and institutionalize an idea that it deems a social innovation, it must pay attention at all times to signals within the system to determine whether this is truly changing Giddens's social structures, and reducing issues such as conflict, or improving diversity and the experiences of previously marginalized individuals and groups within society.

When social innovations are developed by actors within a niche level, and that niche activity leads to the construction of new knowledge and new forms of authority that do not supplant existing authority per se, then a novel proto-regime may emerge around the innovation. Eventually, the proto-regime may follow different paths. In some instances, the proto-regime may become the dominant regime if the existing regime collapses, as occurred in the case of financial derivatives following the collapse of the Bretton Woods institutions. In other cases, such as the national parks, the proto-regime may be quickly absorbed into the dominant regime, simply expanding what was the regime level. Then again, the proto-regime may continue to exist alongside the dominant regime, causing ongoing tensions as the two shape and are shaped by each other. The latter could be the most useful way to characterize the case of the Internet since some regimes have attempted to control and institutionalize rules and policies around the Internet, but most have failed to do this successfully, with open access and anti-authoritarianism still dominating many of the Internet's structures and processes.

THE ROLE OF NICHE–LANDSCAPE AND LANDSCAPE–REGIME INTERACTIONS

Having analyzed the different patterns of social innovation generation within the niche and regime scales, it becomes paramount not to neglect the critical role that the landscape level and its structures of domination, legitimation and signification come to play in the history of social innovations. The landscape scale is often described in only vague terms because it is largely viewed as "an exogenous environment beyond the direct influence of niche and regime actors (e.g. macro-economics, deep cultural patterns, macro-political developments)" (Schot and Geels, 2008, p. 545). Since the multi-level perspective has been developed by scholars interested in the management of socio-technical transitions (Geels, 2002; Smith et al., 2010), it makes sense that those elements that can never be "managed" have not received as much attention as the niche and regime, where the framework deems it more likely that actors exert agency (Van Driel and Schot, 2005; Verbong and Geels, 2007; Geels, 2010).

However, as Westley (Chapter 1) articulates, in a complex system, the view that the landscape scale is entirely exogenous and somehow untouched by deliberate and strategic agency by niche and regime actors at times, and emergent and self-organizing patterns at other times, does not quite fit. Moreover, when examining social innovations that are not just socio-technical in nature, the landscape itself can be understood to involve more than macro-economic and macro-political developments or culture as cited by Schot and Geels (2008), and to include other Giddensian structures.

Taking this view of the landscape scale, four insights about its role in the cross-scale dynamics of social innovation histories are presented by the cases. First, across the cases, the up and down nature of resistance and acceptance of socially innovative ideas appears to be linked to the structures of signification and legitimation at the landscape level. At times, those landscape structures appear to serve as attractors that niche actors are drawn towards. But in turn, these structures then become a type of resource for the niche. As an example, the development of parks had a long history of attaching to the attractor created by various environmental philosophy and romanticism movements, as highlighted by Antadze (Chapter 2). But it was the emerging national economic strategy linked to the development of the railway, the related opportunities this opened for tourism, and the competition the natural phenomena provided when compared with European cultural monuments, that created an important and opportunistic attractor in shaping the legitimacy and significance of the idea of national parks.

These landscape scale attractors lead to very different outcomes across the cases. For instance, the importance of the Euro-scientific-technical paradigm as an attractor and resource was used to justify access to birth control and the creation of national parks, but was also used to justify intelligence tests. Therefore, it is not that there is a "correct" or "best" landscape attractor for social innovations; rather, it is the "bricolaging" of landscape-level ideas and philosophies, combined by actors working within the niche and regime, that are most important for eventually drawing resources or building some support from the regime level.

The second insight is that the most pivotal moments shaping how a social innovation does or does not unfold may occur when the structures of domination at the regime level align with the structures of legitimation and signification at the landscape level. The birth control case demonstrates this most clearly, given that Sanger had shifted through multiple landscape-scale attractors – morality and ethics, women's rights, women's health – before the sexual health risks associated with venereal diseases aligned with the regime scale's interests. The American Medical Association's legitimation, along with key Supreme Court decisions – both key structures at the regime scale – helped further move birth control out of its longstanding niche.

Thirdly, in nearly every case, these cross-scale interactions and the multiple interacting landscape attractors created paradoxical tensions that are sustained throughout the history of the social innovation. As discussed previously, contestation about the values of the national parks system and what it protects would have been ever present as John Muir, Olmstead and others advanced the idea. Are parks for preserving beauty with little human contact or for game hunting? Do they play a role in education and research, or simply serve as a place for recreation? The fact that Indigenous peoples were often displaced as the national parks boundaries were drawn, and their subsistence hunting or use of forestry resources labeled illegal hunting or logging (e.g. Chatty and Colchester, 2002), was not acknowledged at the time. Today, all these tensions persist within questions about the value of parks and how they should be managed (Dearden et al., 2016). In the case of the Internet, the successful innovation involved an unlikely partnering among powerful strangers when those with an anti-authoritarian philosophy and technical expertise attracted resources from the Department of Defense and those associated with CERN – an EU-funded project. Not only did these connections create niche–regime interactions, but the connectivity across scales also embedded a tension in the way the social innovation continues to unfold today. Tensions between the anti-authoritarian philosophy and the state-based interests in technology that support the exertion of authority remain ever present. With that tension, debates are ongoing about individual privacy versus collective security, individual rights to information and state surveillance and censorship, the centralized model of big telecommunications within the neoliberal version of capitalism versus the decentralized possibilities of the sharing economy, and the notion of proprietary business models predicated on intellectual property and patents versus open source software.

Similarly, numerous questions and tensions surrounded the creation of the residential schools, and many of these debates continue in relation to national education systems today. Specifically, tensions remain about whether education has become a training ground for liberal idealism, and even elitism, or whether its purpose is an attempt to generate a certain national identity by assimilating recent immigrants alongside Indigenous peoples. Other questions about education include whether instead it is intended mainly as a place to foster skills amongst all in order to ensure equal opportunities for well-being regardless of class, location and other socio-economic-cultural variables. Each of these has competing underlying goals and values, which are never entirely resolved by a social innovation, but they lead to a fourth insight regarding regime–landscape interactions.

The cases demonstrate that the landscape and its attractors do contribute to reshaping the regime to some extent, when niche-scale actors are able to use the landscape structures of signification and legitimation as resources. But the findings also show that the regime does not necessarily reshape the landscape, since the structures of signification and attractors do not necessarily disappear. Although women's rights to choose and women's health may be protected for now in the birth control and reproductive rights debates, the issue regularly reappears in public debate and discourse, indicating that the attractors are still present at the landscape for some actors. But for now, the regime gives dominance to certain landscape norms and values.

Finally, taking the positive lens of social research that Golden-Biddle and Dutton (2012) assert is essential, it could be noted that the more transformative social innovations – that is, those that fundamentally altered Giddens's social structures across niches and regimes in ways that are durable – were focused on creating hope and protecting beauty and well-being. Examples include the creation of the Internet, which was largely predicated on ideals of open access and equal opportunity for information, and the establishment of national parks. The cases with negative consequences and little positive benefit or transformation are those that focused on "getting rid of a problem" and that, ultimately, suppressed diversity within the system, such as the intelligence tests and residential schools. Even the Dutch East India Company and financial derivatives, which created the benefit of economic wealth for some, led to that wealth being concentrated in the hands of a few. In turn, such innovations eventually contribute to a lessening of the diversity of voices that are included as inequality is increased. Diversity is a characteristic critical to complex system dynamics and suppressing it has negative consequences for the system itself.

CONCLUSION

As Bunnell and Coe (2001) and Marques (2011) contend, innovation needs to be considered as a process that occurs between and across scales, not merely within a single scale. But while this general claim is challenging to refute in a time of extensive connectivity through economies, technology and social ties, the notion of what cross-scale dynamics actually entails has remained either abstract and vague, or overly simplistic in previous scholarship. When applied to social innovation histories, the combination of Giddens's theory of structuration and the multi-level perspective (MLP) framework reveals a multitude of new insights and ultimately a more nuanced understanding of cross-scale dynamics in complex systems. Patterns across several of the cases challenge previous conceptions of how social innovations emerge or which ones may be most likely to contribute to transformative change.

The findings about niches potentially move scholarship in two new directions for understanding social innovation, which will require further study. First, previous innovation studies based on complex systems have considered that crisis or system collapse may present an important opportunity for the adoption of social innovations by a regime (Gelcich et al., 2010). Although protracted crises are present in all cases, the shocks or disturbances that inevitably emerge in any complex system are not the only or even the most important drivers of a social innovation over the course of its history. Equal attention to the process of "slow variables" in social innovation scholarship will open up new possibilities for future research.

Secondly, the most extensive discussions about cross-scale dynamics and innovation that have been undertaken by previous scholars have focused on the role of networks (e.g. Coe and Bunnell, 2003; Olsson et al., 2006; Gertler and Levitte, 2005; Westley et al., 2013). Although important, the cases in this volume reveal few novel insights about networks. Instead, the findings demonstrate that networks are not the only social structure or form of organization to matter to the long-term development of social innovation through history. The patterns of the cases make it clear that innovation studies based on complex system dynamics must move away from the idea that social innovations are *only* likely to result from a small, close-knit group of people working on the fringe of a system. Networks matter for some cases, such as the financial derivatives. In other cases, far more people contribute to the entire process of social innovation, without ever collaborating and existing in the same space or time. The niche itself will expand and contract over the course of its history, indicating fragility but never complete dissolution.

Whether a social innovation achieves truly transformative change seems at least partly to depend on whether it is introduced and led by actors within the existing regime, or whether it is an experimental niche that draws on the structures of signification and legitimation from the landscape scale to become a proto-regime. Across the cases, dynamics vary widely, but those that achieved the most transformative change are those that evolved into a proto-regime based on the construction of new norms, new knowledge and, ultimately, new authority. The proto-regime does not immediately attempt to dismantle the existing structures of domination, legitimation or signification within the dominant regime; instead it exists alongside of, and is shaped by that dominant regime. Furthermore, those that aim to create hope and change of broad social benefit, rather than to fix a single problem that suppresses overall diversity, appear to have more long-term durability.

Perhaps most interestingly, the landscape structures of legitimation and signification differ in their impact in different cases. While a reliance on the logics and evidence developed through Western scientific epistemologies contributed to reshaping a regime's acceptance of birth control for instance, it also was used to justify intelligence tests and discriminatory practices. The historical perspective enabled observations of how an attractor's shadow side plays out across the evolution of different social innovations, sometimes across cases and innovations emerging in the same time period. This is a new phenomenon to understand in and of itself. But this finding also highlights the fact that landscape social structures do not disappear; they are merely given preference or dominance when selected by the niche and regime, for a specific period of time.

Ultimately, the cross-scalar nature of social innovation histories is indeed dynamic. This book illuminates the critical relevance of these dynamics in ways that have not been highlighted so clearly before. While it could be claimed that humans have always undertaken social innovation, history reveals that truly transformative change is rare. How or why transformation does or does not occur can be partly explained by the cross-scale dynamics of the complex systems in which the social innovation emerges.

REFERENCES

Adger, W.N., Brown, K. and Tompkins, E.L. (2005). The political economy of cross-scale networks in resource co-management. *Ecology and Society*, **10**(2), 9.

Audia, P.G. and Rider, C.I. (2005). A garage and an idea: what more does an entrepreneur need? *California Management Review*, **48**(1), 6–28.

Berkes, F. (2002). Cross-scale institutional linkages for commons management: perspectives from the bottom up. In E. Ostrom, T. Dietz, N. Dolšak, P.C. Stern, S. Stonich and E.U. Weber (eds), *The Drama of the Commons*. Washington, DC: National Academy, pp. 293–321.

Biggs, R., Carpenter, S.R. and Brock, W.A. (2009). Turning back from the brink: detecting an impending regime shift in time to avert it. *Proceedings of the National Academy of Sciences of the United States of America*, **106**(3), 826–31.

Bradach, J. and Grindle, A. (2014). Emerging pathways to transformative scale. *Stanford Social Innovation Review, Spring (Supplement)*, 7–11.

Bunnell, T.G. and Coe, N.M. (2001). Spaces and scale of innovation. *Progress in Human Geography*, **25**(4), 569–89.

Callison, C. and Hermida, A. (2015). Dissent and resonance: #Idlenomore as an emergent middle ground. *Canadian Journal of Communication*, **40**(4), 695.

Cash, D.W., Adger, W.N., Berkes, F., Garden, P., Lebel, L., Olsson, P., Pritchard, L. and Young, O. (2006). Scale and cross-scale dynamics: governance and information in a multilevel world. *Ecology and Society*, **11**(2), 8.

Challies, E., Newig, J. and Lenschow, A. (2014). What role for social-ecological systems research in governing global teleconnections? *Global Environmental Change*, **27**, 32–40.

Chatty, D. and Colchester, M. (eds) (2002). *Conservation and Mobile Indigenous Peoples: Displacement, Forced Settlement, and Sustainable Development* (Vol. 10). New York: Berghahn Books.

Coe, N.M. and Bunnell, T.G. (2003). "Spatializing" knowledge communities: towards a conceptualization of transnational innovation networks. *Global Networks*, **3**(4), 437–56.

Collins, R. (1988). The micro contribution to macro sociology. *Sociological Theory*, **6**, 242–53.

Corntassel, J. and Holder, C. (2008). Who's sorry now? Government apologies, truth commissions, and indigenous self-determination in Australia, Canada, Guatemala, and Peru. *Human Rights Review*, **9**(4), 465.

Crossley, N. (2002). *Making Sense of Social Movements*. Buckingham: Open University Press.

Cumming, G.S., Cumming, D.H.M. and Redman, C.L. (2006). Scale mismatches in social-ecological systems: causes, consequences, and solutions. *Ecology and Society*, **11**(1), 14.

Dearden, P., Rollins, R. and Needham, M. (eds) (2016). *Parks and Protected Areas in Canada*. Oxford: Oxford University Press.

Delaney, D. and Leitner, H. (1997). The political construction of scale. *Political Geography*, **16**, 93–7.

Foxon, T. and Pearson, P. (2008). Overcoming barriers to innovation and diffusion of cleaner technologies: some features of a sustainable innovation policy regime. *Journal of Cleaner Production*, **16**(S1), S148–S161.

Frenken, K., Saviotti, P.P. and Trommetter, M. (1999). Variety and niche creation in aircraft, helicopters, motorcycles and minicomputers. *Research Policy*, **28**(5), 469–88.

Geels, F.W. (2002). Technological transitions as evolutionary reconfiguration processes: a multi-level perspective and a case study. *Research Policy*, **31**, 1257–74.

Geels, F.W. (2010). Ontologies, socio-technical transitions (to sustainability), and the multi-level perspective. *Research Policy*, **39**(4), 495–510.

Gelcich, S., Hughes, T.P., Olsson, P., Folke, C., Defeo, O., Fernández, M., Foale, S., Gunderson, L.H., Rodríguez-Sickert, C., Scheffer, M., Steneck, R.S. and Castilla, J.C. (2010). Navigating transformations in governance of Chilean marine coastal resources. *Proceedings of the National Academy of Sciences of the United States of America*, **107**(39): 16794–9.

Gertler, M.S. and Levitte, Y.M. (2005). Local nodes in global networks: the geography of knowledge flows in biotechnology innovation. *Industry and Innovation*, **12**(4), 487–507.

Giddens, A. (1984). *The Constitution of Society: Outline of the Theory of Structuration*. Berkeley, CA: University of California Press.

Golden-Biddle, K. and Dutton, J.E. (eds) (2012). *Using a Positive Lens to Explore Social Change and Organizations: Building a Theoretical and Research Foundation*. Oxford: Routledge.

Hegger, D.L.T., Van Vliet, J. and Van Vliet, B.J.M. (2007). Niche management and its contribution to regime change: the case of innovation in sanitation. *Technology Analysis and Strategic Management*, **19**(6), 729–46.

Kemp, R., Schot, J. and Hoogma, R. (1998). Regime shifts to sustainability through processes of niche formation: the approach of strategic niche management. *Technology Analysis & Strategic Management*, **10**, 175–98.

Lawrence, S. and Macklem, P. (2000). From consultation to reconciliation: aboriginal rights and the Crown's duty to consult. *Canadian Bar Review*, **29**, 252–79.

Levin, S.A. (1992). The problem of pattern and scale in ecology: the Robert H. MacArthur award lecture. *Ecology*, **73**, 1943–67.

Marques, P. (2011). Theories and policies of innovation: a critical review. *Geography Compass*, **5**(11), 838–50.

Moore, M-L., Riddell, D. and Vocisano, D. (2015). Scaling out, scaling up, scaling deep: strategies of nonprofits in advancing systemic social innovation. *Journal of Corporate Citizenship*, **2015**(58), 67–84.

Moore, M-L., Von der Porten, S. and Castleden, H. (2016). Consultation is not consent: hydraulic fracturing and water governance on Indigenous lands in Canada. *WIRES-Water*, **4**(1), 1–15.

Moore, M-L., Westley, F.R., Tjörnbo, O. and C. Holroyd (2012). The loop, the lens, and the lesson: using resilience theory to examine public policy and social innovation. In A. Nicholls, and A. Murdock (eds). *Social Innovation*. Basingstoke: Palgrave Macmillan, pp. 89–113.

Mulgan, G., Tucker, S., Ali, R. and Sanders, B. (2007). *Social Innovation: What it is, Why it Matters, and How it can be Accelerated*. London: The Basingstoke Press.

Murray, R., Caulier-Grice, J. and Mulgan, G. (2010). *The Open Book of Social Innovation*. London: The Young Foundation.

Natcher, D.C. (2001). Land use research and the duty to consult: a misrepresentation of the aboriginal landscape. *Land Use Policy 2001*, **18**, 113–22.

Olsson, P., Folke, C. and Hahn, T. (2004). Social-ecological transformation for ecosystem management: the development of adaptive co-management of a wetland landscape in southern Sweden. *Ecology and Society*, **9**(4), 2.

Olsson, P., Gunderson, L.H., Carpenter, S.R., Ryan, P., Lebel, L., Folke, C. and Holling, C.S. (2006). Shooting the rapids: navigating transitions to adaptive governance of social-ecological systems. *Ecology and Society*, **11**(1), 18.

Promislow, J. (2013). Irreconcilable? The duty to consult and administrative decision makers. *Constitutional Forum*, **22**(1), 63.

Ritchie, K. (2013). Issues associated with the implementation of the duty to consult and accommodate aboriginal peoples: threatening the goals of reconciliation and meaningful consultation. *UBC Law Review*, **46**, 397–438.

Ross, R.K. (2014). We need more scale, not more innovation. *Stanford Social Innovation Review*, **12**(2, Supplement), 18–19.

Schot, J. and Geels, F.W. (2007). Niches in evolutionary theories of technical change. *Journal of Evolutionary Economics*, **17**(5), 605–22.

Schot, J. and Geels, F.W. (2008). Strategic niche management and sustainable innovation journeys: theory, findings, research agenda, and policy. *Technology Analysis & Strategic Management*, **20**, 537–54.

Smith, A. and Raven, R. (2012). What is protective space? Reconsidering niches in transitions to sustainability. *Research Policy*, **41**, 1025–36.

Smith, A., Voß, J.P. and Grin, J. (2010). Innovation studies and sustainability transitions: the allure of the multi-level perspective and its challenges. *Research Policy*, **39**(4), 435–48.

Smith, M.P. (1998). Looking for the global spaces in local politics. *Political Geography*, **17**, 35–40.

Sossin, L. (2010). The duty to consult and accommodate: procedural justice as Aboriginal rights. *Canadian Journal of Administrative Law and Practice*, **23**, 93–113.

Swyngedouw, E. (1997). Neither global nor local: "Glocalization" and the politics of scale. In K. Cox (ed.), *Spaces of Globalization*. New York: Guilford Press, pp. 137–66.

Truth and Reconciliation Commission of Canada (2015). Honouring the truth, reconciling the future: Final Report of the Truth and Reconciliation Commission. Ottawa: Canada.

Van der Laak, W.W.M., Raven, R.P.J.M. and Verbong, G.P.J. (2007). Strategic niche management for biofuels: analysing past experiments for developing new biofuel policies. *Energy Policy*, **35**, 3213–25.

Van Driel, H. and Schot, J. (2005). Radical innovation as a multilevel process: introducing floating grain elevators in the port of Rotterdam. *Technology and Culture*, **46**(1), 51–76.

Verbong, G. and Geels, F. (2007). The ongoing energy transition: lessons from a socio-technical, multi-level analysis of the Dutch electricity system (1960–2004). *Energy Policy*, **35**(2), 1025–37.

Verbong, G.P.J., Christiaens, W., Raven, R.P.J.M. and Balkema, A.J. (2010). Strategic niche management in an unstable regime: biomass gasification in India. *Environmental Science and Policy*, **13**, 272–91.

Vervoort, J.M., Rutting, L., Kok, K., Hermans, F.L.P., Veldkamp, T., Bregt, A.K. and Van Lammeren, R. (2012). Exploring dimensions, scales, and cross-scale dynamics from the perspectives of change agents in social–ecological systems. *Ecology and Society*, **17**(4), 24.

Westley, F.R. and Antadze, N. (2010). Making a difference: strategies for scaling social innovation for greater impact. *The Public Sector Innovation Journal*, **15**(2), art. 2.

Westley, F.R., Zimmerman, B. and Patton, M.Q. (2006). *Getting to Maybe: How the World is Changed.* Toronto, ON: Vintage Canada.

Westley, F.R., Tjörnbo, O., Schultz, L., Olsson, P., Folke, C., Crona, B. and Bodin, Ö. (2013). A theory of transformative agency in linked social-ecological systems. *Ecology and Society*, **18**(3), 27.

Wyborn, C. and Bixler, R.P. (2013). Collaboration and nested environmental governance: scale dependency, scale framing, and cross-scale interactions in collaborative conservation. *Journal of Environmental Management*, **123**, 58–67.

13. Conclusion: recognizing transformative potential

Frances Westley

When we began the project that produced the cases in this book we, as social innovation researchers, were on a quest. Our goal was to try to understand enough about how successful social innovations went from initiating phenomenon to broad institutional change, as well as understanding the nature of that initiating phenomenon. We were intent on finding patterns that would help illuminate the dynamics of this most complex social process. But our quest was not restricted to history. We also hoped to find patterns that could be used to identify contemporary social innovations in their early stages that hold promise of transformative impact.

At any given point in time, there are many initiatives that self-identify as social innovations, from new technologies (portable homes for the homeless) to new forms of old technologies (bamboo bicycles), from social initiatives (Housing First) to social movements (Transition Towns). While all can claim novelty, only a small fraction of these will go on to be "game changers", to transform the system dynamics that created the problem in the first place. Without a historical lens, it is difficult to understand the particular attributes of those that *will eventually be* transformative. Yet in a time of scarce resources, of time, energy, money and even attention, is there anything we can learn from history that can help us to identify those contemporary social innovations with the greatest potential for transformation? This was our quest.

In this concluding chapter, seven patterns will be identified across the cases in the book. We will discuss each of these in turn. We will then introduce four questions, which those seeking to differentiate transformative social innovations from others can use to make judgments for research or action purposes.

PATTERNS GLEANED FROM HISTORY

Pattern 1: The Importance of Meaning in Social Innovation

As we noted in the introduction, this book of cases and reflections was stimulated in part by the work of Arthur (2009), who charted the growth of technological innovation from the discovery of new *scientific* phenomena. For example, the discovery of DNA spurred innovations around genetic technologies that continue today. Discovery of the light spectrum stimulated innovations in art as well as science and technology. We were curious about the originating phenomena in social innovation. Aside from discoveries about human physiology and development, the number of discoveries that have the same "law-like" property around social interactions and forms are relatively few. The closest perhaps are the discoveries of group behavior (group psychology, group dynamics) and power dynamics (the iron law of oligarchy, for instance) that seem relatively invariant across time and space. However as both Durkheim (1915) and Weber (2001 [1920]) pointed out, the power of beliefs to shape behavior is deep and abiding. The beliefs undergirding the great world religions, for example, have had the power to shape behavior over centuries. Durkheim calls ideas with this kind of power *social facts*, social phenomena that could not be observed directly, but nonetheless are able to shape behavior that is observable (*real in their consequences*).

While several of the cases in this book center around a technical breakthrough or discovery of a new phenomenon – notably the Internet, derivatives and the intelligence test – for the most part a breakthrough social philosophy lay at the origin of the cascade of innovation. As Weber pointed out in *The Protestant Ethic and the Spirit of Capitalism* (2001 [1920]), Calvinism in contrast to Catholicism had an *elective affinity* with capitalism as mode of economic conduct. We see the power of these new beliefs illustrated in the Dutch Partnership case – the way in which Calvinism ruptured the social hierarchy and released capital from its tight coupling to land. The legalization of contraception in Western societies had its origins in the work of John Stuart Mill and his 1869 essay on the subjection of women (2006 [1859]). The creation of National Parks was driven by a cluster of ideas associated with the Romantic tradition, about the spiritual and rejuvenating effects of encountering pure nature, in contrast to the "satanic mills" of industry and commerce. The establishment of residential schools, seen as an innovation in its time, had its roots in colonial thinking about the superiority of European civilizations and the inferiority of other races. On the other hand, the Duty to Consult had its origins in a counter-truth or idea: that of the Two Wampum Belt and the harmonious coexistence of different peoples. Even the Internet and the derivatives market had profoundly ideological underpinnings – respectively, the counterculture thinking of the sixties in the USA, and the new definitions of risk made possible by the Black–Sholes–Merton model and the development of modern portfolio theory – which prompted particular paths of innovative permutations. This powerful attraction to a central, radical philosophy (whether ultimately redeeming, damaging or both) is a deeply human characteristic, one that transcends cultures and historical circumstances.

Pattern 2: Social Innovations Take Time to Unfold and Therefore Transcend the Efforts of Individuals

The cases in this book span long periods of time, generally longer than the lifetime of a single individual. The shortest, the development of the Internet, took over fifty years to have a transformative effect. The longest, probably the legalization of birth control, took over three hundred years. Of course these were not periods of continuous change; rather the pattern was one of "punctuated equilibrium" in most cases – patterns of stability punctuated by periods of rapid change. The moments of change might be characterized as regime shifts – simultaneous gestalt reconfigurations of multiple social elements – and are generally driven by an external shock, one seemingly unconnected to the regime in question. So for example the First and Second World Wars created disturbances in many of the cases, the pattern of activity before and after these events seeming quite distinct. In the case of both the intelligence test and the legalization of contraception, the Second World War with its mobilization of "captive" populations of men spurred a sudden growth in the use of the intelligence test and created a loophole in the opposition to legalized contraception due to the sudden epidemic of venereal disease (Westley et al., 2016).

The length of time that these innovations took to transform the broader society is a sobering thought for those who seek a quick fix to the pressing problems of our society.

While some individuals play key roles in the movement of social innovation from initiating phenomenon to social transformation, no one key individual can be held responsible for any one social transformation. In the National Parks case, for example, a number of individuals played key, although distinct roles. The romantic poets inspired explorers like Gatlin and academics like George Perkins Marsh, as well as noted writers/ environmentalists such as Emerson and Thoreau. Politicians, like Senator Connes, pushed bills through Congress. Hayden (1871) led scientific explorations and became an active advocate. Later (1910–15) Stephen Mather played a central role in setting up the national park service and strengthening the infrastructure of the parks. These different agents worked at different times and in different ways to inspire (poets), connect (Muir, Marsh), and organize (Mather), in order to deliver the necessary resources at the necessary time. While key individuals, such as Tim Berners-Lee in the Internet case, are singled out and accorded a hero status (and without a doubt leave their imprint on the innovation), their work is often founded on the work of others and they too will pass the baton in their turn. This is an important reminder – for those who put too much stress on the individual entrepreneur or inventor in processes as complex as these (Westley et al., 2006) – that social and institutional entrepreneurs need to recognize that they may not see a resolution of the problem with which they are concerned in their own lifetimes. They can, however, take satisfaction in moving the change dynamic forward and keeping the momentum going "on their watch" (Westley, 1997).

Pattern 3: Each Situation is Unique: Coherence of Principles, Not Consistency of Practice, is Important

Looking across these cases we see that each has a unique trajectory, based in part on opportunity context, and in part on the particular individuals who "carried the ball" at certain times and for certain reasons. However, despite the variation and change across cases, there is a coherence which distinguishes each initiative. Complex dynamics are like raising a child, each one is different and each one is highly relational – the particulars of who is interacting with whom at any given moment in time play an important role in the emerging dynamics (Westley et al., 2006). For this reason we do not expect consistency ("The quality of achieving a level of performance which does not vary greatly in quality over time" (OED, en.oxforddictionaries.com/definition)) across time and we do not see it in these cases. As noted above, the pattern was much more one of punctuated equilibria – periods of stability of varying duration, punctuated by those of intense activity, also of varying duration. This was in no way a steady march towards transformation. We did, however, discover a surprising degree of coherence ("The quality of forming a unified whole" (OED, en.oxforddictionaries.com/definition)), which in this case seemed to be guided by the thread of the original idea or principles that undergirded it. Although the initiating idea or invention was interwoven with other ideas or threads over time, nonetheless, it remained identifiable in interesting ways. Perhaps the best example of this was seen in the Internet case, where the anti-authoritarian values of the founders remain a consistent quality, an attractor if you will, for diverse activity through time. While many new permutations and associations were added to the original technology and new partnerships took precedence, the notion that the Internet should remain free from top-down interference and control lasted long enough to see much popular opposition to the government attempts to locate and punish Edward Snowden for his wikileaks. The notion that the Internet can be used to solve collective action problems in a participatory way, free from government interference, remains a cherished ideal.

Similarly in the National Parks case, the romantic view of the restorative properties of untrammeled nature, which influenced advocates such as Muir, are still sacred to those who protect and support the National Parks system, despite the interweaving of this idea with other claims: the importance of parks in maintaining biological diversity and as tourist destinations.

This pattern supports the complexity theory notion of the sensitivity to initial conditions, suggesting that how a social innovation begins will have a fundamental impact on how it evolves over time. It may be a solace to some frustrated founders, who watch their initiatives taking wing, transforming in ways that they never anticipated, that the initial prophetic spark continues to infuse the complex dynamics and can still act as a powerful attractor over time.

Pattern 4: That the Adaptation and Pairing with the Adjacent Possible Shapes the Innovation Itself, Over Time Introducing Often Generative Tensions into the Unfolding Innovation

As noted in the chapter on adjacent possibles, one of the key dynamics of all innovation over time, including social innovation, is the necessity of combining and recombining with ideas, resources and routines/technologies borrowed from the adjacent possible. But given our discovery that social innovation is often driven by a radical, even visionary idea, what are the implications of this kind of combination and recombination for that driving idea?

Two cases offer an interesting contrast:

1. In the National Parks case, the initiative formed alliances for political and/or resource reasons with (a) conservation biologists who were doing inventories of biological resources in the "pristine" west; (b) the designer of Central Park and leader of the public parks movement in Europe, Frederick Olmsted; and (c) the railways, who saw the potential for tourism inherent in a growing National Parks system. Each had a motivation: spiritual inspiration and protecting biodiversity, providing access to nature for the (less privileged) urban dweller, stimulating

tourism-related travel. Each association brought with it benefits – political influence (conservation biology, Frederick Olmsted), financial resources (railroads), popular support (railroads) – but seemingly at a cost, as we will discuss below.

2. In the legalization of birth control case, the initiative paired with the medical community and the military in introducing condoms in World War I, when venereal disease became a real problem with the troops. This made condoms an acceptable form of birth control as long as they were distributed only for the prevention of disease. Later, in the depression of the 1930s, Sanger partnered with those attempting to alleviate poverty; the concept of family planning as a response to poverty and starvation became a new window of opportunity for a woman intent on establishing contraception as a human/woman's basic right. Lastly, she partnered with industry actors (who saw a huge market in contraception) in challenging the Comstock Law, which continued to define any contraception as "obscene". Interestingly, these partnerships did not seem to create the same kind of tensions, perhaps because, unlike the National Parks case, there was continuity in agency. Sanger was able to negotiate each of these associations.

Pattern 5: Paradox and Tensions Characterize Social Innovations and Continue to Drive their Development

Paradox has an interesting role in the dynamics of social innovation and innovation in general. Charles Hampden-Turner in a seminal book (1990) suggested that all industries are structured by a number of paradoxes that define or bound the options for innovation. "Value added" innovations are those that find a way to reconcile those paradoxes or dilemmas. For example, one of the paradoxes in the automobile industry is the tension between safety and sportiness/style. Another is that between fuel efficiency and high performance. Industry players who find a way to at least temporarily reconcile these tensions set a new industry standard and this can be measured in profitability.

Hampden-Turner's work is reminiscent of the work of Claude Lévi-Strauss, one of the founders of the structuralism school of social science, especially his work on myths in primitive societies (1976). Lévi-Strauss argued that there are some irreconcilable oppositions in human experience: between high and low, nature and culture, life and death, divine and mundane. These tensions create a kind of cognitive dissonance in the human psyche – a need to reconcile or bring these values closer together. Lévi-Strauss argues that this is the dynamic behind all mythology. While in "reality" these values may never be reconciled, in an act of creation these ideas can be brought together and integrated, relieving the cognitive dissonance. This attempt will be made over and over in a body of mythology, with various permutations and transformations, all of which can be traced back to the original paradox.

Applying these insights to social innovation in general and the cases in this book in particular, we can argue that the tensions or paradoxes that structure these innovations through time and the dynamic of resolution/ synthesis that sets up a new paradox (thesis/antithesis) is part of what moves the innovation forward. For example, the invention of the intelligence test was made possible by insights based on Darwin's theories of evolution and Mendel's discovery of inherited traits. Nature is destiny. However, these insights were in direct opposition to the democratic belief that men were born free and able to shape their own destinies. In an early 20th-century version of the nature–nurture controversy, concepts like Social Darwinism (which undergirded the intelligence test) allowed for the reconciliation of the increasingly popular democratic notion that status should be achieved as opposed to ascribed, with the comfortable sense of an underlying order. The intelligence test also undermined the concept that leadership and authority should be based on class or breeding. Having ruled out the feebleminded, the rest could compete on merit alone, with no advantage accorded to ancestry. Nevertheless, the intelligence test created a new implicit hierarchy, from genius to feebleminded, that allowed those tasked with making judgments to feel more confident of their choices.

The nature–culture paradox at the heart of the National Parks innovation (are we part of nature or distinct from it?) found temporary resolution in a number of ways. First the two were reconciled in the romantic notion that while we are separate from nature we are somehow spiritually connected in a way that feeds the most creative parts of culture. Secondly, that while we are separate, we are conservation stewards, responsible for tending and preserving the garden in all its varieties. Lastly, that while we are separate we can journey to and immerse ourselves in wilderness as tourists (for a price). These visions, as noted above, are not only in conflict with each other, they represent very different strategies for enactment. For contemporary parks they represent an ongoing strategic tension: should people be kept at a minimum in the park or be allowed to enjoy all its beauties? What about the animals? Should they be managed so that they are an attraction for tourists, or should they be protected from those tourists? And should the parks be run like zoos or theme parks, with an eye to supporting park operations through proceeds from the gate? These debates remain alive and well, after over a hundred years. It is likely that the effort to resolve these tensions will continue to characterize ongoing if more incremental innovation.

Finally, in the Duty to Consult case, an ongoing tension/paradox between assimilation/dominance vs. non-interference/equality has seen the use of force to support one horn of the dilemma, and occasional uprisings/ confrontations (e.g. the 1885 Louis Riel Rebellion) to support the other. Treaties as early as the 1764 Niagara Treaty have attempted to reconcile the two approaches ("both subjects and allies of the Crown . . . a conditional subjection in which they ceded some of their original rights in return for being treated as coequal polities in the empire, with autonomy over their own affairs" (Yirish, 2012, p. 9)). Other initiatives such as the Cowichan Petition (1910) offered a passing hope for innovative action. In 1973, the Supreme Court of Canada ruling on *Calder* v. *British Columbia* influenced the Trudeau government to reopen the land claims process. After 50 years the door was once again open to reconciliation. The subsequent series of court decisions on land claims served to strengthen the "equality/ non-interference" horn of the dilemma, opening up real space for social innovation, including the duty to consult itself.

Again, these examples and others in the book point to the fact that in the complex dynamics of social innovation, paradox is a catalyst to evolution. Harmony or reconciliation achieved through innovation is at best fleeting, a spur to further initiatives.

Pattern 6: Conflict and Opposition Stimulate Combinations and Recombinations in Social Innovation

When Brian Arthur explored how technology innovations unfold through combinations and recombinations, he suggested the search for solutions drove the exploration of the adjacent possible. These cases suggest that the same is likely true for social innovation, but most of the challenges that must be overcome are those of resource scarcity, either of political will or financial resources. One of the most vivid examples of this is found in the Legalization of Birth Control case where the Comstock Act became a lasting challenge to those determined to make birth control a woman's right. The legislation, itself stimulated by moral and religious outrage at the deliberate curtailing of human reproduction, raised a barrier that demanded opportunistic strategies to overcome. Sanger partnered with the medical profession, the social work profession and the prophylactic industry in an attempt to piggyback her cause on their greater resources and alternative justifications (we must control venereal disease for the sake of the troops; we must control families to help those at the brink of starvation; we must take advantage of demand). The Comstock Act was a spur to her creative partnership strategies and sharpened her capacity to capitalize on opportunity.

Like technological innovation, these social innovations progress through combination and recombination. However, unlike the technological bricolage described by Arthur (2009), in these social innovation cases the bricolage seems to be driven as much by scarcity and conflict as by opportunity. Over time, social innovations develop new elements through taking on new partners in order to survive or resist suppression. At any point in time, the innovators described in this book deliberately and strategically engaged a number of separate and sometimes unusual partners for resource reasons. In doing so they at times associated the evolving innovation with unusual, even controversial elements that were grafted onto the innovation. The inherent paradox at times created then became definitive, structuring future conflicts and debates (such as the struggles over nature as pristine wilderness vs. rich resource). Once engaged, these different elements remained a part of the social debates that surrounded these difficult issues, threatening always to pull the innovation towards one basin of attraction vs. another – what Hampden-Turner (1990) terms the "horns of the dilemma". Social innovations remain dynamic and potentially volatile combinations of ideas and rarely achieve stasis.

Pattern 7: Positive Policy Changes Create Stable Zones for Development and New Experimentation: Negative Policy Changes Stimulate Shadow Networks and Preparation for Opportunistic Behavior

As a variable in social innovation, policy change has an interesting role. Policy change itself of course is a dynamic interaction between public process and government expertise. It is generally assumed that some history of public or at least lobby group pressure precedes the implementation of new policies. In many cases, such as the treatment of the First Nations in Canada, this legislation was initially detrimental to innovation, reinforcing the colonial/ assimilation pole of the paradox and making any resolution unlikely, other than through armed resistance. However, as we saw with the Comstock Act, such legislation did not mean that all activity in the problem regime stopped. Rather, as our cases show us, there developed a set of shadow networks that continued to act and plan "below the radar screen". When a window of opportunity opened, as in the First World War venereal disease crisis, actors were prepared to trigger an association beneficial to the cause. Similarly, the Trudeau White Paper presented an opportunity for the Nisga'a to challenge the legality of logging operations on their territory.

In other cases, however, we see how positive legislation, even when arrived at through considerable struggle, provided a springboard for the proliferation of innovations. In the National Parks case, for example, the passing of the National Antiquities Act in 1906 heralded a proliferation of parks in the US. The Calder decision in 1973 created an opportunity for an increasing cascade of new legal decisions that strengthened the rights of First Nations. Ultimately, for social innovations that transform, policy shifts play an important role, both in blocking opportunity (intensifying shadow networks and activity) and in creating windows for accelerated innovation and system shifts.

HOW DO WE USE THESE INSIGHTS TO IDENTIFY "PROMISING" SOCIAL INNOVATIONS?

We began this chapter by noting that this book was inspired by a quest: to understand how social innovation resulted in social transformation. Many innovations do not transform. Like new apps on an existing operating system, they in fact merely strengthen and elaborate an existing system. This does not negate their value; not all systems require changing and much benefit can be derived from social inventions, like the portable home for the homeless, for those who use them. But social innovation is often held up as the game changer, the process which holds promise to create a different society in the future, one that is sustainable, just and equitable. For that to happen, new apps are not enough. New operating systems must be developed.

Nonetheless we know from history that that kind of change, particularly if armed conflict and revolution are not the preferred options, meets with considerable resistance from those who benefit from the status quo, and that includes all of us whose identities, livelihoods or values are in any way connected to the current system. Changing the system "from within" is not a fluid or continuous process. As these cases have indeed demonstrated, it is a time- and resource-demanding process that may take centuries. However, it will not happen at all without the catalytic spark, the initial innovation or cluster of innovations that will serve as attractors for resources across time.

Success can be seen in retrospect, but how do we recognize its potential in the innovations around us? With finite resources to expend, how do we select which innovations are most promising?

While with complex processes such as these, there are no definitive answers, the cases in this book and the patterns described above offer some clues about where to look and where not to look. We will conclude with four questions that may aid in making judgments about the transformative potential of any particular innovation.

1. Does the Innovation Contain a Radical Seed?

Transformative social innovations begin with radical ideas. While radical ideas in themselves are not sufficient to ensure social transformation, they are a necessary starting point. Students of technical innovation speak of *disruptive* innovation, ideas that disrupt the current operating markets, undercutting dominant cost structures. While the social innovations in this book may not have an impact on economic markets (with the exception of the derivatives case), social innovations may disrupt or fundamentally challenge the existing rules and relationships that form our social or cultural structures. Continuing with the homeless example, any innovation that does not have at its core a challenge to the dominant concept of private property is unlikely to be transformative of the homeless problem domain. The rules and relationships of private property are that property is the possession of someone who has paid for it or inherited it. The owner pays taxes on the property, and is constrained to some extent by laws of public decency or municipal by-laws as to what kind of behavior is acceptable and what kind of building can take place, but these are minimal, having to do generally with whether the behavior/building impinges on the rights and freedom of other community members. Other than that, ownership entitles the owner to do what he or she likes in the privacy of his or her home. Without private property laws and the built environment that is the urban manifestation of that private property, homelessness is a non-issue. For it to become a non-issue, the rules of private property would have to change.

In general, most of the innovations addressing homelessness – programs that provide sleeping bags, shelter from the cold, even the ingenious portable homes – do not challenge these laws, these rules and even the interaction (homeless people sleeping in portable homes are just as likely as those sleeping on the streets to be asked to move on, as the Roma people in their caravans have long been experiencing). Public space, already a scarcity in urban environments, is regulated to prevent its use for private purposes. An interesting innovation, which at least challenges the dominant rules and relationships marginally, is Housing First, which provides homes/ apartments for the chronically homeless *without preconditions*. No right (such as the freedom to consume alcohol, own pets, maintain a residence during hospitalization) that is available to homeowners or renters with a lease is denied those placed in Housing First apartments. Support services are offered but are not a precondition for continuing in residence. Hence, those housed in Housing First have the same rights as those who own property, but *without having to pay for or inherit* the property. This approach is therefore more radical than most, as at the micro level it challenges the rules governing rights and relationship to property. Much else would have to change if such an initiative were to have a transformative impact on homelessness and the rules of property that created homelessness in the first place. But in the radical challenge to those dominant rules and relationships, there is at least the seed of a new way of doing things. This seed is absent from many "social innovations" in the homelessness domain.

Looking at social innovation through the lens of complexity raises the question: what system is the innovation hoping to transform? In many cases it will be clear that those fostering the innovation are concerned with alleviation or meeting a need as opposed to transforming any part of the system that created the problem in the first place. It is possible that an innovation with radical intent will fail to transform. It is also possible that an innovation may contain a radical challenge that is not apparent to the founders or to anyone in the early stages. But it is safe to say that unless it is there (visible or invisible), those interested in transformation should proceed with caution.

2. Is the Founder or Originator of the Idea Prepared to Make the Necessary Compromises to See the Idea Grow and Expand, Securing More Resources?

One of the most interesting revelations from the cases in this book is the degree to which those moving the innovation forward at any point in time were prepared to compromise and partner with unfolding initiatives that were the "adjacent possible" for the central innovation. This is in sharp contrast to what is often called the "founder's syndrome", which affects many social and business entrepreneurs. A social innovator comes up with a radical and inspirational program to, say, stop bullying in schools. The program has measurable success and attracts many new resources. As an initial step the program responds to demands to "scale out", to be replicated in other communities and even other cultures. But the founder is very attached to the particular model he developed, down to the very last detail. His approach is precise replication, irrespective of pragmatic considerations and the constraints of particular environments. Permutations are not permitted. The program languishes and eventually dies. This is an all too common occurrence.

These cases have indicated that social innovations that succeed have an organic quality, growing and evolving as circumstance dictates. Key elements are retained but other elements are traded off in the combinations and recombinations with other initiatives through time. Knowing what is essential and what to let go is key, and sometimes difficult to establish.

The concept of minimum specifications is useful here. What is absolutely essential, without which the innovation will have lost its essence, and what can be traded away in return for additional resources? This essence often resides in *principles* (the generative and sacred qualities of nature, the freedom of the Internet, separate but parallel societies connected in friendship) rather than in the particulars of *practice* (the particular routines associated with the initial innovation). Bricolage is fundamental to evolving and growing social innovation over time. And yet it introduces an element of mess into the initiative, which is difficult for some founders to tolerate. Moreover, it is the source of the paradoxes that become embedded in the innovation over time and which further drive the innovation forward. Radical innovations that have begun the process of bricolage necessary for transformation, without sacrificing the essential principles that contain the radical spark, will begin to display elements of paradox at early stages. This was the case with the National Parks example. From the very beginning, the paradox of Nature as a resource to be protected from people and Nature as a resource to be used by people was built into the initiative. While it seems counterintuitive to look for inconsistency and tension in early stages of a social innovation, our cases suggest that evidence of combinations and recombination with accompanying inconsistencies and even emerging paradoxes is a sign of a social innovation with the potential to transform.

3. Are those Associated with the Innovation, Even in the Earliest Stages, Aware of the Need for Change in the Broader Institutional Structures (Values, Laws, Routines, Policies)?

Nearly all radical ideas that succeed in transforming a social system act as attractors, drawing people and resources to their call. This is true of all the innovations in this book; only that attraction can draw enough resources to maintain the momentum over time. However, if the founders are also aware of the institutional barriers between initiation and transformation (which of course is more likely if they are clear on what system they are hoping to transform), there is likely to be evidence, from the very early stages, of strategies intended to facilitate not just dissemination (scaling out) but also institutional change (scaling up). There is also evidence of strategic efforts to connect to and influence policy-makers, even at the initial stages. Al Etmanski, one of Canada's leading and most successful social innovators, keeps a constant vigil on the provincial (British Columbia) and federal governments in Canada. His goal is to change the financial, cultural and social institutions that have created a disadvantaged, disenfranchised and dependent group called "the disabled". Irrespective of political persuasion, Etmanski scans incoming legislators and cabinet ministers for those with a disabled family member and seeks to form relationships with each one. This investment in relationships is geared toward the possibility that, in a shifting political and economic landscape, an opportunity may arise for shifting the institutional routines, laws or markets in such a way that an innovation with radical potential can be introduced into the dominant institutional context. For example, in the early 2000s, Etmanski, in partnership with the BC Law Foundation, introduced the concept of the Registered Disability Savings Plan. Modeled after the Registered Retirement Savings Plan, it was a financial instrument that allowed family and friends as well as the disabled individual him- or herself to put aside funds for the disabled individual. In this it mirrored the innovative initiative Etmanski and partner Vickie Cammack had launched at a local level, that of a facilitated circle of friends – volunteers to extend care of the disabled individual beyond the immediate family. But a more radical seed lay behind this innovation: the government would match two to one contributions, and when the individual chose to draw down the savings, *there would be no claw back of disability payments.* This was a truly radical seed as it challenged the association of disability and welfare, the latter kept to a minimum in order to encourage people to return to work, an outcome not possible for most of those receiving government disability pensions. Etmanski may initially have started out responding to a local need, to keep disabled children safe and secure after the death of parents, but soon recognized that to truly give the disabled a good life, the broader system needed to be challenged.

Evidence of this kind of awareness and at least early stage strategies seem an important indicator of the transformative potential of ideas and initiatives. We see it in the cases of the National Parks, the Derivatives and the Duty to Consult quite clearly, and can discern its presence in the Birth Control Legalization and Internet cases. This is one arena where there is often a distinction between innovation in the technical/for-profit sector and social innovation. While the former needs to have a sense of the potential market for the product, the latter needs to be aware of the political will and appetite to institutionalize and resource an innovation, not through a market transaction necessarily, but through support and influence. Just as a venture capitalist would be unlikely to invest in a start-up that showed no awareness of market demand, social innovations that ignore or are unaware of political and cultural barriers and opportunities are unlikely to be on the path to transformation. This is not to say that the social entrepreneur cannot be helped or trained to take on this broad system awareness. In fact, this is where system entrepreneurs who partner with social entrepreneurs can play a key role.

It is also possible that a particular organization associated with developing the initiative does not itself attempt to scale up or even out, but rather carries the torch of a particular radical idea for a period of time. The Working Centre in Kitchener Waterloo has had a profound impact on the community with its ever-expanding bundle of services to the poor, the homeless and the mentally ill in the centre of Kitchener Ontario. It has a radical formula for mobilizing resources both internally and externally. However, despite recognition and demands, it has shown no interest in expanding beyond Kitchener or taking on the broad policy context. It associates, however, with an earlier tradition of the Catholic Worker Movement and seeks to keep that tradition alive while proliferating new permutations in a single community. It also associates with initiatives that are working to create policy change, such as those fighting for a living wage for all Canadians. The engagement with scaling up or scaling deep takes on many different manifestations, but the vision of a transformed system infuses them all.

4. Is there Evidence of the Possibility of Push Back, of Conflict with those who Control the Status Quo? Can that Conflict be Managed?

Radical social innovation, new ideas and products that can transform the system that created the problem in the first place are likely to encounter resistance, push back and conflict, some passive, some active. This resistance is unlikely to be encountered at the earliest stages of an initiative, when it is still "under the radar". But when the initiative begins to take on momentum, resistance is likely to occur. It may not be as dramatic as the Comstock Act, which made the distribution of contraception "obscene". It may be a relatively subtle repositioning of those interests most directly affected, such as the corporate and global food market's response to the growing popularity of organic food. In some cases this can result in the cooptation of the initiative, as Selznick (1953) illustrated in the Tennessee Valley Authority, the first of the authorities to be set up to protect and conserve environmental ecosystems.

The capacity of the social innovation to transform is not about the absence of conflict; it is about how that conflict is managed. With rare exceptions social innovators do not move forward through overt or violent conflict. Rather, the innovators find ways, through alliances with the right supporters, through switching tactics and making new partnerships to manage opposition and even to coopt it. For example, Ulysses Seal, the founder of the Conservation Breeding Specialist Group, an innovative organization working extremely effectively in the endangered species domain, triggered resentment in the conservation community for his unorthodox workshop approaches and its lack of respect for accepted protocols of working with others. He managed this conflict by giving proper deference to those in ultimate authority, and sharing credit and initiative with anyone prepared to join him (Westley and Vredenburg, 1997).

Balfour Mount, who brought the concept of palliative care to Canada and introduced it into the Royal Victoria Hospital, a teaching hospital associated with the McGill Medical School, initially experienced resistance from doctors in the system who felt that a teaching hospital was about cure, not palliative care. His attitude was that only those with power over the resources he needed had to be won over. He concentrated his message on the Chief of Surgery, Chief of Nursing and Chief of Medicine, persuading each to support palliative care for a different reason (Westley, 1992).

Those interested in discerning social innovations with the potential to transform should look for innovators who do not define conflict as an "us vs. them" proposition, but who instead seek to build collaborations with powerful strangers, alliances with unusual suspects and opportunities to coopt the powerful as opposed to being coopted.

CONCLUSION

As the complexity of our world increases, due to the rate of technological change and the interconnections across time, space and systems, so does our need for social innovations. When the locus of control is clear and the order is hierarchical, a social movement framework has promise. But in situations of high complexity such as the social problems that we explore in these cases, it is difficult to locate the enemy. Change requires managing and facilitating the emergence of creative solutions and the marshaling of those solutions to create disturbance and ultimately transformation. Innovating in complexity means understanding the challenge from a systems perspective, recognizing the importance of radical ideas and the equal importance of paradox, conflict, principles and cross-scale dynamics. All are necessary features of transformative social innovations; no one element is sufficient. Patience truly is a virtue, as is constant commitment to originating principles, as is the art of the long view. But as these cases richly illustrate, transformative change can and does occur.

Finally, looking forward, it becomes clear that transformative social innovations, whether ultimately viewed as positively or negatively transformative, become powerful adjacent possibles for other social innovations. Hence, establishing a National Parks System enshrined in law provided an opening for such innovative legislation as the Endangered Species Act, which, when passed almost surreptitiously in the US in 1973, has had profound impacts on development in the US, and on a variety of innovative programs and processes to conserve endangered species and even reintroduce them to the wild (Westley and Miller, 2003). Similarly the legalization of contraception, which has legitimized the woman's right to control her reproductive processes, has opened the door to new reproductive technologies, driven by market demand that in turn is attracting a new round of ethical, religious and moral debate. Finally, despite and even because of their pernicious and destructive effects, the residential schools have changed the conversation in Canada about Indigenous rights, providing for new ways of looking at the relationship between colonizers and Indigenous peoples and opening the door for current initiatives such as the Truth and Reconciliation Commission.

Social innovation is not a fixed address at which one arrives. It is an ongoing process essential to resilient societies.

REFERENCES

Arthur, B. (2009). *The Nature of Technology: What It Is and How It Evolves.* New York: Free Press.

Durkheim, E. (1915). *The Elementary Forms of Religious Life.* London: G. Allen & Unwin.

Hampden-Turner, C. (1990). *Charting the Corporate Mind.* New York: Free Press.

Lévi-Strauss, C. (1976). *Structural Anthropology.* New York: Basic Books.

Mill, J.S. (2006 [1859]). *Liberty and the Subjection of Women.* London: Penguin Classics.

Selznick, P. (1953). *TVA and the Grass Roots.* Berkeley, CA: University of California Press.

Weber, M. (2001 [1920]). *The Protestant Ethic and the Spirit of Capitalism.* London: Roxbury Publishing Company.

Westley, F. (1992). Vision worlds: strategic vision as social interaction. *Advances in Strategic Management*, **8**, 271–305.

Westley, F. (1997). Not on our watch: the biodiversity crisis and global collaboration response. *Organization and Environment*, **10**(4), December, 342–60.

Westley, F. and Miller, P. (2003). *Experiments in Consilience.* San Francisco, CA: Island Press.

Westley, F. and Vredenburg, H. (1997). Interorganizational collaboration and the preservation of global biodiversity, *Organization Science*, **8**(4), 381–403.

Westley, F., Zimmerman, B. and Patton, M. (2006). *Getting to Maybe: How the World is Changed.* Toronto: Random House.

Westley, F.R., McGowan, K.A., Antadze, N., Blacklock, J. and Tjörnbo, O. (2016). How game changers catalyzed, disrupted, and incentivized social innovation: three historical cases of nature conservation, assimilation, and women's rights. *Ecology and Society*, **21**(4).

Yirish, C. (2012). "Chief princes and owners of all": Native American appeals to the Crown in the early-modern British Atlantic. In S. Belmessous (ed.), *Native Claims: Indigenous Law against Empire, 1500–1920.* New York: Oxford University Press, pp. 129–51.

Index